James Home, Lady Louisa Stuart

Lady Louisa Stuart

Selections from her Manuscripts

James Home, Lady Louisa Stuart

Lady Louisa Stuart
Selections from her Manuscripts

ISBN/EAN: 9783337106492

Printed in Europe, USA, Canada, Australia, Japan

Cover: Foto ©ninafisch / pixelio.de

More available books at **www.hansebooks.com**

LADY LOUISA STUART
SELECTIONS FROM HER MANUSCRIPTS

EDITED BY

Hon. JAMES HOME

"Avito viret honore"

HARPER & BROTHERS PUBLISHERS
NEW YORK AND LONDON
1899

CONTENTS

	PAGE
INTRODUCTION	vii
NOTE	1
SOME ACCOUNT OF JOHN, DUKE OF ARGYLL, AND HIS FAMILY	3
NOTES TO THE FAIRIES' FROLIC	153
NOTES TO THE DIAMOND ROBE	175
HISTORY OF THE FORTUNATE YOUTH	203
UNPUBLISHED LETTERS OF SIR WALTER SCOTT AND LADY LOUISA STUART	217
LADY LOUISA STUART TO MRS. LOCKHART	261
LADY LOUISA STUART TO LADY MONTAGU	268
APPENDIX I. THE FAIRIES' FROLIC	273
APPENDIX II. THE DIAMOND ROBE, OR THE MANIA	295

INTRODUCTION

LADY LOUISA STUART, the subject of this volume, was the youngest daughter of John, third Earl of Bute, Prime Minister at the beginning of the reign of George III.

She was born 12th August, 1757, and died unmarried 4th August, 1851, in her ninety-fourth year. The youngest of a large family, for she was only four years old when her eldest sister, Lady Lonsdale, married, and being of a very uncommon and sensitive character, and endowed with abilities far above those of her elder sisters, and in fact of most young ladies of her time, she found her mother, for whom she had the deepest affection, far more of a companion than her sisters, except the one nearest to her in age, her favorite, Caroline, afterwards Lady Portarlington. Her father had retired from public life in 1763, when Lady Louisa was only five years old, and as in doing so he practically secluded himself from general society also, this contributed to the solitude of her existence.

All these circumstances, as she herself describes in her letters in later life, threw her much upon her own resources, one of them being a habit of composition both in prose and verse that began at a very early age.

Though she went through the usual phase of a young lady of her position, that of going out into London society with her mother, she never seems to have taken much interest in it. Much of the year was, in fact, spent at her father's place, Luton, in Bedfordshire, and also at Highcliffe, a villa that he built for himself near Christchurch in Hampshire. Her father died in 1792, and after the death of her mother in 1794 Lady Louisa settled in a house in Gloucester Place, which continued to be her residence till her death. The quiet and retired habits of her youth continued through her long life. Little as she appeared in the London world, she had that power of attracting the notice and affection of women who, like herself, were of character and ability above the common, which is a sure proof of goodness of heart and superiority of mind; thus she gradually became the centre of a select circle of intimate friends, an intimacy that lasted till death removed them one by one from her. Few, however, of these friends were allowed to know of her literary efforts. From her own sisters the secret was most carefully kept. Her great friend from early youth, Lady Emily Kerr, afterward Macleod, was one of the few to whom it was confided. Many of the papers were destroyed by herself shortly before her death: a certain number remain, and those who are acquainted with them have thought that a time might come when a selection of the best might be made known to the world; her own strong shrinking from publicity being one of the chief reasons for hesitation about this. When Lady Louisa was urged by her nephew, Dr. Corbet, to contribute an introduction or some notes to the life of her grandmother, Lady Mary Wortley Montagu, she was very unwilling to agree, owing to an old and strong prejudice against *appearing in print*—a prejudice that she retained through life; for in her early days it was considered a loss of caste for a woman of good position in society to write for publication. She yielded at last to Dr. Corbet's request, partly in order to do him a kindness, and partly to please her relation, Lord Wharncliffe, the editor of the book. The result of her consent was that admirable chapter of "Introductory Anecdotes," that is sufficiently well known. This is the sole specimen of her writing that has hitherto been published. One of her objections to appearing in print —a fear that her peace of mind might be disturbed by the criticisms of the press—is obviously at an end now. It is hoped that her other scruples may also be fairly considered as applying only to her own lifetime, and that after a lapse of nearly fifty years since her death there can be no valid objection to publishing more of her compositions. Her share in Lord Wharncliffe's book has already given such proof of her abilities that it seems to be only doing justice to herself and to the public to take a fitting opportunity of confirming that reputation. With this object the present volume is issued.

The "Introductory Anecdotes" above mentioned are so well known and so easy of access that it seems unnecessary to reprint them here.

The account of John, Duke of Argyll, and his family, which is placed first in this volume, has already been twice privately printed: first in a small volume by itself in 1863, and secondly in 1889, incorporated in the Introduction to the "Journal" of that Lady Mary Coke of whom Lady Louisa gives such an amusing description in the Argyll Memoir. There are two copies of this Memoir in Lady Louisa's autograph: one in the possession of Lord Home, the other belonging to Colonel Clinton of Ashley Clinton; they differ only in unimportant verbal details.

The Notes to the tales of "The Fairies' Frolic" and "The Diamond Robe," which come next in order, are printed by the kind permission of Mrs. Clark of Tal-y-garn, Glamorganshire, the inheritor of the greater portion of Lady Louisa's manuscripts through her great-aunt, Lady Anna Maria Dawson, niece of Lady Louisa, daughter of her sister, Lady Portarlington. The metrical tales themselves will be found in the Appendix. They have been placed there as their merit is considered not to be equal to their prose Introductions—a question that readers may decide for themselves. Lady Louisa's correspondence with Sir Walter Scott comes last in the volume. That part of it which has already been included in Lockhart's "Life of Scott" and in the "Familiar Letters" is not reprinted here. The most interesting of those letters not hitherto published are now given from the originals at Abbotsford, and the editor takes this opportunity of thanking Mrs. Maxwell Scott for her generous permission. Sir Walter's high opinion of Lady Louisa is sufficiently evident from Lockhart's "Life." She was one of the few to whom he intrusted the secret of the "Waverley Novels." He first made her acquaintance at Bothwell Castle through their common friendship with one of the greatest friends of both, Frances, Lady Douglas.

A memoir of Lady Louisa, under the title of "Gleanings from an Old Portfolio," containing a large number of her letters, has lately been admirably edited, and issued privately by Mrs. Clark of Tal-y-garn. The letters contained in it are chiefly to her sister, Lady Portarlington. A great number of Lady Louisa's letters still remain in manuscript. It is proposed before long to submit to the public a selection of these letters beginning from the date of Lady Portarlington's death, at which date Mrs. Clark's book closes.   J. A. H.

BONKYL LODGE, January 30, 1899.

A MEMOIR

NOTE

"The following memoir was written by Lady Louisa Stuart, daughter of the Earl of Bute, Minister of George III., for the purpose of giving to Caroline Lucy, Lady Scott, an account of her great-grandfather John, Duke of Argyll, and of his family. Lady Scott was descended from the Duke, through her mother (Lady Louisa's very dear friend), Lady Frances Scott, second wife of Archibald Douglas of Douglas, created Baron Douglas.

"Lady Frances Scott was sister of Henry, Duke of Buccleuch, and posthumous daughter of Francis, Earl of Dalkeith, by his wife, Lady Caroline Campbell, eldest daughter of John, Duke of Argyll and Greenwich. Lady Dalkeith married secondly the Right Honble Charles Townshend, who died Chancellor of the Exchequer. She was created Baroness Greenwich, with remainder to the issue male of her second marriage; but, a daughter only by Mr. Townshend surviving her, the title became extinct at her death."

Extract from the Preface to the privately printed edition of 1863.

SOME ACCOUNT OF JOHN, DUKE OF ARGYLL, AND HIS FAMILY

I

JAMES, Earl of Bute, my grandfather, married Lady Anne Campbell, the sister of his two chief friends, John, Duke of Argyll, and Archibald, Earl of Islay; and, dying early, appointed them guardians of his children. My father, who went to Eton school at seven years old, returned no more to Scotland till almost a man; but passed his holidays at the home of one of his uncles, most frequently at that of the Duke, with whose daughters he was therefore bred up as a brother.

The early history of the Duke and Duchess, a very singular one, was often told me by my mother, who, besides the fragments of it that general report and family tradition could furnish, had gathered its minutest details from two of their contemporary friends— Lady Suffolk (concerning whom see Lord Orford) and Mrs. Kingdon, a remarkable person, still living in my mother's days, and at past ninety years old retaining all her faculties, although thought "a little ancient,"[1] according to Swift, when maid of honor to Queen Anne.

Mrs. Warburton—respectable young ladies were not yet styled *Misses*—Mrs. Jane Warburton, a country gentleman's daughter, of an old Cheshire family,[2] was maid of honor at the same time. By what means or interest she became so, I never could understand; for, though well born, in a herald's sense of the words, her education had not fitted her for a stately, elegant court. Accustomed as we have now so long been to the quick general communication which throws the whole kingdom together, it is very difficult to carry our ideas back a century or more, to the period when there were no stage-coaches, no post-horses, no turnpike-roads, and when, in the distant counties, men made their wills before they undertook a journey to London. The habits of the town and country were then, of course, much more distinct from each other. Mrs. Warburton, raw from Cheshire, brought with her a coarseness of language and manners which we should hardly expect to find in the dairymaid of her father's equal at

---

[1] "Colonel Disney said of Jenny Kingdon, the maid of honor, who is a little ancient, that the Queen should give her a brevet to act as a married woman."—*Swift's Journal to Stella.* See "Journal of Lady Mary Coke," 24th June, 1767.

[2] Her father was Thomas Warburton, Esq., son of Sir George Warburton of Winnington, Cheshire. Her mother was Anne, daughter and co-heir of Sir Robert Williams, third Baronet of Penrhyn, whose youngest daughter, Gwen, was the "sister Yonge" mentioned in the letter given in the note on the next page, second wife of Sir William Yonge, third Baronet of Culleton, Devon.—ED.

present.¹ Unluckily, she had few personal charms to make amends for the rusticity, ignorance, and want of breeding that soon rendered her the standing jest of her companions in office. The honorable sisterhood then subsisting were as fond of spitefully teasing each other

¹ The following specimen of the literary powers of her mother was found among the Duke of Buccleuch's papers:

Addressed—
"To the Honble. Mrs. Warburton,
Maide of Honer to her Royal Highnesse the Princesse."
"*Sept. 5th,* 1715.

"DEAR CHILDE,—I hope you have recd the 100 Bill wch Mr. Williams drew on his Brother. I did endorse it, & my sister Yonge sed she wod putt it up safe for you in her Box yt was Lockt. The silver Decanter which yr Father gave you is but an ugly thing. I think it weighs 39 oz. ½, & tis charg'd att 7s. an ounce, so yt there wod be great losse in parting with it. Therefore yr Father gives you 20£ in money, wch you must pay yrself. Perhaps at present the money will be most usefull, but hereafter, when you have more of yr own, 'twill be as well to make a show of your Father's guift in a piece of plate. I have been writing this post to Sir Walter Yonge about the Pattens for Chamberlaine,* wch Mr. Justice Cumberbatch has been much too bussy in, & has been writing up to know if the King can't grant yt pattent. If there shod be any discourse of it, 'tis fitt it shod be known 'tis his doings merely for the profitt that accrews to him, for Mr. Warburton never spoke nor once thought of such a thing; and, to be sure, the officers yt belong to the prince will represent it as it deserves, if such a thing be done; & Mr. Warburton will not medle with it, but as the prince has gratiously granted it to him.

"Yr Brother Hugh's fine horse I hope is come to him, but it & the Master will be very unfitt for travel into Scotland. I trust in God there will be no occasion. Wt good can these poor raw men do? There will be occasion for another horse if he goes out of

* *i. e.* The Chamberlainship of Carnarvonshire, Merioneth, and Anglesey. See " Townshend Papers," *Hist. M. S. Commission*, p. 341.—ED.

as their predecessors, celebrated by Count Hamilton, or their successors in Queen Charlotte's train; so what a life poor Jenny Warburton led among them, ever blundering, getting into scrapes, and blurting out vulgar expressions, may easily be imagined. One of her bright sayings remains upon record. The removals of the court (while there was a court) from palace to palace were superintended by a state officer, called the Harbinger. As the ladies consulted together about their packages, on a rumor of the Queen's going suddenly to Windsor, "Well, for my part," said Jenny, "I shan't trouble myself—must not the *Scavenger* take care of us maids of honor?"

This was her situation, when John, Duke of Argyll, arrived from the Continent with all his blushing honors thick upon him, and a military reputation inferior to Marlborough's alone. Trained under King William, who gave him a Dutch regiment before he was seventeen, he had passed his life either in the field or in transacting the public business of Scotland, and mingled with London society rarely, only in the intervals

---

England, but I think not otherways. If Hugh be not oblidg'd to buy everything of yr Rob Riches draper, 'tis best to oblidge Mr. Simson, who indeed I think has us'd us well. Remember the pattern for the cornish of the bed—4 lb. of good fresh coffee. I don't forget yr cheese; it will go next week. I wod not be att the parting, yet I am convinc'd deare Hugh does wt becomes a man & a christian to putt too his helping hand for this service. If my seven sons were liveing, I shod not think it too much for them all to fight in this cause. Deare childe, write some comfortable news if you can.—I am, yr most affectionate Mother,
"A. WARBURTON."
—ED.

between his campaigns. By this means he was a sight, an object of curiosity, to many of the company at a crowded drawing-room on the Queen's birthday, where he made his appearance newly invested with the Garter, the admired hero of the hour. Lady Mary Wortley says that women see men with their ears. He might have gained by being so seen; but he had likewise everything to attract and charm the eye—personal beauty, an expressive countenance, a commanding air, and the most easy, engaging gracefulness of manner. My mother, who was unborn at the time, and could not have known him till five-and-twenty years after it, described him as even then one of the finest-looking men she ever beheld, as well as the most pleasing; and Lady Betty Mackenzie used to affirm that my brother Charles[1] (of whose beauty you have heard the fame) was his very picture.

Thus much premised, you will not wonder that he should have been the chief subject of conversation at a dinner which the Duke of Shrewsbury, Lord Chamberlain of the Household, gave to the maids of honor, according to the usage of Queen Anne's days, upon her birthday. The cloth being removed, and the ladies' toasts called for, while all the rest named old bishops or generals, the men farthest from their thoughts, honest Mrs. Warburton went straight to the man uppermost in hers, and fairly toasted the Duke of Argyll. Her colleagues set up a shout of laughter. "Oh, ho! He was her favorite, was he? Truly she had taken

---

[1] General Sir Charles Stuart, K.B.—a distinguished general, father of the late Lord Stuart de Rothesay.—ED.

care not to choose too humbly: they wished he did but know his valuable conquest; no doubt he would be amazingly flattered—perhaps made rather too vain!" And thus the raillery, or, as we moderns term it, the *quizzing*, went on, till the victim fell a-crying, and the master of the house was forced to interpose and make peace. At night, when everybody met again at the ball, the Duke of Shrewsbury said to Argyll, who stood near him: "My Lord, you little think what mischief you have occasioned to-day. A poor young lady has been shedding bitter tears on your account." "Upon my account! How so?" Shrewsbury told him what had passed. "Oh, poor thing!" exclaimed he; "it was very hard upon her, indeed. I have a great mind to go and talk to her, by way of avenging her cause. Which is she? Introduce me." And the *quizzers*, to their astonishment, and, as Mrs. Kingdon acknowledged, their no small mortification, saw him devote himself to Jenny Warburton for the remainder of the evening. Possibly what they threw out in scorn came nearer the truth than they suspected. No man can help being a little flattered by the sincere, involuntary preference of almost any young woman; and he might secretly imagine that the impulse of such a preference had thrown the innocent girl off her guard. Be this as it might, one conversation gave birth to others; these led to visits. The visits grew frequent, grew daily; and in a short time his attachment to her became notorious, and was as passionate as extraordinary.

The wonder of it, however, lay principally in her

want of beauty. Her other deficiencies were not calculated to disgust a man of very peculiar opinions, whose shining abilities and loftiness of mind did not prevent his harboring the most illiberal contempt of women. At Athens of yore, it is said, all reputable matrons and virgins were nonentities, shut up within four walls to pursue their domestic labors unheard of and unseen; while knowledge, accomplishments, vivacity, everything that can render society agreeable, belonged exclusively to the courtesans. Now the Duke of Argyll thought this just as it should be, or rather as it necessarily must be, and actually was. He had been married very young to a rich citizen, whom he hated:[1] they parted quickly, and the little acquaintance he could be said to have had with women since was confined to the followers of a camp; or, if a few foreign ladies came in his way, you may be sure he passed upon them the same general sentence as Captain Winterbottom,[2] in the *Mirror;* for where inveterate prejudice reigns paramount, the highest mind will judge like the lowest. In a word, he believed scarcely any woman truly virtuous; but held it certain that none could be so who had the slightest share of mental endowments, natural or acquired. And though Jenny Warburton was quite free from these impediments to chastity, yet, trusting to the inherent frailty of the sex

[1] Mary, daughter of Thomas Browne, whose wife, Ursula Duncombe, was sister and heiress of Sir Charles Duncombe of Helmsley, Lord Mayor of London. The Duchess's brother, Thomas Duncombe, was grandfather of the first Lord Feversham.—ED.

[2] "Roman ladies? Ay, they are papists; and they are all——."
—*Mirror*, No. 97.

and the liberty allowed a maid of honor, he at first concluded that she would fall his easy prey. But when on the contrary she proved absolutely immovable, not to be tempted by promises, or presents, or magnificent offers, nor yet to be worked upon by all the arts and powers of captivation, which he could not but know he eminently possessed, his admiration exceeded even his surprise. He remained convinced that he had found the pearl of price, the most virtuous woman, if not the only one in the world; all the while never doubting that this heroic resistance cost her dear, and was the fruit of many a painful struggle with secret love.

Here his own ardent imagination, aided by his vanity, led him into a trifling mistake. Virtuous the good simple soul really was, and from principle steadily observing those plain precepts which her limited capacity permitted her to comprehend; but in the present instance it cost her no struggle at all. Virtue had neither a warm constitution nor a tender heart to contend with; and as for romantic love, its torments, raptures, conflicts, illusions, perplexities—nothing in Sir Isaac Newton's works could have been less intelligible to a mind like Jenny's. She positively would not, for all his Grace was worth (and so she told him), be —— that thing whose proper name it did not abhor her, as it did poor Desdemona, to speak very distinctly. But she had no delicacy to be wounded by the affronting proposal; nor did she see in it any reason for keeping him at a greater distance than before, since she felt herself in no danger; and it was not forbidden by the

A MEMOIR 11

Ten Commandments, nor in any part of the Bible, to let a man, whether handsome or ugly, sit by one's fireside an hour or two every morning. Their intercourse, therefore, continued undiminished; continued so for years. And what was remarkable, but a proof that the world can sometimes be just, it raised no scandalous reports to her prejudice: the town, the court, nay, the sister maids of honor—watchful spies upon all that passed—bore witness to its perfect innocence, and pronounced her character unimpeachable.

On the death of Queen Anne, Jenny would in all probability have travelled back to her father's seat in Cheshire, with or without a small pension, if the Whig leaders whom that event brought into power had not whispered to each other, "We must provide for Mrs. Warburton, that we may secure the Duke of Argyll."

Consequently her name stood foremost in the list of ladies appointed maids of honor to the new Princess of Wales (Queen Caroline), who no sooner arrived in England herself, and began to study the *carte du pays*—the relations of things and persons here—than she also took care to treat the object of his Grace's regard with particular attention.

But in less than two years after the Queen, died the Duchess of Argyll, his separated wife, who had long been a languishing invalid, hopeless of recovery. A fever of gossiping instantly ran through the court. "What would happen? Would the Duke verily and indeed marry Jenny Warburton? or would he now come to his senses, make her his best bow, and seek out a more advantageous match elsewhere?—for he was held to be rather too fond of money, and Jenny had not twenty-pence portion. When Queen Caroline heard the news, the feeling of one woman for another made her say to Lady Suffolk (then Mrs. Howard): "How I pity that poor Warburton! Her agitation must be cruel; and she must so dread appearing in public, where everybody will be whispering, every eye watching her looks! Go and tell her I excuse her from attendance; she need not wait to-day,[1] nor indeed till all this tattle has subsided." Mrs. Howard hastened with the good-natured message; but instead of relieving the person pitied, whom she found sitting, stitching with the greatest composure, it only made her stare. "Not wait to-day! Why must not I wait? What's the matter? Is the Princess angry with me? Have I done anything?" "Done! Bless us, no! My dear Mrs. Warburton, it is her Royal Highness's kind consideration for you. She concludes you cannot like to wait; she is afraid of your being distressed." "Dear! I always like waiting exceedingly, and I a'n't in distress; who told her I was?" "Oh! she is sure it must overpower you; you will never be able to stand it." "Not able to stand! Why, does she think me sick! Pray tell her I am as well as ever I was in my life, and perfectly able to stand: it's the oddest fancy to have come into her head!" And back went Mrs. Howard, laughing, to make the Princess quite easy about the agitations and sensibilities of poor Warburton.

Not so cool was the other party concerned. He flew

[1] The maids of honor then lived in the palace, and there was a sort of drawing-room every day.

to her with ardor, wanted to omit the form of mourning for a woman with whom he had long ceased to think himself connected, and urged her to let their hands be joined without delay. This she peremptorily refused, though, as it appeared, rather from a whimsical kind of superstition than any sentimental nicety: "No, indeed; she would never marry a man who had a wife above ground—not she." And all his arguments and entreaties being answered only with the same words, repeated over and over again, he was forced to relinquish his design. In six months' time,[1] when the decent ceremonial had been observed, and the first wife might be presumed quite safe in her grave, their union took place.

Marriage, you know, is held an eminent breaker of spells, and Time another. Yet, palpably bewitched as the Duke of Argyll was, neither could accomplish his disenchantment. To say he proved an excellent husband would be speaking poorly: he remained throughout life a faithful, doating, adoring lover. My mother told me she had often seen him stop on entering the room, stand a moment or two gazing at the Duchess as at the loveliest object on earth, then come forward and clasp her fondly to his bosom. Upon which she never failed to look round and cry: "Do you see, you young folks? On such a day we shall have been married so many years: will your husbands' love last as long,

---

[1] The peerage books make the first Duchess die in January 1716, and the Duke marry again in June 1717. But both events happened in 1717. Before the New Style began, the year was held to commence in March.

think ye?" Human affections are so wayward that his love perhaps lasted the longer for the comfortable indifference with which it was repaid—an indifference, however, which she could not help. She loved him as much as she had the faculty of loving anything, and Dido or Eloisa could have done no more. His infatuation did literally equal what philtres and sorcery were believed to produce of old; since, over and above the charm of transcendent virtue, she certainly had that of beauty in his eyes, although in no other person's. My mother one day downright affronted him by happening to observe that a picture of her just brought home was very like. "Like?" repeated he hastily; "no, not like at all: how can anybody think it so? It does not do her justice in any respect. But step this way, my dear, and I will show you another sort of likeness"—taking out of his pocket a beautiful miniature without the least resemblance (that she could discern) to her Grace. Much embarrassed, she began to praise the painting. "Yes"—said he, as to himself, not minding her—"this *is* my Jane."

This uncommon passion stood the test of what in many cases has poisoned matrimonial comfort—of a disappointment too apt to put men unreasonably out of humor with their wives. Without undervaluing women as much as he did, it was natural that the head of so great a family should long for a son; and he longed most inordinately; while, as if to tantalize him, daughter perversely followed daughter, to the number of five (one dying a child); and his hopes, often renewed, regularly ended in fresh mortification—not the less bitter because Lord Islay was his presumptive heir. The brothers frequently disagreed about politics, and usually about everything else; at some times were on a footing of intimacy, at others not upon speaking terms. I have heard my father say, that when he was a boy under their joint direction, he could remember occasions where (non-intercourse chancing to prevail) all arrangements respecting him were to be made by letter. At best, there was that direct fundamental difference in their natures which will rarely allow the nearest and even the kindest relations to be partial sympathizing friends. The one was, properly speaking, a hero; the other, altogether a man of this world. The Duke thought Lord Islay undignified and timeserving; Lord Islay thought the Duke wrong-headed and romantic. Yet both were assuredly superior men. John had genius, with all the lights and shades thereunto appertaining; Archibald strong clear sense, sound judgment, and thorough knowledge of mankind. John, a soldier from his cradle, was warm-hearted, frank, honorable, magnanimous, but fiery-tempered, rash, ambitious, haughty, impatient of contradiction; Archibald, bred a lawyer, was cool, shrewd, penetrating, argumentative—an able man of business, and a wary, if not crafty, politician. "I wanted to discuss such an affair with my brother," he would say, "but all went wrong. I saw the Tollemache[1] blood beginning to rise, so I e'en quitted the field."

[1] Their mother, a lady of very high spirit, was a Tollemache, daughter of the Duchess of Lauderdale (Countess of Dysart in her own right) by her first husband, Sir Lionel Tollemache.

To resume the parallel. John took pleasure in wit, poetry, and the belles-lettres; Archibald in philosophical experiments, mechanics, natural history, and what had no name and little existence in his days, but is now called Political Economy. He planted your neighbor Hunt's garden for Sir Harry Bellenden, and made a place for himself (Whitton) out of a piece of Hounslow Heath, on purpose to try what shrubs and trees he could bring the barrenest soil to bear. The Duke of Argyll had a kind of court round him, consisting of a few sensible party-men, not a few Scotch dependants, a set of dull old officers who had served under his command, and a whole tribe of Campbell-cousins. Amongst these was the very handsome, very stupid, Col. Jack Campbell, in future himself Duke of Argyll, and grandfather of the present family. Lord Islay's humble companions were the ingenious men who assisted him in his scientific pursuits, or those whose inventions he patronized. Conversing as he did with all manner of people, yet still keeping his proper place in the best and highest society, the younger brother could not well be supposed to share the elder's prejudice against intelligent women. He saw women (and men too) just as they were, had no toleration for fools of either sex, and felt a supreme contempt for his sister-in-law, who, in return, hated him cordially and delighted in pecking at his friends or picking up nonsensical stories about his amours. Whenever she deplored her ill-fortune in bringing the Duke no male heir, the burthen of the lament was sure to be: "Ay! the estate will go to my Lord Islay, and he will give it all to his ———." If I say his mistresses and his natural children, you will think me sufficiently plain-spoken: the terms *she* used belonged to much more primitive English; for having been so long the companion of a man whose polished language was almost proverbial had not in the least improved her diction. It is true that he never dreamed of correcting it: his beloved Jane's vulgarity passed for uprightness and simplicity with him, and who else might reprehend the Duchess of Argyll?

Her female court, the wives of the cousins and retainers, were of course more obsequious to her than she had ever been to Queen Caroline or Queen Anne. And what homage was paid her by her own Cheshire relations we may conjecture from the reverential style of her very mother, in those letters found among Lady Greenwich's papers.

I do not deny that the good lady seems to have been formed by nature for an old nurse; yet I question whether Eton [1] would have fallen quite so prostrate before you if you had married a Duke of the blood-royal. It is, or it was, an etiquette with Princes (possibly brought from Germany) that, in formally addressing the Sovereign, his collateral relations should alter the term of kindred, if it implied superiority. For example, when Princess Amelia wrote to our late king, her nephew, she subscribed herself "his Majesty's most dutiful niece." Old Mrs. Warburton ought to have adopted this form, and remained "her Grace's most dutiful daughter"; for so completely does the poor woman's mind quail beneath the awful idea of *a Duchess*

[1] A nurse.—ED.

that she can scarcely find words to express her grateful sense of the honor conferred upon her when "*the dear young ladies*" (her own grandchildren) are sent to pay her a visit in the country.

With regard to the acquaintances her Grace made in the world at large, where everybody must make some, they could hardly help having manners more genteel than her own; but as there are always to be found goodies and gossips of very high quality, they were pretty much upon a par with her otherwise, and, like herself, guiltless of any affinity to that proscribed class, "your clever women," whom her lord's maxims authorized her to esteem for the most part no better than they should be. Gladly did she bar her doors against *all such cattle*—one person excepted, who by his express mandate had constant admittance, free egress and regress, and even no small share of authority. This was Lady Suffolk, whose judgment he valued so highly as to insist upon her being consulted in all cases which he felt his Jane incompetent to decide.

I asked my mother how such a respect for Lady Suffolk's understanding could be reconciled to his contemptuous opinion of the sex. "Oh! easily enough," replied she; "you may be confident he thought she had once been George the Second's mistress; therefore had purchased her superiority at the established price, and was an instance to confirm his system instead of defeating it."

It did nevertheless undergo something like a defeat in the latter part of his life, after he had finally broken with Sir Robert Walpole and joined the Tories against the court. Opposition, you may observe, is almost always a much more sociable body than the partisans of Government. The part of attacking raises people's spirits, gives them the spring of a vigorous courser on rising ground, makes them all hope and animation. Ministers have a load of care on their shoulders; they are to do the business as well as to talk about it; they are a little teased and perplexed by their enemies, and a vast deal more by their friends; they give formal dinners, as in duty bound, and rejoice when the task is performed.

Not to mention that, having the solid loaves and fishes to distribute, it is natural they should neglect using lesser means of attraction. In the mean while their adherents, all and each out of humor about something or other, as well as fully occupied with their own schemes and pretensions, are far better disposed to sit still and grumble than to make any lively exertions in support of the common cause. Opposition, on the contrary, who have only the easy task of finding fault, and as yet no bones of contention among themselves, are gay and disentangled, ready to engage in rounds of dinners and suppers, festive meetings, pleasant parties, and all sorts of amusements. It is no slight object with them to render their side of the question the most fashionable. Making their houses agreeable operates as a measure of policy, keeps their troops together, and gains fresh recruits, especially among the rising young men of promising talents. The ladies whom this brings into play, pleased to be of use and consequence, fall to work with their whole souls in behalf of the party their husbands, or lovers, or friends belong to; and though subject to spoil matters by their violence, yet sometimes succeed in managing them by their address.

The Duke of Argyll, now forced to bear his part in such a bustling scene, saw more of the real world and lived more in mixed company than he had ever done before; and thus unavoidably became acquainted with several women of fashion—women of exemplary lives and unspotted reputation—whom, to his great surprise, he found remarkably conversable and well-informed. He acknowledged to the other men having hitherto disbelieved that any character of the kind could exist; and he owned, with candor, that the discovery raised serious doubts whether his former notions of the sex had had a just foundation. Let me tell you, the frank avowal of these doubts was the proof of a great mind; since an ordinary one, equally under the dominion of prejudice, is ever precisely the horse in the proverb, whom one man may bring to the water, but twenty cannot make him drink. Forcing open my eyes, and inducing me to examine the objects placed before them, are quite different things; nor need we go far to light on persons who, supposing them to have the same given prepossessions as the Duke, combated by the same facts, would solve the difficulty by resolving to believe that the ladies in question secretly favored their footmen, and, settling the matter thus, cling to their own opinion as tenaciously as before.

In the Duke's case, conviction or wisdom came too late, as she mostly does. All his daughters, except Lady Mary, were grown up; his lot was cast, his career nearly closed; his home circle past all chance of improvement. My mother said it was absolutely grievous and provoking to behold the society (if society it could be called) of that house; the spirit of dulness predominating; the toad-eaters, the prosers, the chatterboxes, the old housewives and housekeepers surrounding a man not only so eminent, but so peculiarly agreeable, who, with a tone and manner that would have made nonsense pleasing, had such a variety of interesting conversation. But those that (like herself) were capable of tasting it, seldom got leave to enjoy it for five minutes in peace. Either his Jane came up and took the words out of his mouth without ceremony, or else the clack of her tea-table arose, and some tale of scandal, or history of a game at quadrille, or dissertation about buying dishclouts drowned his harmonious voice, and drove him to take refuge in a corner with one of his political or military followers. Among other gifts, he told a story admirably, with particular energy and terseness, and, conscious of excelling, did not dislike to find a willing hearer. Alas! three times out of four, no sooner had he begun than the Duchess's shrill pipe struck in: "No, no; it was not so"; "No, now, my lord, you don't tell that right; let me." Upon which, moving quietly off, he fell into his usual way of walking up and down the room, with his head bent and his hands behind him (a habit which was also my father's), till she had hammered and stammered out as much of the matter as she could recollect; then, turning round with a placid smile, he would say, "There ——, Jane has told it you."

Notwithstanding many similar instances of complaisance, you must not think he was a man governed by his wife. No one could be more master at home, where his decrees, once issued, were the nod of Jupiter, allowing no resistance, nor, indeed, meeting with any; for a sense of duty disposed her to obey; and although she had the obstinacy of a fool in the petty concerns that she viewed as her own province, yet it is but fair to say that she was quite free from any taint of the cunning which often attends weak understandings. Therefore, she never sought to sway him by cajoling or artifice. Plain truth and downright honesty were the principal features of her character; she always trod a straight path, and always meant to take the right one. In a word, she was a good woman, to the utmost of her knowledge and power. On these valuable (or rather invaluable) qualities he used to declare that his strong affection for her was grounded, and who can call such a basis insufficient?

He would, however, as soon have consulted her cat as herself upon any point of importance. When graver subjects demanded consideration, the wife, the woman, was to keep her due distance, and not presume to intermeddle. But then grave subjects and important points are so few, light and unimportant so many, and these latter start up so continually in the course of every common current working-day, that the party to whom they are carelessly (but constantly) yielded creeps on acquiring, crumb by crumb, a wonderful portion of something which, if not actual dominion, does just as well. Nor is this the least apt to happen where she has been held at the outset too utterly insignificant to alarm the pride of imperial man with a suspicion that it was in the nature of things she should ever prove the conqueror. Could a wren possibly possess some glimmering of human intellect, it would have a far better chance of influencing us than a *whole*-reasoning elephant, or one of Swift's Houyhnhnms, who, coming with the wisdom of Solomon, would find us all set in battle array to oppose him. The Duchess was her husband's darling little bird, whom he loved to indulge, dreaded to hurt, and could not have the heart to handle roughly. In addition to this tender feeling, allowances were to be made for the weakness of the sex, and its whimsies and waywardness; and it was idle to argue with women, and women must have their own foolish way. And thus it ended in her having hers pretty generally in all ordinary daily proceedings, which were all she cared for.

On the head of money—that frequent cause of dissension between husband and wife—they did not differ very widely, both being of saving tempers. Not that I was by any means taught to suppose him the "*miser*" he is represented by Lord Orford—ever caustic, and especially bitter against him as the opponent of his father. My authorities pictured him as strictly just, habitually regular and careful, maybe somewhat *too* careful, in his expenses, but never mean; very capable of generous actions, and, when he gave, giving nobly. His table, his equipage, his whole establishment, were as handsome as possible, and as well suited to his rank and fortune. In the lesser domestic details, which he knew nothing of, and she managed as she pleased, Jenny Warburton's head would sometimes peep out over the Duchess's robes. Yet she was charitable to the poor, and on the whole rather narrow than covetous, only retaining here and there fragments of those early habits of frugality which, in her maiden state, had been both necessary and laudable. After his death she remembered with reverence the grandeur of his notions; and though still occasionally disturbed about twopence-halfpenny, was desirous that in the main her arrangements should be such as became the Duke of Argyll's widow.

You are sensible how often things, seemingly of no moment at all, come, in some unforeseen manner, or at some distance of time, to bear strongly on others of the greatest, and it is amusing to detect the concealed chain of circumstances by which this is brought to pass. But we need not trace the course and effects of her Grace's influence through any intricate mazes: it went directly to one point—in most people's opinion sufficiently material. The daughters, being daughters of the useless, mischievous sex—their birth a calamity, themselves an incumbrance—were unfortunately classed among the trifles left to her sole superintendence, their father interfering only with a negative, so curious and characteristic that it would be a pity to pass it over unnoticed. He forbade them learning French, because *"one language was enough for a woman to talk in"*; and the Duchess, who did not know a word of it, had not the least mind to dispute the position. As what they should be taught was a question wholly beneath his attention, and as she was convinced by her own experience and example, ready at hand to refer to, that most other branches of education were equally needless with foreign tongues, the young ladies learned writing and accompts from the steward, and needlework from a governess very little superior to the housekeeper. "For after all," reasoned their mother, "if you had a pack of girls, if you were so unlucky, what upon earth could you do with them but find husbands to take them off your hands?" Well, then, *she* knew nothing of this, and *she* never was taught that; and, pray, had not she married? Ay, and married the Duke of Argyll! No wonder she thought the argument conclusive. Her grudge against them for not being boys (which was yet greater than his), together with the natural indifference of her temper, prevented her concerning herself about them, while children, further than to ascertain that they were safe and well; and she could rest satisfied without constant ocular demonstration of that, seldom suffering them to come and disturb the dogs and cats who occupied her drawing-room, plagued the company at dinner,[1] and engrossed all the fondness she had to bestow. Lady Caroline, the eldest daughter, dined below stairs on a Sunday; and was just so far distin-

---

[1] One poor mortal, a daily guest, had an antipathy to cats. "*To break him of it,*" as she said, she would place a huge he-cat on the back of his chair, as he sat at table. The Duke, after making fruitless efforts to protect him, was forced to laugh it off as a joke not worth minding. Her dogs were always pugs; and down to the end of her days every visitor on every visit was assured that Pug and Puss (pronounced alike) did not live together like dog and cat.

guished in a few other particulars as to let the humble friends of the family perceive that it would be prudent to begin celebrating her charms and perfections. Otherwise she chiefly inhabited the nursery, which the rest hardly ever quitted. At Sudbrook this was the small house built on purpose for them, and called the Young Ladies' House. Here they did what they pleased, nobody caring, and romped as much as they pleased with my father and uncle when the Eton holidays added them to the parties.

If Time would have but stood still, this order of things might have lasted for ever unchanged. But he has a trick of moving onward: the children grew up, as all children do, and the parents—although surprised at it, as most parents are, could no longer exclude them from their society. The seven stages of human life have been the same ever since Adam and Eve commenced peopling the world; yet few persons can slide from the second to the third, from childhood into youth, without amazing their elder friends as much as if the thing had never happened before. This said in a parenthesis, we resume the house of Argyll. Lady Caroline, the eldest child, and in some sort the heiress (for the Duke meant to make her a son by giving her his English estates), was presented at Court, and her sisters were admitted into the parlor, where, for some time, fear of their father kept them all in silence and decorum, Lady Mary excepted, who was too young (being only fifteen or sixteen when he died), and had too much of the Tollemache blood to be afraid of anybody. Her fearless prattle entertained him; and she grew a favorite, to the great detriment of her future disposition. It is strange how very inconsiderate men, sensible men, nay, men of great abilities, will often be in their treatment of children. Reversing the practice of the children themselves, who invariably talk to their dolls as rational creatures, they toy with their luckless plaything as if it were destined never to become one, and had no more to do with mind and soul than a dancing-dog or a monkey. I have repeatedly heard my father impute the ungovernable violence of Lady Mary's temper in after life to his uncle's injudicious indulgence of her at the period when she was just old enough to know she ought to overcome her passions, and young enough to have resisted them with some success. Not indulgence alone; for, exactly as you have seen a schoolboy teach his pony to lash out, and his cur to snap at people's fingers, he took delight to put her in a fury, crying, "Look! look at Mary!" when she flew like a little tigress, screaming, scratching, and tearing; then, after laughing heartily, he would finish the improving lesson by coaxing her with sugar-plums to kiss and be friends.

The timid reserve of the elder ladies did not last long. Lord Strafford, a very young man of large fortune, happening to dine at their father's on his return from his travels, was so charmed with the beauty of the second, Lady Anne, that he immediately asked her hand in marriage. After she was disposed of, all restrictions seemed to cease, all bounds were broken down; the others freely exalted the discordant voices which they all inherited from their mother, and became the most noisy, hoydening girls in London. In my own day, when they were the most unmerciful censurers of young people's dress and behavior, my mother, who had herself a mind far above laying an absurd stress upon trifles, used to laugh at certain of her recollections, and attribute their violent wrath against the gay world to spleen at growing old, and envy of the pleasures they could no longer partake.

I mention my own day. Ere that could well be said to dawn, I remember having seen the last Earl of Lichfield;[1] a red-faced old gentleman, shaking all over with the palsy, who had almost drunk away his senses, and seemed hardly to know what he was saying or doing. Marvellous are the metamorphoses produced by Time. You may suppose I found it very difficult to believe that this object, formerly Lord Quarendon, had been not only handsome, lively, and agreeable, but much more—the most promising in point of parts among all the young men of the Tory (then the Opposition and Patriot) party—a bud of genius fostered by its chiefs as likely to prove the future pride of their garland.

[1] The last but one—George Henry Lee, third Earl of Lichfield, Chancellor of Oxford University. Gilly Williams writes to G. Selwyn, 11th January, 1765: "At the rehearsal on Wednesday night of the speech at Lord Halifax's, Lord Lichfield came extremely drunk, and proposed amendments and alterations, to the no small amusement of the company." Lord Lichfield married Dinah, daughter and heiress of Sir Thomas Frankland, Bart., of Thirkleby, but died *s.p.* 1772, when the title went to his uncle, Robert, fourth and last Earl, who therefore never could have been Lord Quarendon. The first Earl, Sir Edward Lee, fifth Baronet of Ditchley, married Charlotte Fitzroy, daughter of Charles II. by Barbara, Duchess of Cleveland.—ED.

The Duke of Argyll, in particular, caressed and extolled him, made him free of his house, and, one might say, taught his family to admire him. Blind, meanwhile, like many a man in the same case, to the glaring probability that a young lady would not admire long without admitting some warmer feeling, he never asked himself how he should relish so natural an occurrence. Lord Quarendon had a father alive, not inclined to part with his money; a mother and sisters[1] to be provided for;—in short, he was not by any means a great match. Therefore, since it was certain nothing but a great match would do for Lady Caroline Campbell, it never came into his Grace's head that either party could possibly think of the other. But they found it both possible and pleasant to think, and think on; and he remained almost the only person not apprised of their mutual attachment, until Lord Dalkeith's making her serious proposals brought about a partial discovery.

The Buccleuch family had rested in comparative obscurity for two or three generations past. However inclined King William had once appeared to favor the unfortunate Duke of Monmouth, yet a direct attempt to claim the Crown was a fact to be jealously remembered by its successive wearers; and, so far from reversing his attainder and restoring his honors, as was done in other cases (for instance, to the Argylls themselves), William hastened to bestow the title elsewhere, creating Lord Mordaunt Earl of Monmouth. The

[1] Ditchley went to the eldest sister, Lady Dillon, on the death of her uncle, the last Earl.—ED.

Duchess presently married a second husband, Lord Cornwallis, who had his own interests to mind. Lord Dalkeith, her eldest son, died in her lifetime, at thirty years old; and her grandson, now Duke of Buccleuch, a man of mean understanding and meaner habits, did no credit to his ancestry. In his youth a match was settled between him and your grandmother, Lady Jane Douglas,[1] but broken off; and her brother, the Duke of Douglas, fought a duel with him in consequence. Supposing a story true which was current at the time, that she had owned to the Duke of Buccleuch her repugnance, and, throwing herself on his honor, desired to be screened from the anger of her relations, this duel would seem to denote something chivalrous on his part, auguring better things than ensued. He married another Lady Jane Douglas, the Duke of Queensberry's sister; but, after her death, which happened in a few years, plunged into such low amours, and lived so entirely with the lowest company, that, although he resided constantly in the neighborhood of London, his person was scarcely known to his equals, and his character fell into utter contempt.[2]

Yet in spite of the thousand disadvantages of having

[1] *The* Lady Jane of the "Douglas Cause."—ED.
[2] It was believed that not long before his death he married a Windsor washerwoman. Your uncle, Henry, Duke of Buccleuch, told me that when he was a boy at Eton a middle-aged woman of decent appearance one day insisted upon seeing him. She gazed at him earnestly, kissed and blessed him, and, without saying anything more, went away. He had afterward reason to think that this was his grandfather's widow, who received an annuity from his guardians on condition of not assuming the title.

such a father, the son proved a gentleman; far from handsome, it was true—not of brilliant parts, no Lord Quarendon, but essentially good, amiable, and worthy. These qualities, added to great rank and fortune, made the Duke of Argyll readily accept his offer, not at all doubting his daughter's cheerful concurrence. And if (as I grant it probable) he thought she had nothing to do with the business further than to receive his commands and obey them, still you must beware of going headlong, and setting him down as an unfeeling tyrant. To judge fairly of those who lived long before us, or of foreigners, we should put quite apart both the usages and the notions of our own age or country, and strive to adopt for the moment such as prevailed in theirs. He followed hard upon the time, remember, when it was common for mere children to be united, or at least betrothed, by their parents; when Lady Russel, had she been asked, in the midst of her negotiation with Lord Devonshire, whether young Mistress Rachel was enamoured of his son, would infallibly have deemed the question an impertinent, insipid jest, or the inquirer a madman.

Nor were marriages thus arranged among the great alone; the very proverb, framed, as all proverbs are, by and for the vulgar, "Marry your daughter betimes, for fear she should marry herself," is a convincing proof of the contrary. Consult, indeed, an author of much later date, one certainly not too well versed in the manners of high life, one whose theme and object it was to treat of love—Richardson, I mean, the great father of modern novels—Richardson himself cannot help betraying an evident predilection for matches thus soberly settled. In No. 97 of the *Rambler* (written by him) you find his *beau-idéal* of a matrimonial transaction carried on exactly as it ought to be. The young man can see the young woman only at church, where her beauty and pious demeanor win his heart. He applies to her parents through a mutual friend; they acquaint her with his offer; she is all resignation to their will, for perhaps (mark the *perhaps*) she had seen him at church likewise. Then it proceeds: "Her relations applaud her for her duty; friends meet, points are adjusted, delightful perturbations, hopes, and a few lovers' fears fill up the vacant space, *till an interview is granted.*" In plain English, the two persons concerned have never exchanged a single syllable in their lives till they meet as an affianced couple. And this he calls marrying for love! Brush away all the fine words, and how far it differs from Dr. Johnson's scheme of people being paired by the Chancellor I leave you to determine. But I have been drawn into a terribly long digression.

As facts tell themselves, I need not say Lord Dalkeith's addresses were successful; but you will be impatient to hear what resistance they met with, and how it was overcome. When Miss Townshend[1] eloped forty years afterward, a vulgar, abusive newspaper, such as your present *John Bull*, caught this old anecdote by the tail, and, giving a blundering version of it, bade

[1] Miss Anne Townshend, Lady Dalkeith's daughter by her second husband, Charles Townshend. She married, in 1779, Richard Wilson, Esq.—ED.

her mother recollect "that she had nearly been in the oven herself." Upon which, Lady Greenwich thought fit to tell Lady Emily Kerr (Macleod) her own story in her own way. And a very fine one she made it as ever formed the foundation of tragedy or romance: a conflict between passionate love and sacred duty, adorned with tears, fits, despair, and (for aught I know) delirium. She kept her bed, she said, for many days; the physicians gave but faint hopes of her recovery;—yet still her dear father remained inflexible. Then she had such a love, such a profound veneration for him—and, to say the truth, Lord Dalkeith was so unexceptionable. In short, after sufferings not to be described, she was led to the altar more dead than alive, and there plighted her unwilling vows. But in time, becoming sensible of her husband's excellencies, she perceived the great wisdom of her father's choice, which (Heaven knew!) had made her far happier than she could have been had she followed her own foolish inclinations.

Nothing could sound more reasonable; only, something nearer the time of action, my mother heard a different tale from Lady Betty Mackenzie, who, though not wise, was ever a *straightforward* person of strict veracity. She freely acknowledged that a positive engagement subsisted between her sister and Lord Lichfield, perfectly well known to her mother and every other person in the house, saving its master. Even little Lady Mary could give her verdict upon the cause; and she hit right, as children and young folks are sometimes led to do by their natural reason. "I know sister

Caroline must not marry Lord Quarendon if papa disapproves of it; but, to be sure, she cannot marry anybody else." Sister Caroline did cry, as sentiment required, for near a week; and Lady Betty and Lady Strafford cried too, in concern for her distress, and dread of the scene likely to follow when papa should know all. Before this came to pass, however—to the best of Lady Betty's belief—one morning, on opening the unhappy lady's door, she was accosted with these words, "Well, sister, I have consented to marry my Lord Dalkeith," uttered in such an easy, indifferent tone that she protested she stood staring as if a sudden blow had taken away her breath. Thenceforth she saw no more symptoms of grief or discontent: the old lover ceased to be named, the new one was graciously smiled upon, and everybody fell to discussing wedding-clothes and equipages with the usual alacrity.

Very soon after their marriage the Duke did his son-in-law a most material service by obtaining for his father and family the restoration of one of the Duke of Monmouth's forfeited English peerages—the earldom of Doncaster, by which title their descendants now sit in Parliament. I mention this here to avoid future interruption; for we have not yet done with Lord Quarendon, who bore his disappointment so unlike a patient, good Christian as to prove that he put little faith (whoever might put much) in the reluctance of the bride or her agonizing struggles, or her pious submission to parental authority. He was furious: far too angry for any magnanimous feeling. He went about calling her a mercenary jilt to whoever would listen, with all the other epithets which men, whether of high or low degree, are apt to be lavish upon such occasions. Not content with this, he took measures to lay the whole affair before the Duke of Argyll: it is even said, sent him her letters—a severe revenge upon the person least to blame, since, in fact, the Duke had never imagined that anything more than a mere girlish fancy stood in the way of her accepting Lord Dalkeith. And, however great his displeasure might have been on finding her otherwise engaged without his consent, he was the last man in the world to have sanctioned, much less exacted, a direct breach of promise. He thought, like Walpole's Florian—

> "A soldier's honor is his virtue. Gownmen
> Wear it for show, and barter it for gold,
> And have it still: a soldier and his honor
> Exist together, and together perish."

The blow, then, struck at his heart; not solely on account of Lady Caroline's conduct (although that gave him mortification enough), but because it forcibly overthrew his good opinion of the Duchess. She had been privy to all. She had concealed all from him. She had helped her daughter to deceive him. There was an end of his firm reliance on her affection, her truth, her integrity. The cherished illusion of his life was at length dispelled and done away. About the same time his health began to break; a paralytic disorder afflicted his nerves; but my mother said the tokens of a deeply wounded spirit were very distinguishable from the effects of the disease, as was also the change of manner toward his Jane. He did not become harsh to her; but his coldness, silence, and melancholy abstraction were striking—tacit reproaches, altogether unfelt and even unperceived. The good woman, who in reality had erred only from sheer weakness and folly, being the dupe of a daughter cleverer than herself, saw nothing that ailed him but bodily illness; and, to show due concern for that, fulfilled the duty of a faithful wife by fidgeting and fussing about him with a tormenting assiduity which must have been the one thing wanting to complete Job's trials. Tease—tease—tease, from morning till night. "Now, my lord, do eat this." "Now, my lord, don't eat that." "Now, pray put on your great-coat." "Now, be sure you take your draught." "Now, you must not sit by the fire; it's too hot." "Now, you should not stand at the window; it's too cold." "Oh, how well I remember the way of it," said my mother; "and how I used to pity the poor man!" He never spoke one word in answer; seldom raised his head to look at her; but, for the sake of peace, usually did as she would have him, seeming quite unable to contend. In this condition he lingered, with transient gleams of amendment, but in the main drooping more and more, until repeated paralytic attacks carried him off, a twelvemonth after the marriage of Lady Dalkeith.

It has been abundantly shown that the Duchess's nature was not susceptible of very violent emotions. She could grieve (as she loved) only as much as she could. Yet on this event she uttered an expression that was touching, because it implied a meek sense of her own inferiority of character. "Well" (said she, fetching a

A MEMOIR 37

deep sigh), "I have been the favorite of a great man!" She continued to inhabit Sudbrook and the town house in Bruton Street, both of which he bequeathed her for her life; and this outlasted his such a number of years that I myself have a faint recollection of being put into mourning on her decease.[1]

I once heard Lady Betty relate a circumstance that greatly contributed to depress her father's spirits in the last sad year of his life. Lord ―――[2] (I have totally forgotten the name), a very old acquaintance, whom he had not seen since they were both young men, came unexpectedly to Adderbury. The Duke gave him the most cordial reception, showed him his grounds, insisted he should stay dinner, and seemed so cheered by his company that the day passed over uncommonly well. But at parting, when he attended his guest to his carriage, "*that creature*," quoth Lady Betty, suddenly turned round on the step to whisper, "I had orders to give you this," slipped a paper into his hand, leaped in, and drove away. It was a letter from the Pretender, full of high-flown compliments on his Grace's public spirit in opposing the Court:[3] a conduct which, it might be hoped, was a sure sign of his having at last (though late) espoused the rightful cause,

[1] She died on April 15th, 1767, at No. 16 Bruton Street, when Lady Louisa was nearly ten. The Duke died 4th October, 1743.—ED.

[2] James, fourth Earl of Barrymore. This happened in 1742. See H. Walpole, i. 182. Walpole's insinuations against the Duke's loyalty arose entirely from party feeling.—ED.

[3] He had lately resigned all the posts he held, as he did not approve of the policy of the Government.—ED.

and resolved to reinstate his lawful sovereign. Support like his must insure success; and, were that once obtained, what reward could be denied him? He instantly sent the letter to the King, together with another professing unalterable loyalty, and protesting his utter abhorrence of the treason suggested: protestations which were perfectly sincere; for the Hanover succession had no steadier friend.' Yet that its enemies should have dared thus to tamper with him, and have interpreted his political conduct as forwarding their designs, wounded him to the very soul. He writhed under the insult; could not forget it; and Lady Betty affirmed that to his last hour it rankled in his mind.

His English dukedom of Greenwich became extinct; his brother Archibald succeeded to the Argyll titles and estates; and his eldest daughter inherited considerable property, including Adderbury in Oxfordshire and Caroline Park near Edinburgh. So she was rich, prosperous, and, above all, fortunate in a husband. By all I could gather concerning Lord Dalkeith, he belonged to the species of those quiet, silent, dull men

[1] In answering an attack on himself in the House of Lords during the Porteous debate, the Duke of Argyll said: ". . . I have, ever since I set out in the world (and I believe few set out more early), served my Prince with my tongue; I have served him with any little interest I had, and I have served him in my trade; and were I to-morrow to be stripped of all the employments I have endeavored honestly to deserve, I would serve him again to the utmost of my power, and to the last drop of my blood. . . ." During Queen Anne's last illness, he and the Duke of Somerset attended the Council without summons, in their right as Privy Councillors, and frustrated the intention of those who proposed to proclaim the Chevalier de St. George.—ED.

who are overlooked in gay society and seldom mentioned by the world. But I imagine he very much resembled his uncle Charles (the *good*), Duke of Queensberry, in mildness, benevolence, kindness of heart, and extreme sweetness of temper. Like him, too, he fondly loved his wife, and was content to let the government be on her shoulder. Her Grace of Queensberry—a spoiled, wilful beauty, most bewitching, most perverse and provoking, with superior natural parts, but what the Scotch term an enormous *bee in her bonnet*—wanted the control of a far stronger hand than the poor Duke's to curb her innumerable whims and caprices, which ran riot, and would have tired out the patience of any other man breathing. Lady Dalkeith, a woman of a more common sort, could rest pretty well satisfied with having her own way in every particular, and be good-humored (at least while young) as long as she was pleased. Accordingly, her lord and she were reckoned the happiest of happy couples during the brief period of their married life. Placed at the head of the world, and of an age to enjoy its gifts, they spent their time gayly in entertaining their friends at home, or in seeking livelier pleasures abroad.

You may have heard of their acting plays: this was set on foot by the Duchess of Queensberry,[1] who had always some *rage*, some reigning fancy, which she

---

[1] She invited Quin, of whom she was very fond, down to Amesbury. "And now, Mr. Quin," said she, "I have been considering how to amuse you in the country. Suppose we act a play?" "Madam," replied Quin, "if you asked a grocer to dinner, would you treat him with figs?"

carried to excess. For one year she could think of nothing but the stage, and fitted up a small theatre in Queensberry House,[1] where Otway's "Orphan," a good deal clipped and pared, and Young's "Revenge," were each acted three times. The performers were a family party of brothers and sisters, or cousins bred up together from childhood: Lord and Lady Dalkeith, Lady Betty (then unmarried), my father, Mr. Mackenzie, and a beautiful youth, Colonel Campbell's second son, long afterward known to you as that beautiful old man Lord Frederic Campbell; Mrs. Campbell's brother, Sir Harry Bellenden, and two or three elderly dependants of the Argylls and Queensberrys were pressed into the service to fill minor parts; the Duchess not acting herself, but indefatigably managing, prompting, and overlooking the whole. "The Orphan," in particular, succeeded so well through Lady Dalkeith's *Monimia* and my father's *Castalio* that Frederick, Prince of Wales, had his wish to see it intimated to the Duke of Queensberry; and it was therefore performed a fourth time for the Prince and Princess,[2] and the audience they chose to nominate. For then, and down to a much later day, when-

---

[1] Queensberry House, built in 1726, stood in Burlington Gardens (No. 9); the site is now occupied by the Western Branch of the Bank of England. ("Royal Kalendar" and Wheatley's "London.")
—ED.

[2] Behold the whole and sole foundations of my father's "*having been used to act plays for the amusement of the Prince and his Court.*" Had Lord Henry Fitzgerald become a Minister, some memoir-writer would tell the world he had performed *Varanes* and *Lord Trinket* at Richmond House, to pay his court to the present King. [See H. Walpole, ix. 123–126.]

ever any of the royal family accepted an entertainment from a subject, they pointed out the company they would have invited to meet them. The pictures [1] you have seen of your grandfather and grandmother, and those of Lady Betty and Mr. Mackenzie, were taken in their dresses for the characters of "The Orphan." Perhaps I dwell too long on these trifles; in my own youth they pleased my imagination, and I had such delight in getting at all the details of former days that I believe I made my mother tell me every old story a thousand times, and teased her with a thousand questions about every little circumstance.

As I intimated above, the holiday season of Lord and Lady Dalkeith's festivities was destined to have a very short duration. They had been married but about seven years, when the former, going for a few days to Adderbury with Sir James Peachy,[2] his intimate friend, and by alliance his near relation, was seized with a sudden illness. Danger came rapidly on, and the fourth day he died in Sir James's arms, having just had power to dictate and sign a will which his friend took down on the first scrap of paper at hand. This left to Lady Dalkeith ten thousand pounds—all he could dispose of—and constituted her the guardian of his children. Their eldest son had died an infant. There remained living a daughter, Caroline, who survived her father but three or four

[1] Now at Dalkeith.—ED.
[2] Created Lord Selsey in 1794. He married Lady Caroline Scott, daughter of Lord Deloraine, and granddaughter of the Duke of Monmouth—of course Lord Dalkeith's cousin.

years, and three boys—Henry, shortly after Duke of Buccleuch, James, and Campbell. ANOTHER CHILD[1] had not yet seen the light.

[1] Lady Frances Scott, afterward the second wife of Lord Douglas, and mother of Lady Scott, for whom this Memoir was written.—ED.

II

THE circles produced by throwing stones into water, dear Car, are no bad emblem of the influence which generations, as they pass, have on those that succeed them. That of the immediate parents upon the children is strong and visible; the grandchildren show its traces but faintly; when it widens to great-grandchildren it vanishes wholly away. John, Duke of Argyll, is no more to you than his ancestor the Marquis; Lady Greenwich herself very little; yet she, and even her sisters, had so much to do with a subject in which you take the deepest interest, that their characters must be developed in order to render this well understood. Setting her aside for certain reasons, let me give you an idea of the other three.

Lady Strafford was held strikingly like her father, must have been beautiful when young, and when old retained uncommon sweetness of countenance. To quote Horace Walpole's early description of her in his "Advice to a Painter":—

> "The crescent on her brow displayed
> In curls of loveliest brown inlaid,
> With every charm to rule the night,
> Like Dian, Strafford wooes the sight.
> The easy shape, the piercing eye,
> The snowy bosom's purity;

> The unaffected gentle phrase
> Of native wit in all she says,
> Eckhardt, for these thy art's too faint,
> You may admire, but cannot paint."

Whether the "native wit" was truth or compliment, may be doubted. Physical causes prematurely weakened her understanding; but I should suppose it could never have ranked above the *mediocre,* or what the men mean when they say (rather saucily), "Such a one has sense enough for a pretty woman." Although habitually led by her sisters to inveigh, as they did, against all present fashions, she had neither spleen nor bitterness in her own nature; nor was there much resemblance between her and them except in a loud shrill voice common to the four, which gained them a variety of nicknames, such as the Screaming Sisterhood, the Bawling Campbells, and so forth, and made Lord Strafford, who was not without humor, say, slyly: "I can always tell whether any of *my* ladies are in a house by the time I set my foot in the porter's hall."

Notwithstanding this voice, she had a mild, gentle temper; and having been married out of the nursery, and never in her life accustomed to act or think for herself, she was very like an amiable child, looking up to its governor with great respect but some portion of fear, while the said governor, *alias* husband, though extremely fond of her, held the reins of authority tight, and would be obeyed. When I knew her, she loved company and diversions as well as any girl of eighteen, and brooked as ill the restraints imposed by his lordship, who (long since tired of them himself) often forbade her going into crowds, always insisted upon her coming home at an early hour, and (worst of all) usually carried her off to Yorkshire a month sooner than anybody else left town. He was of a selfish temper, yet in this (to give him his due) he chiefly consulted her welfare; for she had that terrible infirmity, the falling sickness, with such an unconsciousness of it that she would say carelessly, "The little faintings I am subject to now and then." Never did I behold my mother so shocked and unhinged as at her return from a card-party, where she had witnessed one of these little faintings: in reality, a succession of the most frightful convulsions, which came on suddenly, and lasted above an hour. The moment assistance was summoned, Lady Strafford's footmen ran in to hold her, a task far beyond women's strength; and they told the company that they had their lord's strict orders never to quit any place where she was, but always to wait below stairs unknown to her, in case their help should be wanted. The next morning we had scarcely breakfasted when Lord Strafford arrived. I left the room, and he opened his heart fully to my mother, for whom he had ever a particular respect.

"I am aware" (said he) "how churlish and tyrannical Lady Strafford's sisters think me for thwarting her inclinations as much as I am forced to do. You know those ladies: they are not convinceable people; if they once take a notion in their heads, no human power can beat it out again; so I cut the matter short, am peremptory, and let them rail at me as loudly as they please. But now, when you have seen with your own eyes what her malady is, can you wonder I wish to hinder its being perpetually exposed to the world? She never goes to a public place but I pass the evening in misery, dreading what may have happened. Hot rooms, noise, bustle, and even the hurry of spirits produced by pleasure, have an evident tendency to bring on these attacks, which are fast undermining her constitution. While she leads a quiet life in the country, keeping good hours, and breathing pure air, they occur comparatively seldom. Am I, then, to blame for shortening her stay here as much as I possibly can?"

Thus far he defended himself well; but he should also have considered the necessity of rendering retirement pleasant to a woman of an uncultivated, vacant mind, unused to reading, and soon tired of working cross-stitch in spectacles. At this time their intimates were mostly dead or dispersed; they had few neighbors, fewer visitors; he was too stiff to make new acquaintances; he hated humble companions; and, in short, Wentworth Castle became a magnificent hermitage, where the Mackenzies and other relations, who sometimes called in their way to or from the farther North, rarely stayed above four-and-twenty hours. Lady Mary Coke, indeed, had been in the habit of paying it longer visits; but latterly her domineering spirit, and his love of his own way, increased in such happy proportion that, after one stormy encounter, he made a private vow she should never invade him again. And poor Lady Strafford, who lived in constant apprehension of their quarrelling outright, and whom Lady

Mary had once or twice scolded into fits, honestly owned she did not regret his determination. *That* sister was beyond control; the others stood in too much awe of him to take liberties, being warded off by a formal civility, an array of bows and ladyships, which nothing less than prowess like hers could attempt to break through.

Lady Strafford delighted in animals of every sort and species; had favorite horses, dogs, cats, squirrels, parroquets, and singing-birds. Nay, I remember to this hour the pleasure it gave me, when a child, to see a couple of tame green lizards, which she kept in a box, set loose to sport and catch flies in the sunshine. She was also passionately fond of children, courting all young mothers to bring her their babies, and even their school-boys and -girls. Indeed, she would have lived surrounded by young people, if her lord had indulged her taste as freely in this respect as in the other. But he protected the brute creation himself, and shrank from the two-legged ungovernables likely to throw his house out of the windows. The truth was this: both of them bitterly deplored their ill-fate in being childless; both (she more especially) felt the want of objects deeply interesting the heart. But, as lesser motives of regret will often mingle with greater, the feeling operated differently upon the man who had longed for heirs and the woman who pined for playthings. Besides, the most complying, most tractable young folks on earth must have put him, more or less, out of his way—that same *way* which is ever the first of all considerations with the selfish.

Poor man! he suffered severely for having clung to it; and, through his dislike to admit any third person as a permanent inmate, forgot how dangerous it was for Lady Strafford ever to be left a single instant quite alone. The servants, on opening her dressing-room door, one winter's day, discovered her lying senseless against the grate, too much burned for recovery, although she lingered near a week in existence. This manner of dying was shocking; the event itself not to be regretted, as her intellects were already impaired by the epileptic disease, and she would probably have become utterly imbecile had she lived a very little longer.

To poor Lord Strafford, however, it was checkmate— the loss of his all. It left him alone in the wide world; nor do I believe he ever enjoyed another moment of comfort during the few years he survived her. But not even his real, deep, and hopeless sorrow could awe the indefatigable spirit of gossiping, or prevent it from finding him a second wife in six months' time; and of all the birds in the air, and all the fishes in the water, whom should it think fit to bestow on him but—Myself!!! Our approaching nuptials were announced in every newspaper. Having always looked on him as an old uncle, I should as soon have expected that the world would marry me to Mr. Mackenzie, if Lady Betty had been the person deceased. Therefore, it was impossible to forbear laughing, in spite of my concern for his misfortune; and when the return of winter brought him to London, I am afraid he made me laugh still more; for no man of five-and-twenty could have seemed more fearful of confirming the report by being seen to speak to me or look at me. I tell you this nonsensical story chiefly for the sake of an admirable *bon mot* (*tant soit peut libertin*) which it drew from Lady Dye Beauclerk, who knew nothing of either, except our ages. "Soh!" said she to Mrs. Herbert, "your friend Lady L. S. is going to marry her great-grandfather, is she? If she can hold her nose, and swallow the dose at once, it may do very well. *But most people would be apt to take a little sweetmeat in their mouths afterward.*"

III

LADY BETTY MACKENZIE'S figure, though always too thin, passed for fine in her youth; her face was even then plain, but not yet seamed and disfigured as we saw it by the confluent smallpox. The older she grew, the stronger those who had known her mother thought the resemblance between them in features, manner, and mind. Like the Duchess, she was honest, upright, well-meaning, good-natured; like her, ill-bred, positive, and anything but wise. She did not, however, inherit her Grace's insensibility: there they were very dissimilar; for Lady Betty had a warm heart, and most assuredly the power of loving. I defy a more devoted attachment to exist than she had to my uncle; and being love of the genuine, sterling kind (marked by a sincere preference of another to self), which always ennobles the character, it raised her above the folly of hers wherever he was concerned. Her constant attention to his wishes, and visible delight in his presence, were not debased by any silly fondness unbecoming their age. If, through youthful flippancy, one sometimes simpered at the looks of affection exchanged between the ugly, wayward old woman and the good man in a bob-wig, one's heart presently smote one; since, in sober earnest, one could not but allow that their steady, cordial, perfect union was a sight beautiful to behold.

Originally, as I have heard, the love began on her side. He could have rested in cousinly—or brotherly—regard and esteem for ever had not her fervent passion at length attracted his notice, and won a grateful return. When people marry on these terms, the wife is sure to be very humble, very submissive; and so was Lady Betty for several years, knowing no will but his: an order of things that had changed before my time. His easiness leaving most matters to her guidance, she ended by having all that influence which, in the long run, foolish women seldom fail to acquire (the Lord knows how) over sensible husbands.

With respect to Mr. Mackenzie, I came in at the fifth act of the play, as he must have been near fifty when I first remember him. But, by all accounts, I should have seen him much the same man five-and-twenty years earlier. The principal change was what time often effects: a temper once impetuous had subsided into calmness, and left him the best-humored mortal alive—always in good spirits, always happy, fond of society and, from his lively, amusing conversation formed to delight it; yet with pursuits in mathematics, astronomy, and all the exact sciences (to say nothing of a close attention to business) which occupied his mind pleasantly when he was alone. Such as I describe him, you may suppose he could make himself very agreeable to the young: only with us, his relations, he had a trick teasing to all except absolute simpletons. You never grew up for him: at eighteen you were five years old; at thirty—nay, forty—not above twelve; assailed with jokes and nursery-stories, "enough," as Miss Hoyden says in the play, "to make one ashamed before one's love." Girl or woman, you found this annoying; but for men——! I have seen my elder brothers ready to knock him down.

At the same time, he felt little indulgence for youthful follies—apparently because his own nature was too placid and steady ever to have known the force of strong temptation, his blood too temperate to have ever boiled. He had been a man of gallantry, we were told; and we could easily believe it. He had liked what is called *flirting* rather more than Lady Betty approved. This, too, was very credible; but in my life I never saw a person I should have pronounced so passionless. A sort of instinct would have made you refrain from giving way to the least enthusiasm in his presence; you would have forborne to speak before him of those emotions that convulse and tear the heart; you would scarcely have risked naming an unfortunate attachment—not through your dread of his frowns and remonstrances, but for fear of being most good-humoredly chucked under the chin. The conclusion I draw is, that in this uncle of mine there had existed two separate, different men; that one soul had at a certain moment quitted his frame, and another of quite distinct properties entered it, and taken peaceable possession. For surely there are extraordinary mental commotions which (once thoroughly experienced) do in general leave as indelible marks behind them as those violent bodily diseases which change the whole mass of our blood; and it would not have been more astonishing to learn that a woman with the loveliest smoothness of complexion had had the same virulent smallpox as Lady Betty than to hear—what was the fact—that Mr. Mackenzie's reason and his life were once upon the point of falling a sacrifice to the wildest and most romantic passion that ever agitated a human bosom.

The object of it was the Barberini, a celebrated opera-dancer, known and admired throughout Europe, of decent manners and uncommon attractions, but in no part of the wicked world held more inflexibly cruel than other ladies of her profession. I cannot tell whether Mr. Mackenzie first saw her abroad, or in England, where she danced for one season. Wherever it was, he became her slave almost immediately, loving her, not as opera-dancers are usually loved, but

"With that respect, that fearful homage, paid her"

which might have gratified an archduchess of Austria, and with a diffidence which made him tremble to propose the only terms he believed it possible that purity like hers could listen to. For what was he?—what had he to offer in rank, wealth, and situation worthy her acceptance? How might he dare to indulge the presumptuous hope of gaining that interest in her heart which alone could tempt so exalted a being to bless him with her hand? When, after a proper interval of difficulty and delay, the prospect of such happiness did open upon him, his raptures were immoderate. He announced his good fortune to my grandmother, Lady Mary Wortley, in a letter which she preserved, informing her that he had reason to think himself the most lucky of men: he was about to marry a woman whose preference did him the highest honor—one infinitely his superior in every particular excepting birth. What his family might say to it he could not tell, and did not care; he only knew they ought to be proud of the connection. But he really thought a man of his age was fully competent to judge for himself, and provide for his own happiness. To the last sentence Lady Mary affixed this pithy marginal note, "*The poor boy is about nineteen.*"

On these occasions relations and guardians are sad, troublesome people. My uncle's uncle, Archibald, Duke of Argyll, such another cool, considerate person as his future self, instead of feeling due pride in the connection, or leaving "a man of his age" to secure his own happiness, officiously took measures to disturb it. Though the lovers were to be united far off, at Venice, where they hoped they might defy his authority, yet, having long hands, and putting many irons in the fire, he discovered that, before the lady formed her present plans of aggrandizement, she had signed articles binding herself to dance that winter at the Berlin theatre. This being ascertained, his friend Lord Hyndford, then our ambassador in Prussia, easily induced that Court to demand of the Venetian Government that she should be compelled to fulfil her engagement. Accordingly she was arrested by order of the Senate, and, on the very day fixed for her marriage, sent off under a guard to Germany.

Mr. Mackenzie had made a friendship in Italy with a very worthy Catholic abbé, an Italianized Scotchman, named Grant, eight or ten years older than himself. This Abbé Grant, when an old man, came over to England to visit him and my father, and stayed near a month at Luton Park, where some of us found great amusement in putting him on the chapter of events long past, and getting at the particulars of the Barberini story. He was at Venice when the thing happened, and was sent for by Mr. Mackenzie's servants, who did not know what to do with their master. He sat up with him all night, expecting every moment to see him breathe his last; for he was quite delirious, and fell from one convulsion fit into another. The abbé declared he never beheld a scene so distressing; the poor young man's throes of anguish, his state of distraction and despair, excited in him such a degree of compassion that he owned he could not have withheld from him the object of his wishes if he had had the power of restoring her, notwithstanding the disgrace and ruin which he, as well as Mr. Mackenzie's other friends, thought inseparable from the marriage.

As soon as the lover regained his self-possession, he followed his captive mistress to Berlin; but Lord Hyndford, aware that this might be the case, had prepared matters for his reception. On alighting from his carriage, he was saluted with a peremptory order to quit the King of Prussia's dominions in four-and-twenty hours; and a file of unpitying grenadiers forthwith escorted him beyond the frontier. Thence he sent a challenge to the ambassador, who laughed and put it in the fire. He vowed eternal enmity to the Duke of Argyll, he renounced all friendship and kindred with my father—in a word, he committed every extravagance which love and rage could dictate, till the conflicts of his mind, overpowering his bodily strength, threw him into a dangerous fever. When, by the aid of youth and a good constitution, he had struggled through it, the news that awaited him on his recovery probably caused that kind of revulsion which paralytic patients feel when a torpid limb (or frame) is restored to action by the galvanic battery. The Barberini was married to another. An artful adventurer, conceiving her to be rich, had passed himself upon her for a foreign nobleman of high rank, as desperately enamoured as the young Englishman, who now seemed "a bird escaped from the snare of the fowler," considerably richer, and with no relations entitled to control him. Duped into eagerness, she made haste to secure the prize.

Thus ended an adventure which yet was not the most remarkable part of her history. She certainly must have had extraordinary abilities, since she drew within the attraction of her sphere something as opposite to an inexperienced youth as it is possible to imagine—no less a person than Frederick the Great[1] himself, of all men the least likely to be fascinated by female charms. Nor did he admire or pursue her as a woman. Jealous of being suspected of such a weakness, he took care always to have eyewitnesses of their interviews. But

[1] Describing Frederick's palace at Potsdam in August 1773, Lady Mary Coke says: "In the room where he writes he has a full-length picture of the Barberini in the attitude of one of her high dances, and a tambourin in her hand. It seems to be extremely well painted, and I believe it is very like, tho', to say the truth, my remembrance of her is very imperfect. . . ."—ED.

he was avowedly very fond of her conversation; a far prouder distinction, and one that, perhaps, no other of the sex ever could boast. She availed herself of his favor to some purpose, when she found she had been entrapped into becoming the wife of a needy impostor.[1] On her representing to him what were the circumstances of her marriage, his Majesty stretched forth his iron sceptre,[2] supreme over law and gospel, to annul it as fraudulent, banished the sharper, and soon after made (or at least sanctioned) a match for her with a subject of his own, a gentleman by birth. As a Prussian lady she passed the rest of her life in good repute and comfort.

It happened one day at our King's *levée* that a young man just arrived from abroad accosted Mr. Mackenzie rather pertly in my brother James's hearing, and told him he had lately seen an old friend of his, Madame la Baronne ———, naming this very Prussian lady. My uncle for a minute looked confounded; but, recovering himself, drew the traveller into a corner, and held with him a long and earnest conversation, seeming to ask

[1] Not quite a "needy impostor" according to Carlyle. Though a schoolmaster's grandson, he was the son of Frederick's Chancellor Cocceji. Carlyle says the divorce was owing to incompatibility of temper. He does not give the name of the second husband, "a Graf of sixteen quarterings."—Carlyle's "Frederick the Great," book xiv. cap. viii.

[2] The witty Prince de Ligne, when dining with Frederick at Potsdam in 1780, pretended to mistake a plate of Berlin porcelain for Dresden, and expressed surprise that the mark was only one sword, and not the usual Dresden mark of two swords crossed. Frederick explained that the mark was not a sword but *his sceptre*. "J'en demande pardon à votre majesté, mais il ressemble si fort à une épée qu'on pourrait bien s'y méprendre."

him many questions. But for this incident I should have supposed he remembered no more of the affair than of any pain or pleasure he had felt in his nurse's arms. I am sure no recollection of it ever appeared to flash across his mind while he was wondering at the indiscretions of his neighbors.

At the time I knew them, perhaps neither he nor Lady Betty could be deemed void of selfishness. It is the vice, alas! of age, and also that of prosperity; and their prosperity had been uninterrupted, for they possessed all the good things of this world, and one might say, in the words of the Psalmist, that, excepting the loss of two infant children [1] (long since forgotten), "no evil had come nigh their dwelling." As her sway over him was unbounded, and he, again, had great influence on my father, she sometimes made a good deal of mischief in our family—not by design, but need I tell you in how many ways want of sense can answer that purpose equally with injurious intentions? Capricious as the wind, or the weathercock it turns, and subject to those whimsical fits of fondness or aversion called in French *engouements* (for which I know no precise English word), she had, even in the passing crowd unknown to her, her charming favorite and her odious anti-favorite of the season, like her summer and winter gowns; while among ourselves there was always some one who could do nothing wrong, and some one other who could do nothing right. The same individ-

---

[1] One died at Turin in 1759, when Mr. Mackenzie was British minister there. See H. Walpole to Conway, Aug. 14, 1759, vol. iii. p. 246.—ED.

ual often acted both parts in the course of half a year—suddenly metamorphosed from white to black: if a woman, for wearing a feather or a ribbon she disliked; if a man, for something of corresponding importance. I myself usually stood high in her favor, but I had a long interval of grievous disgrace on the score of a new-fashioned trimming, yclept by the milliners *frivolité*. Still, bitter as she would be against the present offender, we were more inclined to laugh at these fluctuations than to resent them. Those less used to her could not so well tolerate the peremptory tone she was apt to assume in all places and companies, from meeting with no contradiction at home, and having elsewhere that species of consideration which is acquired by giving excellent dinners. Mrs. Anne Pitt, Lord Chatham's sister and counterpart, who continually met her at our house, being my mother's intimate friend, said, in her pointed, peculiar manner: "Lady Betty takes the *liberty* in society of telling one that—one lies, and that—one is a fool; and I cannot say I think it at all agreeable."

IV

WE now come to that extraordinary person Lady Mary Coke, a study for the observers of human character as a rare plant or animal would be for the naturalist. Her beauty had not been undisputed, like Lady Strafford's. Some allowed, some denied it; the dissenters declaring her neither more nor less than a white cat—a creature to which her dead whiteness of skin, unshaded by eyebrows, and the fierceness of her eyes, did give her a great resemblance. To make amends, there were fine teeth, an agreeable smile, a handsome neck, well-shapen hands and arms, and a majestic figure. She had the reputation of cleverness, when young, and, in spite of all her absurdity, could not be called a silly woman; but she was so invincibly wrong-headed—her understanding lay smothered under so much pride, self-conceit, prejudice, obstinacy, and violence of temper, that you knew not where to look for it, and seldom indeed did you catch such a distinct view of it as certified its existence. So also her good qualities were seen only like the stars that glimmer through shifting clouds on a tempestuous night; yet she really had several. Her principles were religious. She was sincere, honorable, good-natured where passion did not interfere, charitable, and (before old age had sharpened economy into avarice) sometimes generous.

For her friendships, they were only too warm and too zealous for the peace of the mortals upon whom they were bestowed—I am afraid I might say inflicted.

In information she greatly surpassed her sisters, having a turn for reading, and reading of a solid kind —history and State papers, in which she was well versed, as far, at least, as related to England. But she had not a grain of taste for any work of genius. She esteemed Milton and Pope very fine poets, because such was the creed of her youth; but if their verses had been printed pell-mell with Blackmore's, she would not have found out which was which. Nor did she discriminate better in prose; a writer's style, his reasoning and reflections, she scarcely attended to; the language of Swift and Rapin, Burnet and Burke, went down alike; and the Parliamentary Journals pleased her above them all, as most authentic. Thus conversant with the dryest matter of fact alone, she contrived to apply it to the increase of her own self-importance, and heated her brains with history as others have done with romances. Don Quixote became a knight-errant by poring over "Amadis de Gaul"; Lady Mary, an historical personage by studying Rushworth's "Collections" and Lord Strafford's trial. I verily believe that if she could have been committed a close prisoner to the Tower on a charge of high treason, examined before the Privy Council, tried, and of course gloriously acquitted, by the House of Lords, it would have given her more delight than any other thing physically possible. But, living in an age when all this was little less than morally impossible, she had no way of getting upon a level with the Queen Marys and the Lady Jane Greys who were always running in her head, except by striving to magnify every common matter that concerned herself, like the Don when he turned windmills into giants, and carriers' inns into castles. Nothing ever happened to her after the fashion of ordinary life. Not to mention the unprecedented behavior of most men, women, and children whom she had anything to do with, she could not be caught in a shower but it was such rain as never before fell from the skies. The dry-rot that broke out in her house was totally different in its nature from the dry-rot at her next neighbor's; and in case of a cold, or a sore throat, woe to the apothecary who ventured to quicken her pulse and excite her ire by tendering that established consolation, "It is going about, madam, I assure you; I suppose I have now twenty patients with just the same symptoms as your ladyship's";—for all her disorders were something nobody else could judge of, or had ever experienced. I once heard her literally talk of the *exquisite pain* she suffered from pricking her finger.

Cervantes, we know, designed to give his hero a taint of real madness, which he represents as at one time on the point of being subdued by judicious medical treatment. Here the parallel will fail us. However a stranger might have construed some of Lady Mary's visions, she had no insane tendency—not so much as what is familiarly termed a *twist*. Her delusions were altogether wilful, springing from a noble disdain of being nothing more than simply and barely the person she was. Therefore, all the bleeding and blistering imaginable would not have put one of them to flight, nor lowered the distressed princess, the persecuted heroine, into a reasonable woman, of high quality, rich and surrounded with advantages, but debarred from the cognizance of State affairs—in the first place by her sex; in the second by want of power to influence a cobbler's vote at a Westminster election. So much for the portrait. It is time to put the original in action.

Lady Mary's marriage was an affair conducted in the old-fashioned manner; overtures being made by Lord Coke's relations to hers, terms proposed and rejected, others acceded to, and the bargain finally struck for two thousand five hundred pounds per annum jointure and five hundred pin-money, as the fair equivalent for her twenty thousand pounds, which at that time was a larger portion than could often be met with out of the city. Still the Duchess of Argyll demurred in perplexity, averse from the connection on account of Lord Leicester's notoriously dissolute and violent character. Yet the son, though faithfully following his father's footsteps, won her good graces. But this is a matter that a young man may always manage with an old woman, even of a wiser class. Then officious friends brought her favorable reports of him—another thing sure to happen: he had sense, he had good-nature, he had this and that, which, when his wild oats were sown, a prudent woman—according to custom again— might work upon and do wonders. To conclude, Lady Mary, who at nineteen had a very positive will of her own, intimated that she liked and chose to accept him.

Yet no sooner were the conveyancers set to work, and the suitor's visits freely admitted, than she gave all outward and visible signs of a coyness approaching to aversion. He dutifully attended her mother's tea-table, stroked her Grace's cats, listened to her long stories, talked goodness and morality, and kept his countenance admirably throughout; every now and then lowering his voice to its softest tone, and tenderly addressing the lady of his love: while she, bridling with ineffable disdain, turned away her head and hardly vouchsafed him an answer. Those who knew the Celadon could read in his face a humorous enjoyment of the scene, but yet foresee that her airs of scorn would not go unpunished—for he was inwardly as haughty as herself, thoroughly unprincipled and profligate, had abundance of wit and humor, and not the smallest personal liking for her to counterbalance the secret resentment which such contemptuous usage inspired.

As the lawyers' labors advanced, and the day of execution drew near, her dislike to him seemed to increase; she wept all the morning above stairs, and in the evening sat below stairs, the silent picture of despair. "Then, for the love of Heaven," said honest Lady Betty, "my dear sister, why don't you break off the match?—where is the difficulty?" It was a jest, as Lady Betty well knew, to suppose Lady Mary afraid of her mother; but, granting she were so, she (Lady Betty) offered again and again to save her every discussion—to acquaint the Duchess, dismiss Lord Coke, take all the embarrassing part of the business upon herself. "No," replied Lady Mary, as often as this was urged, "no—it will be time enough at the altar." To the altar then she went (in April 1747), and there, instead of an effectual "No," Catherine uttered the irrevocable "Yes," gave Petruchio her hand, and submitted to be sacrificed. *But—but*—a circumstance awkward to hint at is, as you will find, the main hinge of the story. But rumor whispered that the sacrifice remained incomplete. To speak out, the bridegroom, who conceived he had a long score of insolence to pay off, and was predetermined to mortify the fair bride by every means in his power, did not scruple entertaining his bottle-companions with a ludicrous detail of particulars. He found her ladyship, he said, in the mood of King Solomon's Egyptian captive—

"Darting scorn and sorrow from her eyes";

prepared to become the wretched victim of abhorred compulsion. Therefore, coolly assuring her she was quite mistaken in apprehending any violence from him, he begged she would make herself easy, and wished her a very good night.

The happy pair went on thenceforward in a way suited to this promising outset. He almost immediately resumed his former habits of gaming and drinking, and when they were alone together gave her pretty coarse language, although before company it was, "My love! My life! My angel!"—acting the fondest of husbands. More in mockery than hypocrisy, however, since he lost no opportunity of attacking her father's memory, ridiculing her mother, disparaging the name of Campbell, and slyly throwing out whatever else could irritate her most. You will inquire how she bore such treatment. Why, her lawyers answer the question, for they set forth "that she ever comported herself in a courteous and obliging manner; she, the said Lady Mary, being of a sober, modest, chaste, and virtuous conversation, and of a meek, mild, and affable temper and disposition"; which perforce reminds one of the meek spirit ascribed to Humphrey Hoen's wife (Sarah, Duchess of Marlborough) in Arbuthnot's "History of John Bull." But we must remember that the said Lady Mary's teeth and claws were not yet fully grown; besides, people who, like her, fairly love a grievance, always support real evils better than those fabricated by their own imagination. As heroic sufferers they are in their proper element; it is exactly the character they aspire to exhibit, and it inspires them with a sort of self-satisfaction calculated to produce apparent equanimity.

Three months after their marriage, the young couple accompanied Lord and Lady Leicester to Holkham for the summer; and, as all the family travelled together, it brought about a discovery. When the Leicester coach-and-six stopped at Lord Coke's door early in the morning, Lady Mary was dressed and ready, his lordship had not yet returned from the tavern. Finding upon inquiry that such were his customary hours and practices, his father expressed the most indignant displeasure that so fine a young woman should be so shamefully neglected, and took her part in the warmest manner. This, by the by, never does a woman much service. No third person can step in between a married couple without the risks attending those who handle gunpowder; but perhaps it would be safer for the lady to have any other advocate than one of whom her husband stands in awe, whether it be father, master, or prince; above all, the first, whose pre-eminence is most indisputable, and who cannot be asked that stout question, available against everybody else, namely, "What have you to do in my house, and with my subject?" It puts the son in a humiliating predicament, sending him back to the days of his boyhood; and though he may submit to paramount authority, he bears her a grudge for having appealed to it, of which she is sure to rue the effects long after her momentary triumph has ceased. Thus it happened here. The Duchess of Argyll writes to Lady Dalkeith that her sister Mary's letters from Norfolk speak highly of Lord and Lady Leicester's kindness to her, but say nothing of Lord Coke's. In fact, they were upon worse terms than ever. After their return to town, he scarcely kept any measures with her; and in consequence of their declared quarrel she received a most flattering letter from his father at the commencement of the new year, extolling her as an angel, and calling her husband "*brute*" and "*beast*" in express terms. The depraved wretch, who had proved himself unworthy of such a blessing as Heaven had granted him in her, should henceforth be renounced by him (Lord Leicester), and she regarded as his own beloved daughter married into another family.

Upon the face of this epistle—which is long and elaborate, and was afterward produced in proof of her ill-usage—I think you would have said, "The gentleman doth protest too much"; or have quoted the French proverb, *Qui prouve trop ne prouve rien*, for its exaggerated language is very unlike that of a sincere person. In a short time she herself learned to mistrust it; his behavior at their next interview being cold and constrained, and his manner of listening to her complaints discouraging. A second letter soon followed, intimating that he found Lord Coke so truly penitent, so convinced of her merit, and desirous of regaining her affections, that, if she would but agree to a reconciliation, he was persuaded they might still live happily together. Her papers do not show how she replied: it only appears that one day Lord Leicester unexpectedly arrived in a furious passion, turned some relations of his own, who were sitting with her, out of the house, railed at her pride and stubbornness, told her Lord Coke had done her the greatest honor in marrying her; in short, raved like a madman. She sent for her mother and Lady Strafford, to whom he was not much more civil; and the former, she owns, made matters something worse by scolding him in return.

What caused such a sudden change in Lord Leicester's sentiments and conduct she professes herself unable to guess; but I have heard it sufficiently explained. He was, in one sense, impartial, as he cared not a straw who was right or who was wrong: nor had he any very tender paternal feelings to blind him, knowing his son's faults full well; but his heart was set upon having heirs to his title and estate. With a fair prospect of gaining this point, he would have protected his daughter-in-law, whether angel or devil, and supported her against her husband to the utmost of his power; and the indignation he expressed at Lord Coke's neglect of her and abandoned life was but what he really felt as long as these seemed the sole or chief obstacles in the way. But now the case was altered.

"As women wish to be who love their lords,"

the woman did not wish to be who hated her lord. It is possible that, knowing how important the object was to the family, she might take a perverse pleasure in disappointing them; and far from improbable that she might be partly actuated by pique at the affront originally offered to her personal charms, upon which no poor little, frivolous, weak woman of us all could secretly set a higher value. Her motives, however, were best known to herself: the magnanimous vow she made and proclaimed was, never to cohabit as a wife with Lord Coke; and she adhered to it with all her characteristic obstinacy. The moment his father understood this, it converted him into her determined enemy. Making light of directly contradicting his former professions (as indeed he had little reputation for honor or consistency to forfeit), he gave a loose to the brutality of his nature without reserve.

Nevertheless, through Archibald, Duke of Argyll's, mediation, a kind of truce was made. Lady Mary, being much indisposed, had permission to live two or three months at her mother's house in Bruton Street; while Lord Coke, who was also ill, resided with his parents. But he often called to inquire after the health of his beloved spouse, and never once gained admittance, although she received other visitors; in excuse for which she pleaded that her nerves were too weak to bear the agitation that an interview with him would have caused. Meantime, her uncle pressed Lord Leicester to let the ill-matched pair be formally separated; but his arguments and persuasions had no effect: neither father nor son would hear of it; and all he could obtain was, that both should give him (the Duke) their words of honor to treat her more kindly in future.

The husband and wife, once more reunited, then went to drink a mineral water at Sunninghill, and with them her unmarried sister, Lady Betty, whose presence proved no check to their quarrels nor restraint upon Lord Coke's violence. Throwing the mask and the scabbard aside together, he told Lady Mary it was his resolution to make her as miserable as he could, and he should take her to Holkham for that express purpose. She answered that she would not go unless carried by force. Yet go she did; and from that moment the feud was regularly established, and the war of tongues kindled; the families, as well as the individuals, abusing each other to the right and left: that is to say, widening the breach every hour—in this instance without doing much harm, for the animosity of the principals could not be increased. But how often does it occur that some small grain of kindness, some remnant of affection, still lies lurking in the bosoms of a couple whose passions, flaming above their reason, have set them at variance! And then how fatal a step it is to call in even the best-meaning friends as auxiliaries.

A MEMOIR 71

Hitherto we have hardly named Lady Leicester, a peaceable, inoffensive woman, long inured to obedience; who, as the father was yet more ill-tempered than the son, and addicted to the same vices, had borne submissively for thirty years the trials that exhausted Lady Mary's scantier stock of patience in three months. Her lord did not fail to point out the contrast to others, and ask, exultingly, whether a daughter of the House of Thanet, inheriting in her own right one of our oldest English baronies,[1] would not have been quite as well entitled to rebel and give herself airs as the Infanta he now had to deal with? Quiet as she was, her daughter-in-law, treating her as a foe, in some measure made her one. It could not be expected that she should side with her against a son, her only child. Nor was she wholly inexcusable if she thought (even taking his character at the worst) that a wife of gentler mood might have had a fairer chance of reforming him. However, continuing passive as she had always been, she neither prompted nor opposed the decision of the higher powers.

On Lady Mary's arrival in Norfolk, where she was doomed to remain upward of a twelvemonth, the affair might be considered at issue: the parties fell to work in earnest. Lord Leicester and Lord Coke firmly determined to master her refractory spirit; her ladyship equally resolute not to be overcome. First they skirmished with her, saying and doing whatever was most slighting and contemptuous, and letting all their dependants perceive that the fewer marks of respect they

[1] The barony of De Clifford.

showed her the better they would pay their court. This produced bitter resentment, but no humility; she was not to be mortified into surrendering at discretion. She retreated to the citadel of her own apartment, and declared herself too ill to leave it; which the Leicesters, discrediting, regarded as a pretext adopted to cast odium upon them and excite compassion in the neighborhood. I own I have heard old Lady Cecilia Johnstone say, that when she and her sister Lady Diana Clavering (then young ladies) were at Holkham, with their father Lord Delawar, Lady Mary used to invite them up to her room, and be very merry, and, to all appearance, very well, though muffled in a night-cap and sick-dress, and refusing to associate with the family. For some months she persisted in thus secluding herself; nor could the medical men she consulted ever prevail upon her to stir out of doors or breathe the fresh air—a way of life which, together with fretting and vexation, brought on real nervous disorders. But her antagonists, believing, or choosing to believe, all her complaints affected, proceeded to turn this voluntary confinement into downright compulsory durance. They demanded her keys, seized her papers, and opened the letters she wrote and received; previously taking the opinion of counsel how far they might legally go, and putting this query in particular, viz., "Whether a wife's obstinately denying her husband his conjugal rights did not justify his placing her under unusual restraint?" Lord Leicester, in a letter written about this time to her sister Lady Betty, lays a great stress upon the same point, as "contrary to the laws of God and man." And it was so publicly known and canvassed that it became a standing jest among his very servants to nickname her (profanely enough), "*our Virgin Mary.*"

Now began to peep forth and to be seen her propensity to give things a high *historical* coloring. Her actual situation, with all the terrific power that a husband may exert by strictness of English law about to thunder on her devoted head, was sufficiently grievous; and no very common case either. Yet still it wanted a certain grandeur of peril, which her imagination sought to supply by stretching beyond the locking up and other severities threatened, and directing her apprehensions to assassination and poison. When I first commenced observing my fellow-creatures, Lady Mary's humor had long been so well understood that the dangers which perpetually menaced her life from one deadly enemy or another were things of course that startled nobody. We were almost too much used to the fancy to laugh at it. But in these early days, before even her nearest friends had *found her out* (pardon the expression), they naturally imagined she could not admit such horrible suspicions upon any other than good grounds; therefore, the dreadful fate she had reason to fear was hinted, and whispered, and told in confidence; till the rumor, growing loud, reached the ears of the parties accused, whom it only served to exasperate and impel to acts more decidedly hostile. In March 1749 Lord Coke absented himself, empowering his father, by a letter of attorney, to take certain strong measures, beforehand agreed upon between them: to dismiss Lady

Mary's maid without warning, place about her another of their own choice, remove her from the new house at Holkham into the adjoining old one, and strictly forbid the domestics to admit any of her relations who might attempt to visit her. That she was now in bad health and pitiable distress is credibly testified; yet she continued fighting upon her stumps with all the bravery of Witherington. She would not let the new maid approach her person. "Mighty well," said Lord Leicester, "then she may wait upon herself!" She refused paying the apothecary's bill. It was well, his lordship said again; as he knew her illness to be "all d—d affectation." If she did not choose to defray the expense of it out of her pin-money, she might do without doctors and physic; and he prohibited the man's further attendance.[1]

In this state of persecution and imprisonment she lived five or six months, finding means, however, to correspond with her family all the while, whether by the assistance of servants, or by that of the apothecary and the chaplain—whom compassion partly won over to her side—I am ignorant. By this time Lady Betty was married, and Lady Mary had acquired a zealous, active protector in Mr. Mackenzie, who consulted the

[1] "Went to the Princess Amelia. . . . The Princess said Lady Sarah Bunbury's conduct was still more surprising . . . her running away from him (her husband) would give him a right to lock her up for the rest of her life. I told H.R.H. that times were alter'd, & I was persuaded she wou'd not be locked up, tho' I remembered when people were locked up for no fault at all. The Princess smiled, & said that some people had been locked up for being too virtuous. . . ."—Lady Mary Coke's "Journal," Feb. 23, 1769.—ED.

best lawyers, transmitted her their advice, sent her queries to answer and papers to sign: in a word, took unremitting pains to effect her release. Not without difficulties to combat at home. It was his task to spur the Duchess of Argyll into action, and to hinder her acting foolishly: neither an easy matter. Nay, once —if not oftener—he encountered a sudden squall from that point of the compass whence it seemed least that any adverse wind should blow. Plainly speaking, the captive lady herself wrote him a furious letter, full of bitter reproaches, enclosing another to Lady Betty equally violent, and pretty nearly desiring him to meddle no more with her affairs. With great consistency, she next wondered he had not meddled much further; asking why he omitted doing this, or that, which *she* thought expedient! A proof that then, as well as ever after, she knew better what was to be done than all her friends and all the lawyers in Westminster Hall, Chancellor and Judges included. In my uncle's first amazement he begins his answer with "Madam"; but soon seems to soften toward her; and afterward, on her making him some little apology, assures her, with manly good-nature, that his displeasure had not lasted half an hour, as he attributed all she had said to the irritating effects of misery upon her spirits.

At length a decisive step was taken. The Duchess, attended by Mr. Mackenzie and a solicitor, went down to Holkham, demanded, before witnesses, to have access to her daughter, was refused it, made affidavit of the fact on her return to town, and obtained from the Judges of the King's Bench a writ of Habeas Corpus, enjoining Lord Coke to produce his wife before them on the first day of Term in November. Lady Mary, when thus brought up, swore the peace against him, and instituted a suit of divorce on the score of cruel usage, the Chief Justice declaring her to be under the protection of the court in the interim, and ordering that her near relations should have free admittance to her, together with her lawyers and physicians.

I have often and often heard my mother describe the ceremony of Lady Mary's public appearance. The court was crowded to excess, the bench filled with ladies, for the Duchess and her daughters not only assembled those related to them, but engaged all the most respectable of their acquaintance to countenance her by attending. Her male kindred and friends assisted likewise. On the other hand, Lord Leicester and his son, having no great interest with respectable women, gathered together a numerous *posse* of lively, clever, wild young men; all the rakes and all the geniuses of the age came to back Lord Coke, or rather to enjoy an exhibition in their eyes very diverting. Lady Mary's faction found it far otherwise; the poor old Duchess was crying bitterly, Lady Strafford repeatedly fainting away, and my mother said she never saw a more moving scene in any tragedy. If one durst form such a surmise, perhaps it distressed her and the rest of the troop more than it really did the chief actress; for I cannot but suspect that there was something in the dignity and solemnity of the transaction wonderfully consonant to Lady Mary's inclinations. However, she came forth feeble, squalid, and in a wretched plight, dressed almost in tatters, which (by the way) the Leicesters maintained that it was her good pleasure to wear, since her pin-money had never been withheld, and she had spent it as she thought proper. I should wrong you greatly by omitting one incident. The mob, which was prodigious, pressing to gain a sight of her, broke the glass of her sedan-chair. "Take care!" said the tender husband as he handed her out of it. "*My dearest love! Take care and do not hurt yourself.*"

While the suit was pending she resided in the garret of Lord Leicester's town-house, about which garret again were two stories. She affirmed that they would allot her no better apartment; they, that she perversely preferred it to any other, in order to appear cruelly used. Her friends daily clambered up to it, notwithstanding its inconvenient height, and my mother was present more than once when Mr. Mackenzie and the lawyers labored to extort from her the information necessary to form the base of their proceedings—

"——labor dire it was, and weary woe."

Reclining on a couch, Lady Mary returned this comprehensive answer to all their interrogations: "Never was any human creature treated as I have been." "That we do not doubt, madam; but the law requires of us proof. We must go upon specific grounds. Will you please to enter into particulars?" "It is enough to say that in every respect my usage was most barbarous." "But how and in what precise respect? Cannot your ladyship state some one act on some one day?" "Oh!

a thousand acts every day." And in this mode of answering she would persist, maugre argument and entreaty, till the learned gentlemen visibly gave some of Lady Townley's gulps to swallow wrong words; and one may safely presume they said to each other, as they went downstairs, "Well! if her husband did thresh her, he was not without excuse."

But all she could bring forward in the article of battery was this, that once, in a violent passion, Lord Coke struck her on the arm, and tore her lace ruffle. It was once too often, to be sure; yet even among gentlemen and ladies, who certainly ought not to war with their fists, one blow can no more constitute inhuman usage than the one swallow of the proverb make a summer. In short, law, like arithmetic, passes assertion through so fine a sieve that a considerable portion of it is apt to stick by the way. And when you read poor Lady Mary's memorial, or, technically, *libel*, addressed to the Spiritual Court, you need be no deep civilian to perceive how little beside assertion it contains. As may be expected, it tells only her own story, and makes the most of that, leaving you quite convinced that she had the ill-luck (which betides many a woman) of what is vulgarly called catching a Tartar, or lighting upon a very bad husband. But neither bad husbands nor bad wives can be easily got rid of in our stiff, strait-laced country, whose austere old statutes invest the former with an authority which Lord Coke had taken care not to overstep, save in a single instance, *i.e.*, when he denied her mother the permission of seeing her. Had the doors been freely opened to the Duchess, they might have continued fast closed upon Lady Mary for ever.

To prove her life endangered, the libel states that Lord Leicester had *talked* of sending her to the Hundreds of Essex, or some place equally unwholesome. The law, fortunately for most of us, does not mind what nonsense people *talk*. Yet this formal legal document records other sayings which one is still more surprised to see there. For example, what, I suppose, Lady Mary herself held too heinous an offence to be omitted—that, once upon a time, Lord Coke, finding her employed in reading Locke upon the "Human Understanding," told her she could not understand a word of the book, and was an affected b—h for her pains. Doubtless a most rude, affronting speech, and sorely grating to the ears of a wife (a wise woman, too!); but if the judges preserved their gravity on hearing it repeated, they did all that decency could demand of mortal men. Another time, it seems, Lord Leicester said she was a piece of useless lumber, fit only to be locked up in a garret, out of the way. Useless, you will observe, had a comical meaning, a sense in which it was true. And again the bench must have been tempted to smile.

I am uncertain whether the cause ever came to a hearing, or was given up without one; but it fell to the ground so completely as to leave Lady Mary at the mercy of her enemies; and she would have had no choice but to fly her country or return to her prison, if they themselves, satisfied with their victory, had not grown a little tired, perhaps a little ashamed, of persecuting her further. Lord Hartington (in after days Duke of Devonshire), the friend of Lord and Lady Strafford, offered himself as a mediator, and the Leicesters, by his persuasion, consented to let her live at Sudbrook unmolested, upon condition that she should withdraw her suit, pay its expenses herself, never set her foot in town, and have no separate maintenance but her pin-money. Hard terms, yet softened down from those stipulated at first, which were, that she should on no pretence come within twenty miles of London, and should publicly give herself the lie—that is to say, acknowledge, through her lawyers, in open court, that her complaints had been totally void of foundation.

No Turkish prince, yesterday living immured in the seraglio, and to-day placed upon the Ottoman throne, ever experienced a more agreeable change of situation and prospects than Lady Mary, when Lord Coke's excesses, producing an early decay, brought him to the grave only three years after their separation.[1] At six-and-twenty she emerged from a very dull retirement, a state of constant humiliation and fear, into the perfect freedom of an independent widow, with a jointure of twenty-five hundred pounds a year, fully equivalent to what five thousand would be at present. Re-entering the world, too, with the advantage of its good opinion; for she had been generally pitied, and everybody but a few friends of the Leicester family rejoiced at her deliverance. She conciliated further good-will by her decent behavior on the occasion; not affecting a con-

[1] August 1753.

cern she could not feel, but wearing mourning, and abstaining from amusements for the usual space of time.

When she left off her weeds, the Duke of Argyll and Colonel Campbell, as I have heard, wished to bring about a match between her and *Young Jack*, the latter's eldest son, who was passive, if not assenting. But she said she could not possibly marry a man whom she had always viewed as a brother. Indeed, her uncle's robust constitution set the dukedom and marquisate at such a distance from this young heir of the family that he had then nothing to tempt ambition, though perhaps everything to inspire love. Now *Love* was affirmed by Lady Temple—a very sensible woman, who knew Lady Mary well—to be "the only passion that had no place in her composition." The same Lady Temple wrote a complimentary portrait of her as follows:—

> "She sometimes laughs, but never loud;
> She's handsome, too, but somewhat proud:
> At court she bears away the bell,
> She dresses fine, and figures well:
> With decency she's gay and airy;
> Who can this be but Lady Mary?"

So dignified a person, though extremely willing to receive homage from admirers, held out no encouragement to the younger brothers, the inferior fortune-hunters, who pursue rich widows in serious earnest. They must have perceived that such an aim was hopeless; and I never heard that any adorers of a higher class laid titles and estates at her feet. If they had, it is not an utter impossibility that their offers might have been taken into consideration. At least, I know a story which seems to imply thus much; and as it is entertaining, and I can quote the best authority for it, chapter and verse, you shall have it at full length. By certain dates, I conjecture that at the time she must have stood upon the verge of thirty.

The Duke and Duchess of Queensberry had two sons, both of whom lived to be men. The eldest, when travelling through Yorkshire with them and his new-married wife, rode onward, and either shot himself or was killed by his pistol going off, almost within view of their carriage. The second died of a consumption the following year. And thus the Duke's nearest collateral relation—Lord March (the *Old Q.*, whom you remember)—became his next heir. He was then the most brilliant, most fashionable, most dissipated young man in London, the leading character at Newmarket, the support of the gaming-table, the supreme dictator of the Opera-house, the pattern whose dress and equipage were to be copied by all who aimed at distinction, and (need we add?) the person most universally admired by the ladies. Naturally a male coquet, he made love to every pretty woman of his own class, and bought it ready-made (in Quin's[2] phrase) from every one of a lower who set it to sale. He would have been

[1] October 1754.—ED.

[2] Alluding to Quin's famous repartee when the Duchess of Queensberry asked him, "Pray, Mr. Quin, do you ever make love?" She meant upon the stage, where he commonly acted tyrants, villains, etc. ; but, giving her question a different turn, he answered, "No, madam, I always buy it ready-made."

held a great matrimonial prize notwithstanding—as a duke's heir, with an earldom and a good estate in present—could any young lady have had reasonable hopes of winning him; but prudent mammas, frightened, sought to keep their daughters aloof, and it was pretty plain that whoever dared the adventure must pursue it at her own peril.

The Queensberrys, overwhelmed by the load of calamity which thus fell suddenly upon them, had retired to Amesbury,[1] and there lived a year or two secluded from the world, keeping up hardly any correspondence with their friends. My mother was much surprised, therefore, when she received a letter from the Duchess, to say that, particular business calling them to town, they earnestly wished she would drink tea with them on the evening of their arrival. Of course she obeyed the summons, and the meeting passed as it usually does between people so circumstanced, when pain has been deadened by time, and both parties strive to converse as if they had forgotten what the sight of each other never fails to recall. Presently Lady Mary Coke appeared, who was welcomed with extraordinary kindness, and seemed to have been expected. She was all graciousness in return, but august beyond her usual dignity, like a person wound up to act a solemn part on some important occasion. Next entered the Earl of March, looking excessively out of humor. He paid his respects sullenly to their Graces, made her Ladyship a very grave bow, then, spying my mother, cleared up his countenance, as if thinking, "Ah! here will be

[1] Their place in Wiltshire.—ED.

a resource "; and sitting down by her, he began to rattle away upon whatever news occupied the town at that moment. The Duke and Duchess joined in the conversation whenever they had an opportunity, and were visibly anxious to make Lady Mary bear a part in it also; but they toiled at that pump in vain: dry monosyllables and stately bows of assent being all their utmost efforts could draw forth. I need not describe the pantomime, for you have seen it a hundred times, and I a thousand. At last, the Duchess, perceiving my mother about to rise, caught her by the sleeve, and whispered: "No, no; don't go; pray outstay them. I want to speak to you." In the second that whisper lasted, Lord March contrived to turn on his heel and escape, without looking behind him. Lady Mary stayed a little longer, still magnificently silent; then departed, high and mighty as she came.

When the door was fairly shut upon her, "Now," said the Duchess, "do, I beseech you, tell us the meaning of all this?" "The meaning of what?" asked my mother. "Why, of these two people's behavior to each other." "Nay, how can I tell you anything about it?" "Why, are not you in the secret? Don't you know they are going to be married?" "Not I, indeed; it is the last thing I should have thought of." "Why, truly," rejoined the Duchess, "it would not have occurred readily to *me;* yet so it is: behold it under Lady Mary's own hand!" And she produced a letter in which Lady Mary announced that Lord March had been pleased to make his addresses to her: his preference assuredly did her great honor, and so forth; but her high respect for their Graces induced her to defer giving him a favorable answer till certain of their entire concurrence: should either of them have the slightest objection, she would instantly put an end to the treaty. "You may be sure we did not hesitate," continued the Duchess; "the object nearest the poor dear Duke's heart is that March should give over his pranks and make a creditable marriage; and none can exceed this for birth, fortune, and character. She has her foibles, undoubtedly; but, perhaps, a spirit like hers may do best to cope with his wildness. At any rate, that is *his* affair. I wrote by return of post to say how very happy the news had made us, and to assure her of our heartiest approbation. The Duke wrote the same thing to March; and without loss of time here are we come trundling up to London. We thought that you, as her relation and our friend, would be just the right person to meet them and prevent any awkward embarrassment. But they seemed determined not to exchange a word. What can possess them? Have they been quarrelling already?"

My mother, who thought within herself that Lord March's marrying at all was half a miracle,[1] and his pitching upon Lady Mary a whole one, could give no clew to the mystery; which grew more incomprehensible day after day, and week after week. The Duke and Duchess were at their wits' end. The lover in-

---

[1] See the Selwyn "Correspondence," i. 318–343, for a rumor of his engagement to Lady Anne Conway, and Lady Mary Coke's "Journal" for Miss Pelham and Lady Susan Stewart's desire to marry him.—ED.

geniously eluded most of their invitations; but whenever they did force him into the company of his mistress, the same scene presented itself over again: he was as distant, she as imperial, as at first. Another thing was much stranger yet: he had for some time *protected*, as your precious modern delicacy styles it, a certain Madame Arena,[1] the *prima donna* of the opera. This protection, instead of being withdrawn, or modestly concealed, was now redoubled and paraded. You never drove into the Park, or through St. James's Street, without meeting him with the Arena in his chariot. The Arena sat at the head of his table; the Arena hung upon his arm at Ranelagh: his attentions to the Arena on the opera stage were conspicuous in the face of the audience, and under Lady Mary's own nose if she chanced to be present. Tired out, the Duchess of Queensberry resolved to attempt fathoming his intentions; but set about it very gently; for even she was afraid of him.

"She hoped nothing unpleasant had occurred between him and Lady Mary?" "No; nothing that he knew." "And yet he must be sensible that there were circumstances which wore an odd appearance. If one might put so home a question, Did he in earnest design to marry her?" "Oh! certainly: he should be quite ready at any time; that is, if her Ladyship choose it." "Nay, my dear March; this is no answer." "Why, what more would your Grace have? I can't marry her unless she chooses it; can I?" "Now, do be serious one moment. You know very well what I allude

[1] The real name was Rena apparently. See Selwyn, i. 210.—ED.

to. Plainly, what must she think of the Arena's remaining in your house?" "The Arena, ma'am? The Arena? Pray, what has Lady Mary Coke to do with the Arena's living in my house, or out of it?" "Bless me! how can you talk thus? Do not common decency and propriety require——" "My dear madam, leave propriety and Lady Mary to protect themselves. She is no girl: she will act as she pleases, I dare say, and so shall I."

The springs of this impertinence could not be divined; but its drift was manifest; and the Duchess, having a real regard for Lady Mary, next undertook the nice task of representing to her how poor a chance of happiness she would have with such a volatile husband; and delicately hinting that it might be her wisest way to give the matter up, and draw off while she could still retreat with the honors of war: all which good counsel fell upon the ear of a statue. The lady, impenetrable and stately as ever, "could not by any means permit herself to doubt of my Lord March's honor; nor had he given her any cause of offence." Thus baffled on both sides, the poor Duchess had nothing for it but to sit still and wait the event.

As far as her nephew [1] was concerned, however, the whole club at White's could have expounded the riddle. To them he was abundantly communicative, vowing vengeance against Lady Mary, and swearing she had played him the most abominable trick that ever woman played man. He saw, he said, that she had no dislike to admiration: she was a widow, inde-

[1] *Welsh* nephew. Lord March was son of the Duke's first cousin.

pendent; of an age to take care of herself; so, thinking her tolerably handsome, to be sure, he supposed he might try his fortune in making a little love. If it pleased her, why, well; if not, she knew how to repulse him. But the big, wicked word MARRIAGE had never once entered his head, nor issued from his mouth; nor yet anything ever so distantly tending to it; and would any woman in England past fifteen pretend she took him for a marrying man? To go, then, and bring him into the hazard of disgrace with the Duke and Duchess of Queensberry, by catching up his first civil speech as a proposal, was an exploit she should pay dear for. With all his impudence, he durst not give *them* this explanation; therefore let her help him out of the scrape as she had thrust him into it; the whole burthen should rest upon her own shoulders.

He understood his antagonist ill. No chilling demeanor, no neglect, no affront, even with the Arena-flag openly hoisted, could provoke the enemy to leave her entrenchments. Finding her steadiness invincible, he had recourse to an opposite mode of warfare. He paid her a morning visit: what passed never fully transpired; but he got what he wanted, an outrageous box o' the ear, and a command never to approach her doors again. Overjoyed, he drove straight to Queensberry House with a cheek still tingling; put on a doleful face, and was mortified beyond expression at having unwittingly incurred Lady Mary's displeasure. Who could account for the capricious humors of ladies? Though quite unconscious of any offence, he had tendered the humblest apologies; but she would listen to

A MEMOIR 89

none: and since everybody knew the noble firmness of her determinations, he feared, alas! he must look upon his rejection as final. Blind as you may think this story, he met with no cross-examination or perplexing inquiry into whys and wherefores; for the good Duke and Duchess had been so teased by the conduct of both parties, and by that time were grown so sick of the whole affair, that they rejoiced almost as much as himself to see it at an end.

Possibly his Lordship's version of its origin should be received with grains of allowance: for, though one may well believe he neither mentioned nor thought of matrimony, yet it is likely that his professions of love had been more direct than he chose to allow. But granting them such as she might fairly take for a proposal, it was easy to ask him whether he had consulted his friends; and I suppose no woman but herself would have proceeded to inform them of it without his participation.[1]

And now let us quit love and marriage for things more congenial to Lady Mary's disposition. She no sooner began to chalk out her own path after regaining her freedom, than it became her chief object to connect herself with the Court, and acquire at once the favor

[1] "Dined at the French Ambassador's. Lord March sat by me at dinner, & expected, I believe, that I should be flatter'd with his attention, instead of which I endeavour'd to convince him he was not so delightful a creature as some Ladys made him believe, & as I never had contributed to give him that false notion of himself, I shou'd be enough his friend to tell him he had many faults. He seem'd much surpris'd & more mortified than I expected. . . ."—Lady Mary Coke's "Journal," 14th June, 1767.—ED.

of Princess Amelia (or Emily), George the Second's daughter, and that of the person her Royal Highness most disliked, his declared mistress, Lady Yarmouth. His mistress!—You are startled. It is not among the smallest praises of our late King that, "*By his long reign of virtue*"—to use Walter Scott's words—he rendered such a sound strange in our ears; that we, who were to *his* manner born, naturally recoil at the thought of reverencing a woman so designated. But for near a century before he ascended the throne scarcely any sovereign in Europe had ever been without a female favorite thus publicly acknowledged. All did not lead the profligate lives of Charles the Second and Louis the Fifteenth. Some few, if married men, forbore giving the lady an obnoxious title, and left the question of what was her real place about as dubious as it is with us whether we should view the Head of the Treasury as Prime Minister. Otherwise, a Master of the Horse or Captain of the Guard could not be a more regular part of the State establishment. Even the ungallant William, as if for form's sake, appointed Lady Orkney to the post after Queen Mary's death; and after Queen Caroline's, George the Second's bestowing it on Lady Yarmouth neither surprised nor scandalized the gravest of his subjects. Nor, indeed, bating the name (which they were so well used to) did there appear anything very scandalous in the connection; for if he had been a private person nobody would have entertained an evil thought of the stiff old gentleman and his respectable housekeeper, who led together a life "dull and dignified" as that of your ancestors in Tantallon Hold.

Lady Yarmouth was a quiet, orderly, well-behaved, well-bred, honest German; long past her youth, and without the least pretension to wit or beauty. She treated the King with profound respect, and every one else with great civility; entered into no cabals, did no mischief, made no enemies; and though she had a daily intercourse with the ministers, like Queen Caroline, never, like her, meddled with their business, but listened silently to what they said, and faithfully reported it to their master—without giving, or perhaps forming, any opinion of her own. The only sin the nation could lay to her charge was, that she sold a few places, titles, and ribbons; and in this she acted by his Majesty's express consent and advice—having refused the first offer made her, and, when she told it him, being asked in his German-English, "And why was you such a great fool?"

Yet pray do not misconstrue my meaning: when I say Lady Yarmouth held the place of Queen, and received the homage due to it, I am far from seeking to justify your aunt on the poor pretence of her having swum with the stream, and done but what she saw others do—the last error she could ever be accused of falling into. Nor yet must you take her to have been at this period less outrageously virtuous, or more lenient toward frail women, than when you knew her fifty years later. No such thing. But, by some revelation or inspiration granted to her alone among all the mortals subject to King George either in Britain or Hanover, she had acquired a positive certainty that he and her spotless friend were privately married. And from this faith, to do her justice, she never swerved to the end of her days. It could not but gratify the person chiefly concerned; add to which, that the favorite lady, although bowed down to with equal respect by the whole crowd of great and small approaching St. James's, must have discerned Lady Mary to be perhaps the only person there who literally courted her for her own sake; wanting none of the good things she could dispense, excepting her gracious smiles in public, and a gruff word or two extraordinary from old Squaretoes (as he was most irreverently called) at the Drawing-room. Such a disinterested attachment claimed, at least, the return of good-will; notes and letters passed between them, and presently Lady Yarmouth's hair, or her picture, I forget which, shone on Lady Mary's arm in a magnificent bracelet set with diamonds. It is but fair to add that the King's decease no way diminished the devotion vowed by the wearer of the bracelet to the giver, though the latter left England directly, and therefore it could only be testified at a distance.

Princess Emily, a woman of quick parts and warm feelings, but without Lady Yarmouth's *bonhomie*, saw further into Lady Mary's character; for her Royal Highness knew more of the world than princesses usually do; partly from native sagacity, partly from keeping better company and having a mind above that jealous fear of the superior in understanding which so often leads them to prefer associating either with people of mean capacity, gratuitously dubbed *good creatures*, or else with those who can cunningly veil their sense and act the part of butts and buffoons for interested purposes. As Bishop Watson [1] once told me that he had wisdom enough of his own, and would rather meet with something a little more amusing in his acquaintance, so might she have said of *dignity*. She had quite enough of her own; therefore the solemn grandeur of the mock princess often tired the real one, and always struck her as very ridiculous. Unluckily, too, her favorite friend Caroline, Marchioness of Lothian [2]— as yet Lady Ancram—had a wicked wit, prone to disconcert all ultra-gravity; and was the person in the world whose jokes Lady Mary most dreaded encountering. Many a trick, I fear, did these able confederates play her; but she obliged them by playing herself one that surpassed all the rest.

You have seen at Newbattle the whole-length portrait of Lady Ancram, holding a large lute. Lady Mary Coke chose to be painted with a large lute also. Now, the individual lute,[3] that sat for its picture bodily in both instances, belonged to the former lady, who played upon it very agreeably. The latter borrowed it from her, took a lute-master, labored and strummed, and made nothing of it, because she had no ear, and,

[1] Bishop of Llandaff, 1782–1816.—ED.
[2] Lady Caroline D'Arcy, sister of the last Earl of Holdernesse. Their mother was the daughter of Meinhardt, Duke of Schomberg.
[3] The lutes are *not* identical. Lady Ancram's is an ordinary lute, held in the hands, a feat difficult to perform with the one in Lady Mary's portrait. The correct name for this instrument is apparently a Theorbo or base lute—Italian "Chiterrone." Both pictures are by Allan Ramsay. Lady Ancram's is at Newbattle, Lady Mary's at Mountstuart.—ED.

like Hortensio's pupil in Shakespeare, was subject to mistake her frets and fingering.[1] After a reasonable time, Lady Ancram wished to have her lute back again; but Lady Mary, equally loath to buy an instrument for herself, or to give over strumming as a lost cause, found twenty excuses for still keeping possession, in spite of repeated billets, serious and comic, that came to dun her in English, French, and Italian. As a last resource, Lady Ancram resolved to try dunning her in German—a language she knew her to be intently studying (with much the same success as the lute) for the sake of their royal friend and that of Queen Yarmouth. This required Princess Emily's assistance. She wrote a proper note for Lady Ancram to copy, and remained in good hope of seeing some curious Anglo-German jargon in answer. But the event was better still, and far exceeded their expectations. Lady Mary arrived with an air of inward satisfaction, and soon fell to moralize on most people's aptness to overrate their own talents. Then proceeding to *apply*—as it behooves a pious preacher—" Why, now, madam, between ourselves, there's my Lady Ancram. She *is* very clever— no dispute of that; but, really, she can't do *every* thing, as she will fancy she can. In strict confidence, I'll show your Royal Highness a note I have had from her in what she takes to be German. Do but look at it. German, indeed! Your R.H., who knows what German is, will be amused with the bungling, blun-

---

[1] "I did but tell her she mistook her frets,
And bowed her hand to teach her fingering."
—" Taming of the Shrew."

dering attempt she has made to write a language she knows nothing of." The Princess, not daring to move a muscle for fear of betraying herself, shook her head pityingly over her own note; and confessing what was strictly true—but *how* true the other little suspected— "that, to be sure, poor Lady Ancram could not write a word of German," allowed Lady Mary to go off in triumph.

All this while a youth was growing up in the same high quarter, whose name Lady Mary would not willingly have had left out of her history. You are aware I mean Edward, Duke of York: and curious, I do not doubt, to inquire his character. As people will take liberties with their own relations, it was given very concisely by his aunt Princess Emily, when, in after days talking to a friend of mine, she described his late Majesty's brothers, all in a lump, as "the best-humored asses that ever were born." With regard to one of them—Henry, Duke of Cumberland—the expression, however strong, was happy, almost picturesque; no alteration could mend it. Not so for the Duke of Gloucester, who, though a weak man, with many failings, had good qualities and princely manners, and could not justly be pronounced a fool. Nor did the Duke of York's folly, I believe, approach the towering height of his brother Cumberland's; but I have always heard that he was silly, frivolous, heartless; void alike of steadiness and principle; a libertine in his practice, and in society one of those incessant chatterers who must by necessity utter a vast deal of nonsense. Horace Walpole's letters record the laugh that arose on

Prince Edward's asking a lady [1] how she liked Young Clackit in the farce.[2] You see the cause. Young Clackit struck the company as so precisely his Highness's very self that it got the better of a respect which daily familiarity with royalty, here and there and everywhere, had not then worn away. He was the first of his race who began the good work of demolishing it, by running about giddily to all sorts of places with all sorts of people—of course, principally the worst sort—until his frolics won the public attention, and the Duke of York's *crew* grew a phrase used, as the lawyers say, in common parlance.

The friendship—or call it league—he formed with the Delavals, a family renowned for their wild profligacy, spread his fame through the northern counties, where he more than once visited Sir Francis Delaval and his sister Lady Mexborough at their country-seats; and Yorkshire rang long and loudly of the orgies therein celebrated. The most innocent of their pastimes consisted of practical jokes played on each other, and, if possible, on some luckless stranger of an age or character to render such pleasantry an affront. This man saw his bed sink through the floor just as he was stepping into it; that was awakened before day by a sluice of cold water from the ceiling. The gentlemen

[1] The Duchess of Richmond. See Walpole's "Letters," vol. iii. 221. "Prince Edward is grown very fickle. Lady Millbank is already forgot, & given place to the Duchess of Richmond, who he pursues with great earnestness, but meets with so little encouragement from her Grace that I fancy he will soon grow weary. . . ."—Lady Mary Coke to Lady Dalkeith, 8th April, 1758.—ED.

[2] "The Guardian" by Garrick.—ED.

started out of closets to catch the ladies at their toilets; the ladies stole and hid necessary parts of the gentlemen's dress in revenge. Mr. Wedderburne, afterward Chancellor, passing near one of these enchanted castles when going the circuit, thought it proper to pay his duty to the King's brother, and was received with much civility; in secret with exultation, for he and his wife were fresh game, of the right breed. But a fearful figure in a white sheet appearing in the middle of their bedchamber, which, upon examining it, he found full of trap-doors, he took Mrs. Wedderburne away betimes next morning, without the ceremony of bidding his Royal Highness farewell.

Among the motley tribe of gamblers, jockeys, boon companions, fiddlers, singers, and writers of *good* (*i.e.*, infamous) songs who enlivened this illustrious association, Foote, the famous mimic actor, held an eminent place, and paid no less than one of his limbs for the honor. He rode very ill; therefore it was an excellent joke to mount him upon a vicious horse, declared gentle enough to carry any lady. The animal threw him, as might be expected; and the surgeons could save his life only by instantly cutting off a leg which he had fractured in a horrible manner. However, the accident made his fortune: since the Duke, feeling some compunction on the occasion, engaged the King to give him the patent of the little theatre in the Haymarket, the source of all his future affluence.

Considering the inglorious nature of the Duke of York's brief career, you will wonder to hear that high expectations of him were entertained in his childhood

—at least by his parents: I know not whether by any one beside. But he was decidedly their favorite son, and their preference of him to his eldest brother a feeling openly avowed. Some distinguished foreigner praising the latter—"Oh, ay," replied the Prince of Wales coldly—"Yes; George is a good boy; but Edward has something in him, I assure you. Edward will be somebody. You will hear of him one of these days." And even when both were advancing to the age of men, the Princess Dowager took little pains—not enough—to conceal the same partiality. The reasons of it I have a mind to make Dr. Johnson assign instead of myself; his words being so much better than mine, and the passage I shall quote so apposite; although beginning with a position cruelly discourteous:

"Women, by whatever fate, always judge absurdly of the intellects of boys."

I am afraid this comes nearer the truth than one would wish to admit. But then I maintain that the mind has a sex, notwithstanding a common saying to the contrary; and mind may occasionally be misplaced —lodged in wrong habitations. A voice I once dearly loved to listen to used to assert that there were in the world almost as many he-women as she-women, instancing particularly a whole flourishing family of brothers and sisters who had not anything like a MAN among them. With this caveat let Dr. Johnson go on:

"The vivacity and confidence which attract female admiration are seldom produced in early life, but by ignorance at least, if not by stupidity; for they proceed not from confidence of right, but fearlessness of wrong.

Whoever has a clear apprehension must have quick sensibility, and where he has no sufficient reason to trust his own judgment, will proceed with doubt and caution, because he perpetually dreads the disgrace of error. The pain of miscarriage is proportionate to the desire of excellence; therefore till men are hardened . . . diffidence is found the inseparable associate of understanding."

Here Johnson, without knowing it, was drawing an exact picture of the royal house, and pointing out accurately how the heir of the crown, silent, modest, and easily abashed, differed from his next brother, whom brisk animal spirits and volubility of speech, added to that first of gifts, a good assurance—hourly strengthened by encouragement—enabled to join in or interrupt every conversation, and always say a something which the obsequious hearers were ready to applaud. If the other ever faltered out an opinion, it was passed by unnoticed: sometimes knocked down at once with: "Do hold your tongue, George: don't talk like a fool." And everybody knows that young persons—or any persons—under the curse of bashfulness, will talk below themselves when afraid to hear the sound of their own voices, and fearful that whatever they utter will be treated with scorn. Let alone conversing, it requires considerable self-possession, if not some share of impudence, to carve a leg of mutton, if you see all around you ready primed to laugh at your failure. Yet, when thus abruptly silenced, George the Third did not brood over it with the dark sullenness pretty sure to follow where early shyness conceals, as it often does, a haughty temper, and a high, though smothered, self-esteem. "Pride and sharpness were not in him." It only tended to augment, perhaps create, the awkward hesitation we remember in that most excellent Prince; whose real good sense, innate rectitude, unspeakably kind heart, and genuine manliness of spirit were overlooked in his youth, and indeed not fully appreciated till a much later time.

You will think I have diverged most widely from the main point: but never fear, Lady Mary will appear again by and by; and, as this may not be the last time I shall fly off at a tangent, you must use yourself to digressions and *prosing*. On Prince Edward's first setting out, hardly yet freed from a governor's control, the underlings of his mother's court praised and puffed him as far as they durst for shame; and the highest company were ready to give him welcome, because, by the then received notions of society, he did them an honor in seeking their acquaintance. So thought even Mr. Walpole, whom (with the good leave of a swarm of magazine-critics that never saw his face) no one who knew him in his lifetime would ever have accused of servility. Kings and princes were no rarities to him: nor was he really elated by their notice; he took it at its current value, neither more nor less, as we accept the sovereign proffered us for twenty shillings without troubling ourselves to weigh it. When he knelt in form to kiss the Duke of York's hand at his own door,[1]

[1] He performed this ceremony twice within an interval of twenty-eight years to two Dukes of York—the uncle and the nephew (see H. Walpole, iii. 347 and ix. 150), and gives his reasons for doing it to Lady Ossory, ix. 152.—ED.

he probably had a politic view quite unsuspected by the aforesaid critics; that of warding off too close an intimacy, and preventing the illustrious young gentleman from skipping in and out of his house at pleasure. To keep at a profoundly respectful distance from our superiors is the true way, as he perfectly knew, of keeping them at a convenient distance from ourselves. Let each man stand in his proper place, and none can press heavily upon another.

All this is now so changed that I seem to be speaking of the world before the Flood. But who has changed it? *They* have, the Great themselves. "*Tu* l'as voulu George Dandin."[1] It is their own act and deed. Whatever you hear about the diffusion of light, and the downfall of prejudice, and the march of intellect, and many more fine things, set forth in fine writing, and retailed in speech by innumerable parrots without feathers; did princes associate chiefly with persons of superior rank and consequence, such persons would still jealously value the privilege of approaching them. Were eminent merit and shining talents the principal exceptions, it would become a mark for merit and talents to aim at. And this because it is, and ever was, and ever will be the nature of man to prize highly what he cannot easily obtain; independently of the thing's intrinsic worth, or its want of it. For mere eating, how little does a blackcock excel a chicken? Yet nobody wonders that a sportsman should waste the livelong day in pursuing the one "o'er moor and mountain": whereas, if he rose early to go into his

[1] Molière's "George Dandin."

own farmyard and shoot the other, his heirs, in case they were aggrieved by his will, would perhaps bring it forward as a legal proof that he had lost his senses.

To proceed. In days when royalty was yet a gem for few to cheapen, you may conclude it could not fail to shine brightly in the eyes of one who had such a natural bent to admire it as Lady Mary Coke. She addressed the Prince still more respectfully than Lord Orford; but tempered her respect with all the attractive smiles and graces which could make the handsome young man feel himself flattered by the handsome woman's curtsying so particularly low to him. Honestly speaking—observe—the young man was *not* handsome. As described to me, he had a little, mean figure, and a pale face, with white eyelashes and eyebrows, and a certain tremulous motion of the eye [1] that was far from adding to its beauty. Their ages at this time stood as follows:—his barely twenty, hers thirty-two; a disparity which would spoil a romance, but in real life spoils nothing; on the contrary, gives a zest and spirit to flirtation, by gratifying the vanity of both parties. The lady who at two-and-twenty would have despised a boy of nineteen finds something mighty soothing in his attentions when conscious of being rather past her

[1] Frederick, Prince of Wales, was questioning a gentleman newly come from Germany about the family of a Sovereign at whose Court he had been Minister. "Have they turned out well-looking?" said he. "Oh Lord, sir, hideous; they have all white, shaking eyes." "Ah!" replied the Prince, very composedly, "to be sure that must disfigure them; it is the case with some of my children, as you will see presently."

bloom: while the boy, looking down upon insipid misses—*Anglicé*, pretty girls of his own age—is exalted above measure in self-estimation by the preference of the fine woman whom he sees others admire, and believes to stand on the pinnacle of fashion.

In this way probably commenced the friendship, or whatever it was, we speak of. Lady Mary, however, having a reverend care of her reputation, kept upon high ground, admitted his Royal Highness's visits but sparingly, and wholly avoided any suspicious familiarity. In consequence his letters (which are boyish enough) abound with complaints of the prudish strictness that holds him so far aloof, and inspires him with such awe that he hardly dares hazard the most innocent expressions, for fear of being misunderstood, and giving her nicety a causeless alarm. "Strong symptoms of love-making," you cry. I do not deny it; yet one of these letters betrays, I think, some nearly as strong of *Quizzing*. How the world went on so long without that useful verb I cannot imagine: it had early acquaintance with the mischievous thing. He tells her he has been studying the History of Scotland, and is wonderfully struck with the resemblance of character between herself and Queen Elizabeth. Nobody can question that this was the most deliciously palatable compliment he could have concocted, considering the peculiar taste of her he sought to please. But the woman whom it did please to be likened to Queen Bess by a lover must have known little of love and its whimsical ways, and, indeed, just as Lady

Temple affirmed, have had no such passion in her nature.[1]

But the presumptions of quizzing do not rest here. Lady Susan Stewart,[2] the Lady Augusta's lady of the bedchamber and favorite, used to tell my elder sisters, Lonsdale and Macartney, who were her intimate companions in their youth, how the Duke of York daily diverted her mistress and her with accounts of Lady Mary's pomposity, of the awful reserve maintained and the distant encouragement held out by turns, and, more

[1] The following is the text of the letter referred to:

"*Friday Morn.*

"P. Edwards complts to Lady Mary Coke, and cannot help making another attempt to enquire how she does. Is provok'd with himself for not remembering the fashionable hours better than to send to enquire after a lady's health at so early an hour as must oblige her to send back word she's asleep, out of compliance and conformity to an idle, dissipated, unthinking age.

"This is an offence I have the more reason to plead an excuse for, as my life is far spent in my morning occupations before this time, and being at present employ'd in the Scotch History, where Queen Elizabeth makes her name of so great importance, that, sway'd by some part of her behaviour (which always strikes me with a great resemblance to my present correspondent, and wou'd not at all be unworthy of her, were it not for that duplicity in her conduct and cruelty to Queen Mary, which is a blemish that must always attend that great Princesses memory), the resemblance of the rest of the character made me forget for a minute the age I live in; I otherwise should not have been so old fashion'd. However I have suffer'd enough from my reiterated absurdity, and flatter myself to that alone I owe the anxiety I am in concerning the health of her to whom these lines are address'd."—ED.

[2] Daughter of Lord Galloway. She married Granville, Earl Gower, created Marquis of Stafford, in 1786, and was mother by him of Lord Granville, Lady Georgiana Eliot, the Duchess of Beaufort, and Lady Harrowby.—ED.

than all, of her evident intention to become the wife of his bosom. Nay, Lady Augusta [1] herself seldom spoke to them (my sisters) at the drawing-room without making ludicrous inquiries after *her sister* Mary. "What is sister Mary about just now? Is she disturbed at this or graciously pleased with that? Come! you must tell me something of my dearly beloved sister." And, with all possible respect be it spoken, the simper I was wont to see stealing over King George's countenance long after, whenever he heard Lady Mary's name mentioned, seemed to betoken that in early life he too had had his full share of the diversion. In short, I can have no doubt that her lofty aims were a standing jest with all the royal family.

Not that this precludes the possibility of the Duke's having felt a great degree of liking for her, and believed in the reality of hers for him. Men—men of the idle world at least—are so made that their turning a woman into the most cruel ridicule is nothing to the purpose. They may still be extremely vain of her partiality, and inclined rather to overrate it than suppose it feigned. Of course, they will think of her with a good deal of kindness; perhaps with more than they

[1] The late Duchess of Brunswick. Frederick, Prince of Wales, who studiously affected English manners (perhaps in a spirit of contradiction to his thoroughly German father), revived the old English custom of styling his daughters the Lady Augusta, the Lady Elizabeth, etc.; justly deeming this, our national title (like the Madame of France or Infanta of Spain), more dignified than that of Princess, so common on the Continent, and there so far from being confined to Royal persons. But Queen Charlotte saw the matter in another light: the *Lady* wounded her ears, and she re-established the (German) *Princess*.

care to own; but that a very dissipated man—in plain English, a rake—should continue long harboring in the depth of his heart a romantic passion, a faithful, fervent attachment, to a pattern of rigid virtue, one dozen of years older than himself——! Do but consider the likelihood of such a thing!—

"——for aught that ever you could hear,
Could ever read in tale or history."

We all may have known instances of such extraordinary affection subsisting where there was a considerable difference of age on the wrong side; but then either the women have been otherwise than virtuous or else the men have not been rakes. Take the former supposition: it implies the existence of consummate skill and powers of allurement, which, aided by the force of habit, have riveted the chains that chance or caprice originally forged. In the latter case (a far rarer) habit may operate too: but the best feelings of an honest, affectionate heart are usually engaged; and esteem must have helped to ripen the man's sentiments into something more like the strongest degree of brotherly or filial tenderness than love properly so called.

Lady Greenwich once told Lord Haddington that she really believed the Duke of York and Lady Mary were secretly married. Why she thought so, or chose to say so, I shall not pretend to conjecture. I should never have guessed this to be her opinion. I am certain it was not that of her other sisters, or their husbands; for they were sufficiently explicit upon the subject: sometimes laughing like the rest of the world; sometimes wishing they could deter Lady Mary from exposing herself. It is past my power of belief that she would ever have destroyed one scrap of paper tending to prove, I will not say a marriage, but a promise, an engagement, an undefined connection, an obscure and nameless tie between them; since she preserved his veriest notes of three lines, written in a great schoolboy's scrawl, to hope her cold was better, or to recommend a tuner for the lute of famous memory. The longest and latest epistle of all, dated from Rome in 1764, and subscribed "Your affectionate friend, Edward," instead of containing a single phrase trenching on the tender or the mysterious, is rather what sentimental folks would spurn at, as a mere matter-of-fact letter. Any gentleman might have addressed it to any lady, young or old, or even to one of his own sex. It simply tells where he has been, whom he has seen, and how he has been received by the Pope and other princes; concluding with a grumbling comparison between his own situation and income, and those of his "*brother Sosia*," meaning the Cardinal of York.[1]

[1] The following is the letter referred to:

"ROME, *April 25th*, 1764.

"DR LY MARY,—Nothing having happen'd worthy troubling you with a further account of than what report of newspapers wou'd suffise, has made me defer writing till now. The attentions I have met with everywhere were what I might flatter myself with receiving in some degree. The manner of showing them has been conducted in the most friendly or respectful manner to the King, according to the different situations from whence they came: all in the most obliging, *some* even with affectionate tenderness towards me. I need hardly tell you I mean those paid me by the King of Sardinia. Enquire of G. Pitt, who will give

Upon his death, which happened at Modena[1] in 1767, Lady Mary's affliction was excessive; and it was

you a full account of it. The D. of Modena & Madame Zimonetta did all they cou'd to make Milan as agreeable as possible, in which they succeeded so well that I promis'd the Duke to meet him at the Fair at Regio. My tour to Naples was interupted by the famine riot and disorder, that I fear will still prevail there for some time. This made me stay at Florence & the environs till the Holy week brought me to Rome. Sr Horace Man did the honours of the last place. It is requisite to know the good nature, good humor, good sense and real well understood hospitality he possesses, to know how agreeable he can make himself. I desire you will tell his friend H. Walpole how much I am pleas'd with him. At my arrival here I receiv'd the same attentions as elsewhere from the foreign ministers and nobility of the country. The Pope pays me every mark of distinction possible. I have assisted at all the functions. The very Tribune in St Peters which us'd to be fitted up for the old Chevalier was transferr'd to me. The Governor of Rome is my particular friend. Cardinal Albani gave me a ball last night, an event not seen these two years, and forbid then by the Pope, but approved of on this occasion. There is another tonight at the Corsini Palace. Tomorrow there's a horse race in the town. I visited yesterday the Castle of St Angelo, which was lin'd from top to bottom with soldiers. The officers saluted me as I passed. As for Brother Sosia, he has gone to reside at his Bishoprick: whether he is the true or the false one is not for me to determine, but I am sure, "Il est celui chez qui on devroit diner," for he is a Cardinal with £40,000 a year. I have no chance of ever being a Bishop. His private establishment is at present £15,000 for life, & will be more when his father dies; alas! mine is but £12,000, and that only during pleasure. I think of returning to Florence in a few days. I cannot conclude without acquainting you I never knew Ldy Spencer so well as at present. Your friendship for her I am sure will make you rejoice at hearing so good an account of her. Adieu. I find I must be very soon among you in the autumn, when I hope to assure you in person of the esteem & regard with which I am—Yr very affectionate Friend, E." —ED.

[1] By mistake for *Monaco*.

affiché—for I must borrow a French word—displayed and proclaimed to all hearers and beholders. His body being brought home for interment, she went down into the vault as soon as the funeral was over, attended by Colonel Morrison, his groom of the bedchamber, to kneel and weep beside the coffin. This Morrison, whom I remember an old general, was a tall, lank man, with a visage uncommonly rueful and ugly. "Umph!" said George Selwyn, in his grave, slow manner; "if her ladyship wished to enact the Ephesian matron, I wonder she did not choose a better-looking soldier." For some years she constantly repeated these visits to the Duke's remains whenever the opening of the royal vault on the demise of a prince or princess gave her an opportunity:[1] but all her acquaintance were expected to know that the hallowed building containing them must never be named or alluded to in her presence. Lady Emily Macleod, while still a girl in a white frock, got into a sad scrape on this account. Her father and mother had a very pretty villa near Blackheath, which Princess Emily one morning drove down to see, carrying Lady Mary Coke with her. As Lord Lothian was absent, and Lady Lothian not quite well, her Royal Highness took the young lady to show her the walks and prospects. Now they stopped to look at a fine view of Greenwich Hospital, now at a noble reach of the river crowded with shipping. "And here, madam, this way, your Royal Highness may catch a glimpse of Westminster Abbey." "My dear!" exclaimed Lady Mary, rather sharply, "if you please do

[1] See "Journal of Lady Mary Coke," 21st May, 1768.—ED.

not talk of Westminster Abbey before me." The Princess laughed; and they walked on and on till they came to an eminence, where poor Lady Emily, forgetting the injunction, pointed out the Abbey, as it seemed to rise in awful solemnity from a grove of elms within the place. "Child!" cried Lady Mary in her shrillest key, "what do you mean? Have you a mind to make me faint away? Did I not forbid you to say anything about the Abbey?" People of warm tempers are subject to mistake in the mode of expressing their feelings, and confound one kind of emotion with another: so the girl went home and asked her mother why that lady always flew in such a passion at the sight (or sound) of Westminster Abbey.

Nothing could be more characteristic of both parties than the first interview between Princess Emily and Lady Mary after the Duke of York's decease. The one, neither feeling concerned nor seeking to feign it, talked on common topics as usual, resolved not to notice the other's mournful silence, bows, and monosyllables. A violent burst of tears ensued. "Dear Lady Mary!" quoth her Royal Highness, "do not make yourself so miserable about my sister" (this was the Landgravine of Hesse-Cassel, who had a fit of illness); "I assure you my accounts of her are quite satisfactory." Here the paroxysm redoubled. "Nay, but surely you may trust me; I am not in the least uneasy now; by yesterday's post I received a letter from herself to say how fast she was recovering." At last Lady Mary, taking none of these hints—for broad hints they were meant to be—sobbed forth the name of York; and at last also Princess Emily, losing patience, broke out with all the rough bluntness of her father: "My good Lady Mary, if you did but know what a joke he always used to make of you, I promise you you would soon have done crying for him." I presume this abrupt dialogue induced Lady Mary to send the incredulous aunt all his notes and letters, in order to show her what his sentiments had been; but the packet came back with only one brief dry sentence in answer as follows: "*I thank you for the letters, which I return, and wish I could prevail on you to burn them all.*—AMELIA."[1]

In three or four years, ere the wound was well healed, two surprising public events took place; ostensibly not at all concerning Lady Mary, yet felt by her as personal injuries and mortifications to herself. These were the Duke of Cumberland's marriage, and, what it probably hastened, the public avowal of the Duke of Gloucester's. I was then beginning to open my eyes and ears, and to attend to the conversation of my mother's visitors; and I can bear witness that Lady Mary lost her rest and appetite, and ran some risk of losing her wits upon these royal misalliances. She foamed at the mouth as she declaimed against them. Knowing the whole affair, certainly one can conceive nothing more irritating to a great lady, duchess-dowager of York by her own creation, yet, with all the Campbell blood in her veins, unable to prove herself so, than to behold two such persons authentically Duchesses of Gloucester and Cumberland. Lady

[1] The packet still exists, with this note attached in Princess Amelia's writing.—ED.

Waldegrave was a most lovely woman; not of much sense, but blameless in character and conduct. She had the manners of the high society in which she had always moved; she was the widow of a distinguished man of quality; but—there was no disguising it—the illegitimate daughter of Sir Edward Walpole, by a mistress whom, if report spoke true, the keeper of some infamous house, descrying her uncommon beauty, had fairly beckoned in from the top of a cinder-cart. The widow Horton had no such stain of birth, but in every other respect was far less fit for a princess. Her father, Simon Luttrell,[1] might be pronounced the greatest reprobate in England. He once challenged his eldest son, the late Lord Carhampton, who in return sent him word that if he (the father) could prevail on any gentleman to be his second, he would fight him with all his heart. Such was the style of the family. The daughters had habits suited to it; vulgar, noisy, indelicate, and intrepid: utter strangers to good company, they never were to be seen in any woman of fashion's house, though often leaders of riotous parties at Vauxhall or Ranelagh. Yet Mrs. Horton was not accused of gallantry. She belonged to that disgusting class of women who possibly spread wider corruption than many of the more really, or—let me say—more *nominally*, vicious: women who have never blushed in their lives; who set modesty and decency at defiance in cold blood; and, because they have *done* nothing, take the liberty of saying everything; as if desirous to proclaim that it is not principle, but want of sufficient temptation alone,

[1] Created Lord Irnham, and afterward Earl of Carhampton.

that hinders their walking the Strand. Lady Margaret Fordice said, very aptly, that after hearing the Duchess of Cumberland talk for half an hour one ought to go home and wash one's ears.

The King, highly offended with his brothers on this occasion, forbade them his sight, and notified that no one who frequented their courts should be received at St. James. So had William and Mary done to Queen Anne, and George the First and Second to their refractory sons. But their successor was much too goodnatured to enforce his edict; especially against the Duke of Gloucester, whom he loved. Were you ever at a trial by the Peers in Westminster Hall? When first proclamation is made that "our sovereign Lord doth strictly charge all manner of persons to keep silence on pain of imprisonment," everybody is struck totally dumb for about five seconds: then our fair sex (if not the other) recover their fright, and go on whispering and clattering just as before. His Majesty's prohibition had like effects. It overawed people for the first month; in the second they stole a visit to Gloucester or Cumberland House,[1] went to Court early in the third, and, being spoken to as usual, troubled their heads no more about the matter. It soon grew a dead letter, which nobody pretended to mind but the household, the ministers, and their wives. Meanwhile, as it pointed out to the Opposition a cheap and

---

[1] Gloucester House, now Grosvenor House, was purchased from the Duke of Beaufort in 1761. Cumberland House was built for Henry, Duke of Cumberland, in Pall Mall, and is now part of the War Office. (Wheatley and Cunningham's "London.")—ED.

safe way of showing disrespect to the Crown, their zeal instantly flamed high for the Princes in disgrace; and never were Princesses so reverenced and Royal Highnessed by patriots as the ladies whose consequence Aunt Emily overturned with one careless word. "Well! to talk no more of my nephews and their women——"

Neither of the proscribed houses, then, was at all deserted; but they differed materially from each other in point of society, for the Duchess of Gloucester maintained a degree of state, approved of by the Duke, that gave some stiffness to her parties, which were commonly rather select. Unbounded freedom reigned at Cumberland House, as its mistress, laughing forms and etiquettes to scorn, was better pleased that tag, rag, and bobtail (pardon the vulgar phrase) should flock in than that numbers should ever be wanting. This did not spring from humility.—Query, does it in any case? She was not honestly indifferent to the honors she affected to undervalue; but she had sense enough to know that nothing could ever place her upon the same level with the persons born in purple: therefore she bore them an inveterate hatred, and made whatever appertained to rank, birth, or dignity the object of her contemptuous sarcasms. Her sister, Miss Betsy (or Lady Elizabeth) Luttrell, who had a great deal of real, though coarse, wit, and was more precisely what the Regent Orleans entitled a *Roué* than one would have thought it practicable that anything clad in petticoats could be, governed the family with a high hand, marshalled the gaming-table, gathered round her the men, and led the way in ridiculing the King and Queen. Buckingham House served as a byword—a signal for the onset of Ho! Ho! Ho!—and a mighty scope for satire was afforded by the Queen's wide mouth and occasionally imperfect English, as well as by the King's trick of saying What? What? his ill-made coats, and general antipathy to the fashion. But the marks preferably aimed at were his *virtues;* his freedom from vice as a man; his discouragement of it as a sovereign; the exclusion of divorced women from his court; beyond all, his religious *prejudices*—that is to say, his sincere piety and humble reliance upon God. Nothing of this scoffing kind passed at Gloucester House: the Duke respected his brother and himself too much to permit it, and the Duchess, however sore on her own account, saw nothing ridiculous in conjugal fidelity, nor yet in going to church and saying one's prayers— superstitious practices to which the unenlightened woman was greatly addicted herself.

Now, upon my statement, would not you conclude that, of these two obnoxious couples, the Cumberlands must have been most the objects of Lady Mary's abhorrence? Yet was it quite the reverse. She regarded them with supreme disdain; but at the name of the Gloucesters her eyes struck fire, and her teeth absolutely gnashed together. I hope for the honor of history, and for hers, that no paltry female feeling lay lurking at the root of this bitter animosity—no original grudge against the beautiful Lady Waldegrave for having, on her first appearance, eclipsed other people who were far less young, and never had been half so handsome.

Perhaps the mere circumstance of a slight common acquaintance between them operated disagreeably. It might be more galling to have a person put over one's head who a moment ago stood in the ranks by one's side than to see a stranger promoted from another brigade. In short, I only warrant the fact—I cannot tell the reason. The unconscious Duchess of Gloucester seemed to run pins and needles, goads and stings into her, drawing blood every day by some fresh piece of arrogance or sauciness; though all the while, notwithstanding the airs she—that woman—chose to give herself ("*that woman*"—not pronounced in the cool tone of Princess Emily, but with a killing emphasis), the woman was *not* MARRIED: the Duchess of Cumberland was.

To explain this to your comprehension. The widow Horton, when she had secured her idiot-prince—by means, it was said, of some stern hints from a resolute brother, "*un certain Alcidas qui se meloit de porter l'épée*" (see Molière's "Mariage Forcé")—took especial care to be wedded in the face of day, and have register, certificate, and witnesses all forthcoming. The Duke of Gloucester, who at first intended to keep his marriage a profound secret, found himself hampered by the precautions he had used for that purpose, and in consequence could not produce his proofs so readily. But the King, though angry, ever upright and honorable, as he had no manner of doubt on the subject in his own mind, would not suffer any to be started in Council, and I believe none was entertained by the world at large: so Lady Mary stood out alone—as she had the glory of doing against the foolish notions of her ignorant fellow-creatures in many another instance.

A year or two after these marriages, Lady Mary resolved to leave the land where such monstrous acts could be committed, and breathe a while the pure air of countries more strictly governed. It was not her first sally abroad. She had made two or three excursions into Germany since his late Majesty's accession, and formed intimacies with sundry German princesses —Mary of England, in particular, Landgravine of Hesse-Cassel—her professions of attachment to whom had authorized that wicked, wilful mistake of Princess Emily's recorded above. The Royal and Serene Highnesses in question (most of them her correspondents) were now to be revisited at their respective courts for the refreshing of friendship: then she purposed paying her respects to the hero Frederick of Prussia, and then pushing on to Vienna. The hero proved not only inaccessible but invisible. At Berlin his brothers and sisters and his poor cipher queen were as civil to her as could be wished, and she saw many of the generals who had gathered laurels in the Seven Years' War; but vainly did she spend a whole week at Potsdam, go to the opera, and attend the parade. Frederick, rather than meet her eyes, forbore enjoying his music and exercising his troops, and continued obstinately shut up in his private apartments till assured of her final retreat. Seriously, she persuaded herself that there was something in his seclusion during her stay that did regard her, and was too marked not to be intentional; therefore, as distinction is all in all, she remained nearly as well satisfied as she would have been with a favorable reception. The King of Prussia, she thought, did not take pains to avoid an insignificant person, one of no political importance.[1]

Ample amends awaited her at Vienna, where the British envoy, Sir Robert Murray Keith,[2] was then all-powerful; being universally popular, and cherished as a familiar friend by the Emperor Joseph. Our ambassadors at foreign courts had not yet learned to dread invasions from their countrywomen: travelling boys and tutors frequently gave them a great deal of trouble, but English ladies did not at that time go swarming all over Europe. The arrival, then, of a woman of high quality and unstained character, like Lady Mary Coke, was an incident rather acceptable to Sir Robert, who, by paying her particular respect himself, insured her obtaining attention from the crowned heads: to whom he made her birth and rank fully known, and introduced her in the most advantageous manner. A duck—or why have not I the grace to say a Swan?—

[1] Frederick was always present at the daily exercise of the troops at Potsdam. When Lady Mary was there he did not come, upon which she said to Lord Marischall, in the presence of one of his (the king's) aide-de-camps, "that I hoped his Lordship would tell him, that altho' I allowed him to be a very great Hero and a great King, I prefer'd the Heros of Antiquity, for they had complaisance for Ladies, and that his Majesty had none, which I looked upon as a great defect in his character." ("Journal," 4th August, 1773.)—ED.

[2] The British envoy in 1770, when Lady Mary first visited Vienna, was Lord Stormont. Sir Robert Keith was not appointed till 1772, on Lady Mary's second visit to Vienna. He had the difficult task of steering clear of her quarrels during her third visit in 1773.—ED.

A MEMOIR 119

takes the water by instinct, swims proudly along, and is happy. Thus in a court Lady Mary found her natural element. Here, making a graceful curtsy, playing her fan with a good air, and dressing magnificently, were all things of some moment; and her knowledge of history and pedigree, foreign and domestic, turned to still better account. The Empress-queen received and treated her with all her habitual graciousness; Joseph, ever a most agreeable man in society, was well-bred and courteous to Sir Robert Keith's friend; Prince Kaunitz, the prime minister, followed his example; Count Seilern, who had been ambassador in England, welcomed her as an old acquaintance; the Thuns, the Lichtensteins, the Esterhazis, invited her to superb entertainments; and, on the whole, I suppose the months she passed among them were decidedly the happiest of her long life. When about to go away, she had a private audience of the Empress, who, with many flattering expressions of regret for her departure, desired she would accept a fine medallion set with jewels, and wear it for her sake.

All this was so much sunshine beaming on Lady Mary's mind. In extraordinary good-humor, breathing nothing but admiration for the perfect beings she had left, she came home to recount her *prosperities*, as Madame de Sévigné would have said, to a set of cold, incredulous hearers. No doubt her descriptions were pompous, and people laughed at her, as they had the confirmed habit of doing, let her talk of what she would; but I shall confess that, for once, I had no inclination to join them: her conversation interested me more than it ever did before or since. First, it was fluent—an epithet that seldom belonged to it, unless when anger prompted her to pour out invectives. In the next place, she had something worth talking of— the mountain did not now bring forth a mouse: heroic language suited an heroic subject, and when she expatiated on the talents and virtues of the great princess by whom she boasted herself favored—on her spirit, her despatch, her penetration, her magnanimity, her justice, her clemency—to listen "I did seriously incline": for I was very young, and very enthusiastic— to speak the truth—and had in my heart a greater *hankering* after heroes and heroines than I durst openly acknowledge, for fear of becoming as good a joke as Lady Mary.

I still retain a lively remembrance of her painting the scene she said she had witnessed during an illness, in which the Empress lay for some days seemingly at the point of death, the physicians giving scarcely a hope of her recovery. Every church was crowded, day and night, with persons of every class from the highest to the lowest: all kneeling promiscuously, and praying with such fervency, as if each individual had been petitioning the Almighty to spare the object dearest to his own bosom. The multitude who thronged round the palace-gates stood watching for the moment of their opening in breathless, silent anxiety; not a sound to be heard but now and then a sob that could not be suppressed—the soldiers stationed to prevent the populace from rushing in weeping the most bitterly of all. For the courtiers and nobility—if asked after her, they

A MEMOIR 121

began their answers in due form, with "Her Imperial Majesty," but melted as they went on, till her high titles sank into "*Notre chère Marie Thérèse,*" uttered in that tone of true affection, that voice of the heart, which can neither be feigned nor mistaken. It was at length judged necessary to administer the last sacraments; and as the Emperor, her son, advanced to receive the priest bearing the Host and holy oil for extreme unction, the tears were seen streaming down his cheeks. But men are men, and power is power: on another day the symptoms of universal despondency drew from him a remark which betrayed that he did not view it without an inward sensation of jealousy—" This excessive despair," he said, "looks not only as if they loved her, but as if they were afraid of her successor."[1] Very probably no unjust inference.

Besides such anecdotes of Maria Theresa, I had pleasure in learning particulars concerning Prince Kaunitz, considered as the wisest statesman in Europe; Laudohn, esteemed by the King of Prussia one of its greatest generals; Marshal Lacy, long the leader of the Imperial armies; and many other remarkable characters. Then the grandeur of the Hungarian nobles, their ancient descent, their magnificent palaces, even their plate and diamonds, and feasts and balls and shows, went for something with an imagination hardly yet weaned

[1] This attack (smallpox caught from her son Joseph's second wife, who died of it) took place in 1767, three years before Lady Mary's first visit to Vienna. Madame Cobenzl, wife of the Prime Minister at Brussels, gave Lady Mary an account of what Lady Louisa describes. See "Journal of Lady Mary Coke," 18th July, 1767.—ED.

from the enchantment of the Arabian tales. So, I repeat it, I was for the first and last time an attentive, gratified auditor. Others, less captivated by the theme, grew sooner tired of its constant recurrence, and, besides, felt a strong impulse to rebel when poor old England was unmercifully run down, and declared to have nothing in it worthy to be seen or spoken of. It was true, nobody could say much in behalf of the tarnished tapestry at St. James's, or of that wainscoted ballroom which would have made a decent figure if seated over the market-house of a country town, and lit with tallow candles. We had always a woful deficiency of regal splendor.[1] But what were the Duchess of Bedford's suppers and the Duchess of Norfolk's concerts to those of the Princess Something with half a dozen hard names? And you might see more massive gold-plate at Prince Esterhazy's table than the

[1] "Your saying you wish'd I had been at the Christening [*of Princess Amelia, youngest daughter of George III.*] made me smile. You had at that time forgot how many great courts I had been at, & had seen Royal marriages and a royal christening in magnificent Palaces, performed with all the pomp & ceremonies of the Church of Rome. Judge, then, how poor a sight a christening in the dirty rooms of St. James' must appear to me! & indeed I don't know what part I have not seen: The rooms I have often seen lighted up: The table with a piece of red velvet over it I have seen, as also four gilt candlesticks upon the table; an Archbishop in his lawn sleeves performing a ceremony; a great deal of bad company, which you know must always be the case where Privy Councillors' wives are admitted; &, after all, I fancy I have as good a right as anybody who goes there, tho' I never intend to claim that new pretension of being a Privy Councillor's wife. To say the truth, I know of but two ceremonies worth seeing in this country—a Coronation and the trial of a Peer. . . ."—"Journal of Lady Mary Coke," 4th October, 1783.—ED.

whole peerage of the three kingdoms could furnish pitiful silver!

This, however, is a traveller's trick, not peculiar to Lady Mary. "Disable all the benefits of your own country, or I will scarce think you have swum in a gondola." But as such assertions are sure to be stoutly combated, contradiction, often carried beyond the truth, whetted her zeal to the sharpest edge, and trebled her passionate fondness for Vienna. Unfortunately, the natural consequence of this was a longing to return thither, which it would have been more prudent to resist than to gratify. Our second visit to a place that has extremely charmed us on a first very rarely answers. I suppose, because a certain lapse of time enables that busy artist, imagination, so imperceptibly to color and improve the sketches drawn by memory that, no longer distinguishing the handiwork of each, we ascribe the whole picture to the latter. Then, upon again viewing the real objects, and finding the likeness unfaithful, we call them to account for our disappointment, and insist that they are themselves altered and disfigured.

How far this occurred in the present instance I cannot pretend to say, nor do I know the exact details of what passed. I only understood generally that Lady Mary, being now quite at home at Vienna, acted as she was prone to act at home, and very shortly either took a warm part in some feud she found raging, or else declared a war of her own against a court-lady, near the Empress's person, and long established in her favor. The Empress was so unreasonable and unjust as to side with her Grande Maîtresse; perhaps, too, to think that an officious foreigner had no business to come and meddle with the intrigues of her court, much less to lead parties and stir up dissensions. No more audiences or medallions were to be obtained; the sovereign's frown had its accustomed effect upon the courtiers; and there was no doing what might so readily be done in England, if the King had spat in your face, or, for that matter, you in his; no leaguing yourself with the friends of freedom, and holding your head higher than ever. Lady Mary left the territories of her enemy in complete, thorough, perfect *dudgeon :* with only one consolation, *videlicet,* as perfect a conviction that Maria Theresa, the last of the illustrious line of Austria, the Empress of Germany, the Queen of Hungary, the leading power of Europe, was *her* enemy—HERS!

I remember hearing it suggested that some rumors respecting the deceased Duke of York might have reached the Empress's ear, and, as she was much surprised at Lady Mary's unlooked-for appearance a second time,[1] led her to suspect the wandering heroine of evil designs on the heart and hand of Joseph. This I utterly disbelieve. I dare say her Imperial Majesty knew mankind better than to apprehend any danger for her son (a man of full age, already twice married) from the wiles of a fair traveller, considerably on the wrinkled side of forty. But the surmise was not a little agreeable to Lady Mary, as I myself ascertained ten or twelve years afterward. I must defer telling you how, for it would be too long a parenthesis at present.

[1] It was really the third visit.—ED.

From Vienna she pursued her way through the Tyrol into Italy, at every step meeting with those difficulties and disasters which seem to beset us, by some fatality, whenever we ourselves are prodigiously out of humor; just as every species of food is nauseous to the taste when our stomachs are loaded with bile. Italy would not do at all; so, bending her course homeward, she next visited Paris, but only to undergo additional evils. The young King and Queen of France had but lately assumed the crown destined to be torn from their heads in so cruel a manner, and were now in the zenith of apparent prosperity, enjoying that brilliant, deceitful calm so finely pictured by Gray—

"Fair laughs the morn, and soft the zephyr blows,
While proudly riding o'er the azure realm
In gallant trim the gilded vessel goes,
Youth on the prow, and Pleasure at the helm."

In those days one of the unfortunate Queen's chief sins appears to have been a want of attention to that resentful part of the Creation, *Old Women,* and consequent disregard of all the forms, etiquettes, decorums, and nice observances which old women value and recommend—not always unwisely, as her melancholy history may prove. Now, imagine a tall, elderly, English noblewoman, full fraught with all these offensive things, wearing a large flat hoop, long ruffles, and a sweeping train, holding herself very upright, speaking very bad French, and, to crown all, abusing the Queen's mother without mercy. I say, imagine such a wight arriving amidst the revelry then reigning at Versailles, and judge whether the giddy crew and their leader were likely to receive her with open arms? Probably poor Marie Antoinette rejoiced to have so fair a pretext as this grave personage's recent disgrace at Vienna for declining to be annoyed with the *vielle cour* of England, in addition to that of France, which it was not in her power to shake off. But Lady Mary along with the smart had at least the balm of thinking that the daughter acted by the special injunctions of the implacable mother, whose couriers went and came to and fro for no other purposes than what concerned her. So all was well—or ill—as you choose to term it.

One of the most memorable consequences resulting from this last luckless expedition was a breach between Lady Mary and Horace Walpole, once her intimate acquaintance, her correspondent, the poet of her praise.[1] He had always been more or less guilty of laughing at her, it is true; but that was what most of her friends took the liberty of doing, and his printed letters show you it might be done with impunity, for she was so cased in self-satisfaction that the keenest raillery, if couched in civil language, would pass upon her for a compliment. So their intimacy remained unaltered. But he had gradually cooled toward her ever since she took the field so fiercely against his niece, the Duchess of Gloucester; and now, when life's flowery season was closed for both, when she was of the middle age and he a humorsome old bachelor, her imprudence put his remaining regard to a test it could

---

[1] Walpole's praise had not begun in 1746. "Lord Coke is to have the youngest of the late Duke of Argyll's daughters, who is none of our beauties at all." (To Sir H. Mann, vol. ii. p. 49.)

not stand. When you approach the confines of fifty, dear Car, avoid, as far as you may, having any kind of difference with a young beauty. If it cannot be helped, manage it by yourself, meekly and silently, and never —oh! never!—expect a MAN, an old acquaintance, an old friend, even an old lover—no, not if parson of the parish, not if your confessor (supposing you a Catholic)— to espouse your cause with zeal or readiness. Lady Mary's malignant stars, or her genius for quarrelling, led her to fall out with Lady Barrymore, a daughter of the famous Lady Harrington—"*daughter every way*"— but as yet only just entering on her career: very pretty, very lively, bold as a lion, and highly admired at Paris, the fashion there, which is saying everything. This did not particularly concern Mr. Walpole, who was by no means one of those old fops or fools who vie with younger fops for the favor of ladies; yet when summoned to act as champion on the opposite side, to wage war with the fashion, he quailed, or, what was worse, presumed to investigate the merits of the cause, point-blank against all the laws of chivalry and friendship; at least, so it appeared to Lady Mary.

We had not the details of the business from herself. She returned to England in no communicative mood, touching either that or her greater wrongs; commonly sitting rapt and absorbed in awful, portentous silence, or, at most, throwing out hints, very significant, but not explanatory of particulars. "Well, Lady Mary," my mother began, "I suppose you saw Mr. Walpole at Paris?" "Yes, I saw him, as FALSE as ever he could be." "Why," returned my mother, who had known him from a boy and did not herself think sincerity his constant characteristic, "you might now and then have seen cause to suspect that before, Lady Mary." "I know it pretty certainly NOW!" and, as if too indignant to say more, she folded her arms, threw herself back in her chair, and looked the rest. We got no further information till he arrived from abroad, when he very soon came to tell us his own story; how fairly, I do not know; how entertainingly, you shall judge.

"My dear Madam!" said he, "do but conceive that I was fast asleep in my warm bed, at peace with the whole world; when my Swiss valet-de-chambre comes, in his nightcap, sputtering and fussing, to wake me at five o'clock in the morning. I must get up immediately. 'Oh Lord!' cried I; 'is the house on fire?' No; but there was a lady in distress. *Miledi Coke—il lui est arrivé quelque malheur; elle est tout éplorée*—and she must positively see Monsieur that instant. So Monsieur was forced to comply, sorely against his will. I huddled on some decent clothing, and hobbled into my salon, where I found her ladyship, *tout éplorée* indeed, pacing up and down the room in such a *taking* that I trembled to ask whether she had been robbed or ravished. She had bid me adieu, you will observe, and was on the point of setting out for England; so the scene amazed me the more. I could make neither head nor tail of anything she said for some minutes. At last, when it transpired that Lady Barrymore had enticed away her confidential courier and factotum, I fetched my breath once more; and, I am afraid, made a sad slip of the tongue. 'Is that all?' said I. I

own I deserved to have my ears boxed; and truly I
was near getting my deserts, for I wish you had heard
the tone in which ALL! was thundered back again. I
drew in my horns as fast as possible, humbly admitting
the loss of a useful servant to be a very serious evil,
and his leaving her at the eve of a journey a most
vexatious circumstance. I did not say, how could *I*
help or hinder it? I only proffered my best services
in looking for another fit person to fill his place; and
then, like a blockhead, I begged her to compose herself, take a few drops, go home, and lie down; and at
noonday I would wait upon her to concert further
measures. I might have guessed that this would
throw oil on the fire. Mercy! what a blaze followed!
She fell into the most absolute *Tantrum* you ever beheld; wrung her hands and tore her hair. She was
betrayed, abandoned, devoted to destruction, had not a
real friend on the face of the earth. If I were the
tenth part of one, I should go and scold Lady Barrymore, and bring back the courier *vi et armis*. She expected no less from my former professions, but now she
saw nobody was to be relied upon; there was neither
faith, truth, nor humanity existing. She next proceeded to unveil mysteries, and told me the true state
of the case; which, if it *had* been true, would, to be
sure, have rendered *my* interference vastly easier and
more efficacious! Lady Barrymore, it should seem,
was but an instrument, a tool, in the hands of the
Queen of France; and she again only executed the
commands of her mother, the Empress of Germany,
who had projected the whole affair long beforehand.

Lady Mary was to be assassinated on the road between Paris and Calais; and to that end this faithful courier— the sole obstacle to their murderous designs—by whom her life had already been defended two or three times from the Empress's myrmidons, was to be wiled away at any price. I thought to myself, it would have been the shortest way to poison him, as the thieves sometimes serve one's house-dog at Twickenham; but I durst not utter such a word. Now, dearest madam, what could I possibly say? If I had attempted to convince her that the Empress did not know, and the Queen did not care, whether she and her courier were at Paris or at Pekin, and that their Majesties were as likely to plan the murder of my favorite pussy-cat, you know I should have acted as simply as the good clergyman who comforted the penitent author by assuring him that no mortal had ever heard of his writings. And, besides, my person might have been endangered. I am not built for a hero, and she is for an Amazon. I confess to you those two fists of hers struck no small terror into my cowardly soul; and, as she flounced out of the house, I could hardly believe I had escaped without a scratched face or a black eye. I caught a little cold from my air-bath in the morning, and it brought on a little gout; but that did not much signify."

As I said above, I will not answer for the strict accuracy of the narrative; but one part of it—that respecting the Imperial plots conjured up by Lady Mary's imagination—Lord Orford neither invented nor exaggerated. She left us in no doubt on this head, as you shall see when I have finished the chapter of Coke and Walpole.

The flames of discord subsided more quickly than you would have expected after such an explosion. Not that peace was ever formally made, much less familiarity renewed; but Mr. Walpole only withdrew to a civil distance; and Lady Mary, though she hated him from that day forward, felt an awe of him that bridled her temper. To break with him totally would have been to quarrel (in the child's phrase) with her bread and butter. For he was intimate with almost all her friends; she could not exclude him from Princess Emily's card-table, nor lessen his influence over Lord and Lady Strafford. Therefore, they soon began again to play at Loo together, like well-bred Christians; and I really think he viewed her with more indifference than enmity. She presented herself to his mind merely as a ridiculous, wrong-headed woman; the less one had to do with whom the better.[1] But that his love of laughing at her increased I cannot deny. Many years after the time I speak of he one day said to me —I forget on what occasion, it was something relating

[1] Lady Mary thus speaks of him in 1780:—"24 *July* . . . I mentioned in my last Journal my intention of going to Park Place this week, but having wrote to Ly Aylesbury on Saturday to know if they were to be at home, I this day received her answer to beg me to fix some other time, for this week their house was full, tho' when she named them there was not so many as there were last year when I was there; but I suppose there is one she did not name, who never chuses to meet me, and that is Mr. Walpole." By his letters of this date Walpole does not appear to have been at Park Place at this time.—ED.

to her—"Lady Louisa, I will teach you to make verses —good, regular verses—and we will address them to Lady Mary Coke, who, you know, is famous for always scolding the Living and crying over the Dead. I will make the first line of the couplet, and you shall make the second. You shall not be able to help it. Now, mark mine—

> "The more you scold the less you'll kiss.
> . . . ."

You may believe I was as little able to help bursting into a most improper fit of laughter.

While Lady Mary was still abroad, somewhere in Italy, Lady Betty Mackenzie came to us, one morning, in serious alarm at a letter she had just received from her, giving most deplorable accounts of her health and situation. Lady Betty read us the greater part of it aloud. It said she was miserably ill, and without a human creature near her whom she could trust. Her maid—who, she saw plainly, was in other interests than hers—treated her with the greatest insolence; well aware she should be supported and rewarded—no need of saying by whom. Not to enter into her various causes of complaint against this wretch—perhaps, indeed, it might be hardly safe in a common post-letter—let it only be mentioned that there was every reason to believe she had robbed her of her fine pearls.[1]

[1] ". . . My pearls being found at Notting Hill has given me the greatest disquiet, as 'tis a proof beyond all doubt Deehens" (her servant) "has been in England, and likewise in my house, which I always feared would be the case. . . . I have all the reason in the world to think the French maid was in all his secrets. . . .

Lady Betty knew not what to think or to do; but the particular purport of the letter being to desire she would fetch certain keys from Coutts's, and search a certain trunk for such and such papers, she did so immediately; and lo! the very first thing apparent in the trunk was a case containing the identical pearls the maid had been purloining in Italy under the auspices of Maria Theresa,—the nameless personage thus mysteriously glanced at, and the saucy Abigail's secret protectress. In this predicament it availed Lady Mary nothing to dismiss that individual waiting-woman; for, as fast as she could turn away men and maids, the Empress was sure to supply her with others; every new one ten degrees worse than any of the old: besides heaping upon her all the injuries that could be inflicted through the medium of postmasters, innkeepers, blacksmiths, custom-house officers, sentinels at the gates of fortified towns, and vendors of the necessaries of life. "Kings have long hands," says the proverb; of course, the greatest sovereign in Europe might well have the longest, beyond the reach of which it was impossible to travel. Imagine what it was to be the object of such a persecution! That is, imagine the pride and pleasure of it. For hate, like love, has an equalizing power; and our inveterate foes, however loath, cannot avoid raising us, by their very hostility, to a

She acknowledges that he must have stole the Pearls, and that he or his wife must have carried them to Notting Hill, for she does not in the least deny my having wore them at Berlin. In short, the treachery and baseness of almost all my servants is shocking to think of. . . ."—Lady Mary Coke to Lady Greenwich, Paris, 5th May, 1774.—ED.

level little beneath their own. To have, then, not a lion, but an empress, always in the path, and, nevertheless, so far to defeat her malice as to bring off life and limb as safe as if one had never offended the House of Austria—what a triumph! So Lady Mary felt it. Through all the multiplicity of her grievances and the gloom they caused we could descry a wonderful increase of self-importance. To use a familiar expression, she came home a foot taller, and looked down upon common things and common mortals more scornfully than ever.

One circumstance puzzled me a good while. She often complained of rheumatic pains in her arm and shoulder, and when a pang seized her would grasp the part with her other hand and cry: "Ay, there it is— going on as usual, for fear I should forget. Ay! I suppose I am to be reminded by this token as long as I live—Ay, Ay!!" All this uttered with a bitter laugh, "*un cotal riso amaro,*" and the air of a high-minded sufferer resolved to contemn somebody's malignity. I did not know what to make of it. The pains, it seemed, were not to be brought in "by the visitation of God": yet Lady Mary was no believer in sorcery, nor had she ever, as far as I could learn, been cast into any damp dungeon. And how one's worst enemy, whether Empress-queen, or Grand Signor, or Great Mogul, could give one the rheumatism otherwise I was at a loss to comprehend; but by putting hints together and listening heedfully to all she said of her travels I caught the right clew at last. As she traversed the Milaneze, her post-boys, dutiful subjects of the Empress, purposely mistook the road, and drove her full into the middle of a river, or a mill-stream, where it was their mistress's design she should be drowned. That they themselves must have been drowned the foremost, their loyalty or their villany set them above minding; for Maria Theresa had her creatures in as good order as the Prince of Lebanon his assassins of old. Lady Mary's sole protector, the faithful courier, afterward seduced by Lady Barrymore, rode forward, produced his pistols, and compelled them to stop; but could not induce them to relinquish their purpose until chance sent to his aid some foreign travellers, who by main force turned about the horses' heads and escorted Lady Mary to the next post-house. While the dispute lasted she sat up to her knees in water, the least ill effects of which was the rheumatism aforesaid.[1]

Let me relate one other instance of this relentless pursuit of her, and then have done. She had always been a good economist, and now, growing more and more attentive to pounds, shillings, and pence, did not scruple taking some small trouble to save a few even of the two latter. The furniture of an ordinary house in her neighborhood was to be sold by auction; she went to reconnoitre it, and among the useful articles spied and fixed upon a walnut-tree chest of drawers likely to go for about twenty shillings; but, instead of

[1] This adventure is fully described in Lady Mary's "Journal," 7th November, 1773.

In her "Journal," 20th July, 1774, Lady Mary says, "I have had a very violent pain in my right arm almost ever since I return'd to England, which I think I catch'd with sitting with my back to a window open."—ED.

sending her butler or her carpenter to bid for her, she went in person and in full majesty—a sure signal inviting all the brokers to bid against her. This was done with such perseverance by one swarthy, shabby-looking fellow that he raised the sum to a ridiculous height. "I now perceived the meaning of it," said she: "the matter being so trifling, I protest it had not occurred to me before; but nothing escapes the vigilance of THAT PERSON, nothing is below *her* attention. Oh! I could tell you such stories, ha, ha, ha!" (and again came the scornful laugh). "I gave the man a *Look* which I fancy he could perfectly understand, and then said to him significantly: "Well, sir, I see you are determined you will have it, and you must; I contend no longer." THAT PERSON we all knew to be the omnipresent Empress of Germany, whose restless spite, grudging Lady Mary's housekeeper a cheap second-hand or tenth-hand chest of drawers, had commissioned forth Moses or Nathan, from the Seven Dials, to bid the old walnut-tree affair up to the price of new mahogany. The look darted at the Jew broker must have been worth seeing; and oh! that Maria Theresa, while actively governing her extensive dominions, and (one grieves to add) busy in partitioning Poland, could but have known the minor feats she was supposed to perform in England! Perhaps she lived the longer for her happy ignorance. I heard much of her from the Marquise di Circello, long the Neapolitan ambassadress at Vienna, who said she was not always grave, but, like most persons of real ability, could laugh most heartily on a fair occasion; therefore on this she might have risked breaking a blood-vessel, and expiring in the literal sense of the word.

Everybody knows how quickly after her death the various changes devised by the philosophic genius of that very arbitrary monarch, her son, embroiled all his affairs, and drove part of his subjects into open rebellion. Yet at first it was the fashion here to applaud everything he did or attempted to do; and while that humor prevailed, the late Lord Stafford laid a comical trap to disconcert Lady Mary. "So, madam,"—he began over the whist-table—"I am quite charmed with your Emperor Joseph; he fulfils all you used to promise for him—so liberal, so enlightened! And then what he has done for Prince Kaunitz is admirable." "Prince Kaunitz!" repeated she, much pleased, "what of him?" "Why, have you not heard?" "No, nothing of Prince Kaunitz." "Oh, then I am so glad to tell it you. You know that nasty, cross, bigoted old woman never would let the poor Prince have a mistress. Well, the Emperor has declared him at full liberty, and now he keeps *three*." The other men present set up a roar, and poor Lady Mary looked as people look when civilly patting a great dog they are afraid of, and dare not kick out of the room. A joke was a thing that always puzzled, even if it failed to offend her; but she took a magnanimous tone with regard to the deceased Empress, giving you to understand she had buried her just resentments in her great adversary's grave, and was willing once more to recall her merits, only premising, "this it is but fair to say—thus much I must acknowledge—justice compels me to bear testimony"

—and such other candor-breathing sentences by way of preface or apology.[1]

Now for the incident I would not introduce sooner. Once upon a time, as the fairy-tales say, I took a fancy to divert myself with going, well disguised, to the house of an acquaintance who saw masks on the night of a great public masquerade. I was then past my girlhood, but not past my *shy-hood*, if I may coin such a word; the eyes of my fellow-creatures still had power to cast a spell over my tongue, which a mask seemed to set free by giving me something like the sensation of the little woman in the nursery-ballad—"Sure enough, it's none of I"—for this very reason, those most used to me were the last to discover me. "Three great oaths would scarce have made them believe" I could be the mask who found so much to say; Lady Mary Coke in particular—though she came to us five days in the week, and stayed, and stayed, and stayed, Heaven knows many a wearisome hour—knew my face better than my voice, and minded my presence no more than that of the round-cheeked marble boys that sup-

[1] On Dec. 23d, 1780, Lady Mary says in her "Journal":—"I must once more return to the subject of the late Empress Queen, whose death is still talk'd of, though the news is now a fortnight old: when I first learnt it I felt exactly as you and Lord Strafford imagined I shou'd; her former graciousness and kindness not only revived in my mind, but represented themselves in lively colours; her unjust persecutions were buried in her grave: as to my admiration, it had never ceased: the great qualities and virtues I knew she possessed, her very engaging manner, such as I never saw in any other person, must excite admiration in everybody, & as she has now closed the scene with uncommon greatness, nothing remains to deprive her of it."—ED.

ported the old-fashioned chimney-piece. If they, or if I, had begun battling a point with her, her surprise would have been but equal. Safe, then, upon the sheltered ground of insignificance (which, by the by, is a much more convenient comfortable post than most people are disposed to think it, and infinitely the best for observation), I challenged her boldly to compare notes about *our mutual friends at Vienna*. I had all their names and histories by heart; could remind her of everything that passed at Prince Such a one's *fête*, given in honor of such an Archduchess's marriage; lament the untimely death of the beautiful Countess ———, to whom he was supposed to be secretly attached —" wonder whether her daughters had grown up pretty? were there two of them, or three? Did Lady Mary know their aunt, the Chanoinesse,[1] who so hated returning to her chapitre at Prague? Did she recollect the hunting-party at Baron ———'s country-seat? And the fright some of us were in when the wild boar made toward the grove of firs?" She was quite enchanted; so was I when I heard her peremptorily silence the company's guesses at the mask with: "Pshaw! you are all wrong. It is somebody who has lived a long time at Vienna; she knows the whole society there—that *I* can answer for. She has mentioned things about which it would be rather difficult to deceive *me*." Ah! thought I, I may try fortune-telling next, since I see how easy it is to make people believe you have told them what they have told you. Thus encouraged, I fell to discussing

[1] Comtesse Canal. See "Journal of Lady Mary Coke," 24th August, 1773.—ED.

the national character of the Hungarians; thence diverged to the conduct of Joseph; and lastly, ventured to say outright that I understood from good authority he had been so captivated by a certain English lady, not far off, that nobody knew what might have happened but for his mother's tyrannical interference. Lady Sackville, who was sitting by, opened her eyes very wide and stole a fearful look at Lady Mary, concluding, I believe, that she would rise in a fury and tear off my mask. No such matter, indeed. She bridled, simpered, fanned herself, almost blushed, and, I assure you, looked as prettily confused but as well pleased as ever was boarding-school girl on hearing her charms had smitten the Captain in quarters.

With this last extensive tour Lady Mary's voyages and travels closed; for if she ever went abroad again (which I doubt) it was only for a few weeks, to Spa or some place of the same kind.[1] She had therefore no more opportunities of being at deadly feud with any foreign potentate. But as Sir Arthur Wardour, who could remember having once been guarded to the Tower by a troop of dragoons, lived to see himself in his old age carried to jail for vulgar debt by a couple

[1] Lady Mary was in Paris in 1775, and at Spa in 1781. Walpole says to Lady Ossory in 1781: ". . . Lady Mary Coke has had an hundred distresses abroad that do not weigh a silver penny altogether. She is like Don Quixote, who went in search of adventures, and when he found none imagined them. She went to Brussels to see the Archduchess, but either had bad intelligence, or the Archduchess very good, for she was gone when Lady Mary arrived; so was the packet boat at Ostend, which she believes was sent away on purpose, by a codicil in the Empress Queen's will. . . ."—H. Walpole, viii. 81.—ED.

of bailiffs, so was it her lot to stoop from braving the enmity of empresses and queens, and live to dread the revenge of John and Betty, leagued with an atrocious cheesemonger. Plots against her still abounded, if you would believe her own report; but now she ascribed them to the servants she was perpetually changing, and the tradespeople she accused of roguery. I dare say you recollect the set of ragamuffins composing her household, people who, for want of a character, could get no other place. The only one among them that stuck long and gained a vast hold of her favor was a certain *Claire* from the French West Indian Islands, a mulatto in hue, but well-shaped, and it may be presumed no fool. A fancy sometimes seized the watchmen of Berkeley Square to cavil at Claire's proceedings, merely, Lady Mary said, because rather late in the evening she had just stepped out to see a sick friend, or had been suddenly sent for by a San Domingo cousin. Since all she did could be so well accounted for, I wonder they ever parted; but everything must come to some end. Claire left her mistress, and dived under the earth for aught any of us knew. She was no more heard of till, fifteen years afterward, at the very least, up she started, the favorite sultana of Sir Harry Englefield, whose friends were never tired of complimenting him on his taste for the black princess—the Queen of Sheba—"the glowing dames of Zama's royal race"—and so forth. He bore their raillery as a great philosopher should do, gravely maintaining that beauty consisted wholly in form, and was quite independent of color.

Claire, then, during Lady Mary's reign over her, or

hers over Lady Mary, stood acquitted of robbery and murder, and everything else; but the rest of the crew kept their lady in constant alarm for her throat, or her casket of jewels. However, any mortal foes were better than none: these suspicions filled up chinks in her mind, or relaxed it from its greater cares concerning the nation, about the government of which she took more trouble than the whole Cabinet Council. In politics she always adhered to the loyal side of the question, yet at the same time generally disapproved of the ministerial measures: the opposition was sure to be wrong, but the others never right; by which ingenious mode of viewing things she kept herself richly supplied with subjects of disturbance and objects of censure all the year round.

Matters went yet worse in that more frivolous world which was equally honored by her superintendence. Say what she would, protest, argue, and harangue, sacks were left off, ostrich-feathers worn, and a thousand fantastic dresses invented. Nay, in process of time, the hoop vanished after the sack, and, like Tilburina's confidante, everybody ran mad in white linen. Of all these abominations, there was no sin so crying as the feathers, which Lady Mary, and I must own many calmer older ladies, deemed a positive badge of depravity—a test of virtue or vice. Perhaps she might abhor them the more as in some sort the test of youth or age; for, in spite of the wisdom added by increase of years, she had no relish for growing old. Twelvemonth stealing after twelvemonth, however, this inevitable evil would come; and as she grew sourer in consequence of it, more overbearing, more contradictious, less regardful of common civility, temper at length got such an entire mastery of every other feeling that she put the finishing stroke to her absurdities by contriving to hatch a quarrel with Princess Amelia.

It is an ugly lineament in human nature, but certainly friendships, or what the world calls so, are subject to the wear and tear of time, as well as things less precious. Old companions (sometimes including old husbands and wives) do insensibly grow tired of bearing each other's faults and infirmities and suppressing their own; as if on both sides ill-humor, waxing larger, wanted more elbow-room, and rejoiced to get rid of what confined it within decent bounds. The Princess and Lady Mary were almost arrived at this dangerous point. Nobody could be easier to live with than the former, but she would have the respect due to her observed: if Lady Mary was great, she was much greater; if old, much older; therefore she had every claim to a deference which the other's turbulent spirit would no longer yield; and, as dispute and contradiction now and then went the length of downright impertinence, her Royal Highness's patience began to be on the ebbing tide.

In such cases you may observe that the actual cause of rupture is usually next to nothing—a drop that makes the full cup run over—a spark that lights upon a pile of combustibles, you scarcely perceive how or when. Lady Mary sat down to cards one evening in a mood of superlative perverseness; sought occasions to squabble, found fault with the Princess's play, laughed her assertions to scorn, and finally got a very sharp reply for her pains. In lieu of recollecting herself, she took fire, and retorted more sharply still. The Princess declined further altercation, with an air that said, "I remember who I am," and the company gazed at each other in silence. When the party broke up, Lady Mary departed unspoken to, and all concluded she would be admitted into that house no more. But Princess Emily gave her fairer play than they expected: she desired to see her alone, and calmly entered upon a good-humored expostulation. "We are such old friends," said she, "that it really is too foolish to fall out and part about a trifle; but you must be conscious you were very provoking the other night. As I lost my temper too, I am the readier to forgive; only say you are sorry, and I will never think of it again."

Here was a noble opportunity to display unyielding firmness of character. Lady Mary drew herself up to her utmost height, and answered, with all the dignity of Charles the First at his trial, or Algernon Sidney confronting Judge Jefferies, or Cornelius de Witt quoting Horace upon the rack, or any other pattern of inflexible virtue you can name: "Madam, I respect your Royal Highness, as I ought; my loyalty to your illustrious house has been sufficiently proved, my attachment to your person is beyond dispute; but I cannot give up my integrity and honor—I cannot retract the opinions I have once delivered while I continue persuaded they are just. Your Royal Highness yourself would be entitled to despise me, did I act so meanly; I am no sycophant—no flatterer; adulation will never flow from me——" "Pooh! Pshaw! Nonsense!" cried the Princess, interrupting her—"where's the use of all these heroics about nothing? Who wants you to retract, and flatter, and I know not what? Can't you say, as I say myself, that you are concerned for this very silly business, and so let us be friends?" "No, madam; my honor—honor, which is dearer to me than life——" and then followed another *tirade*. After one or two more vain endeavors to bring her down from her stilts, the other rose to *her* full height likewise, and, assuming all the King's Daughter: "Well, madam," she said, "your Ladyship knows your own pleasure best. I wish you health and happiness for the future, and at present a good morning. Here!" to the page in waiting, "Order Lady Mary Coke's carriage"; then, gravely bowing in token of dismissal, turned away. From that moment they never met again. The loss was altogether Lady Mary's, and also the mortification. This she betrayed by a constant fidgeting anxiety to know whatever passed at Princess Emily's parties, who came and who went, and what her Royal Highness said or did. The Princess survived their final rupture but two or three years.[1]

[1] The quarrel took place probably in 1781. The "Journal" for 1781 begins on May 25th. The last mention of intercourse with the Princess Amelia before this apparently is on January 13th, 1780, when Lady Mary entertained her at dinner at Notting Hill. So the quarrel must have taken place between January 1780 and June 1781. Among a few letters from Princess Amelia is the

Very little remains to be added. After the Prince of Wales grew up, his conduct engrossed almost all Lady Mary's attention; you may suppose not often winning her praise: and as for his connection with Mrs. Fitzherbert, it went near to make the old Gloucester and Cumberland fever rage in her veins anew. The Regency question in 1789 kindled, if possible, a still fiercer flame, and enabled her to do something more than scream her Anathemas; since then, for the first time in that reign, ladies obtained a power of meddling with State affairs which—lady though I am who say it —may they never have again. While the poor King held the reins in his own hands, he resolutely kept

following in her writing, undated: "The Charter House Petitioner has brought me Ldy Mary's letter—one so greatly born must allwais be well come at my Table, & is constantly expected of Tuesdays, provide she will be a little less contradicting and hide her great ability's from those she thinks are inferior to hers. . . ."

(*3d June*, 1781.) "*Sunday.*—Some days ago I had a card from the Dutchess of Marlborough to invite me the seventh of this month to meet the Princess Amelia. How this happened I can't tell, but I wrote my excuse, which I seal'd up, where I told the Dutchess that as the Princess Amelia was to be there I thought it improper for me, which was my only reason for not waiting on her Grace. . . ."

On January 27th, 1785, Lady Mary says: ". . . The game of Lu is in its last stage: 'tis rarely play'd excepting at the Princess Amelia's two or three times in the week. The great losings & winnings are generally conceal'd, but I heard by accident Ly Margaret Compton lost one day last week a hundred & fifty guineas. I have always thought the same of high play, & therefore disengaged myself from that party. . . ."

Princess Amelia died in 1786. Lady Mary expressed sincere anxiety, and made constant inquiries after her during her illness. —ED.

petticoats aloof; but now his calamity forcing the Queen into the front of the battle, every woman belonging to court, lady or lady's chambermaid, arose and was busy. The opposition *Shes* took care not to fall short of them in activity, and, as a peaceable stander-by, I saw enough to convince me that female whisperings and caballings greatly envenomed the public contest: a good work which Lady Mary forwarded with all her might; besides blowing the coals in some private families divided in opinion (as many were) upon a subject that produced more bitterness and ill-blood than any other within my remembrance.

Here, then, I think I may pause, as I have nearly brought my recollections down to the place where yours may be expected to begin. I need not tell you how Lady Mary passed the latter years of her life, nor assist you to piece what you witnessed with what I have related, as you will find it all dovetail together perfectly well. Her character was thoroughly singular, if not *unique;* but never contradictory: you always knew in what direction to look for her, although sometimes your imagination might not stretch far enough, or soar high enough, to overtake her.

It may be worth while to bestow a moment's consideration on the manner in which that character affected her relations and familiar society. People who plod straight along the beaten road of life leave no mark of their passage; but the footsteps of those uncommon travellers who go tramping over strange ground are in general traceable. You can distinguish the effects of their influence, whichever way it operates. If directly, as with some, it founds a sort of school: their example and spirit continue to bear sway even after their existence is at an end. With others, on the contrary, it works, and strongly, too, in an inverse ratio to what they would have wished. This was the case with Lady Mary, who preached us out of good-breeding, regular economy, respect for authority, and many other commendable things, by dint of incessantly preaching us into them; and as her notions were ordinarily more exaggerated than erroneous, one was at times half tempted to regret the certainty of their summary condemnation without appeal. You may have heard it observed that Cervantes brought about an unfavorable change in the character of the Spanish nation, because, while he demolished what was fantastic and absurd, his resistless attack overthrew the chivalrous spirit itself, and with it much that it would have been desirable not only to preserve but to cherish. The very same thing might be said of Lady Mary, who, without doubt, was the person of all actually treading on earth that came nearest to the Hero of his work. She lowered the tone of thinking in those connected with her as Don Quixote did in his readers. Every act or opinion bordering on the great, the noble, the dignified, everything elevated above the conceptions of the common "worky-day world," had a chilling shadow of ridicule cast over it, as "just suited to Lady Mary Coke." And the fear of being pronounced like her frequently led one to stifle one's real sentiments, if not force a laugh, on occasions when one's young heart beat quick, and inwardly glowed with feelings very opposite to derision.

In another respect, too, this anti-influence of hers had mischievous consequence. It became the ready shield of protection for a degree of housemaidish ignorance which people would otherwise have blushed to avow. If you were caught supposing Lord Chatham and Lord Clarendon to have flourished together, or concluding that James the First was Queen Elizabeth's eldest son, you had but to shrug your shoulders and cry, "Well, for my part, I don't pretend to Lady Mary Coke's amazing knowledge of history," and you came off with flying colors. So likewise for the time present: you might confound the offices of Chamberlain and Chancellor, and ask whether the Secretary of State usually voted with Ministry or Opposition, yet have the laugh for you instead of against you, as soon as you declared yourself "no profound stateswoman like Lady Mary Coke." There might sometimes be malice in the matter, I own: a mischievous contention who should scandalize poor Lady Mary most. Her skill in genealogy and etiquette made one flippant girl think it a pretty air not to know how she was related to her first cousins; and another assert she could not see the use of bowing and curtsying to the King and Queen: the men, indeed, only grew a trifle more bearish after one of Lady Mary's lectures, resuming tolerable good manners as the taste of it wore off. To wind up all with something like a moral, be it remembered that we do the worst office possible to whatever is serious or praiseworthy by carrying it to an extreme which must inevitably excite laughter; but at the same time be it confessed that we cannot habituate ourselves to look constantly and exclusively at the ridiculous side of almost any object without in some degree injuring, if not debasing, our own minds.

Finished at Ditton Park in March 1827.

NOTES TO THE FAIRIES' FROLIC

NOTES TO THE FAIRIES' FROLIC

To ———,

with the foregoing tale, 1830 [1]

You may have seen people contemplating with a sort of tenderness the old doll or plaything of their childhood, by chance discovered in some trunk brought from the lumber garret. Just such a foolish feeling of partiality led me at a very mature age to undertake remodelling and completing this tale, the first part of which I wrote when I was barely seventeen!—though not exactly as it now stands. To speak truth, its identity is like that of the miser's famous stockings, darned with silk till every thread of their pristine worsted had disappeared. But the idea was the same. Two fairies visited the London world for the purpose of shining as a female wit and a fashionable beauty. What to do with them when they had performed their parts I did not know; so they went back to Oberon's Court abruptly and awkwardly enough, without attempting to leave any lesson behind them.

Some trifling particulars relating to Zirphe's dresses and tradespeople remain unaltered. Fashions in dress

[1] For the metrical tale, see Appendix, p. 273.

being pretty sure to come round again in a course of years, and Madame Beauvais sounding as well as the Madame of 1814, or even as Madame Maradin Carson herself, I thought it useless to modernize such matters in my *rifacimento*. The expensive sedan-chair indeed may require a word of explanation, since the enormous magnitude of our present town has made the thing (once so common and convenient) almost as much a theme for the antiquarian as Louis the Fourteenth's huge coach with a couple of *portières*. But while Bloomsbury and Portman Squares, Hyde Park Corner and Whitehall were the farthest points at which we had to seek our acquaintance, sedan-chairs were the usual vehicles for women. Maiden ladies and those of narrow fortune had no other. The rich and great always kept two, a plain one for constant daily use, and another magnificently decorated, which, with two, three, or sometimes four footmen before it, carried them to court, to formal visits and public entertainments.

With regard to the state of society, that in which Zirphe is supposed to move may seem to have undergone some change; but it only *seems*, for, unlike the metamorphosed worsted, its warp and woof continue the same. There was then *a very fine set*. Is there not now? And has there not always been one as far back as the days of Ben Jonson?—a certain number of persons, some of high rank, some distinguished for beauty, some few for ability, some for nothing at all, who, by linking themselves together and assuming superiority, obtain, if not the reality, at least the reputation of it; who sit fastidiously apart looking down upon the rest of the world (nobody presumes to ask why), despising all attempts to rival them, and cherishing mysteries in dress, language, sentiment—ay, and in morals too—above the comprehension of the uninitiated? Collegiates (see Ben Jonson's "Silent Woman"), Leaders of the ton, Exclusives, Exquisites, Dames du Chateau, Merveilleux and Merveilleuses — the cant name flits by, grows first vulgar, then obsolete, and gives place to a newer; the class remains permanent, or rather reproduces itself in every succeeding generation. This fact of its being only reproduced, not new and fresh created, is ever a stumbling-block to young people, who cannot at first sight discern any affinity between that precious object now denominated a *Dandy*, and my Lord Foppington with his full-bottomed wig, embroidered coat, and gold-clocked stockings, mincing the letter *o* into *a*, and going to church to ogle the ladies. Yet they would readily acknowledge a horse to be a horse and nothing but a horse, whether "barded from counter to tail," glittering with gilt caparisons, or simply bridled and saddled after the modern manner. And I am apt to believe that in both cases the difference lies solely in the outward trappings of the animal.

Orinda's world may perhaps have varied more essentially—I will not say for the worse. A certain portion of knowledge is more generally diffused among women; and men are inclined rather to wonder when they do not find it in a lady than to stand astounded when they do. Authoresses are likewise become too abundant to be either worshipped as divinities on one side, or ranked with learned pigs and bullfinches on the other. You still hear the epithet bluestocking, but it is uttered playfully, not in rancor and scorn, unless by those below the average height of sense and information. In my time it was a bitter reproach with some, resented as bitterly by others, according to the company you fell into. The set at whom it was principally levelled made head boldly against their maligners by gathering together all who had literary talents, pretended to them or admired them, in select parties sacred to rational conversation alone—that is, without cards, dancing, or music. I am afraid this was not always productive of what Pope describes, in a line which they were particularly fond of quoting, "The feast of reason and the flow of soul."

For Reason she might predominate, or might not; but you may judge how there could be any flow of soul where most of the company came with a set purpose of shining, and all were well aware that they could not pronounce a word which would pass unscrutinized. Mercy on the people who understood what they were about so ill as to vent the first whimsical thought that chanced to come into their heads! I have known it happen (for incorrigible *naturals* do exist), and seen it disconcert the whole assembly, as it would a band of musicians if "Roy's Wife" should be suddenly struck up in the middle of an intricate concerto. Everybody stared and nobody knew what to answer, nor how to get back again into regular order.

This reminds me of a French anecdote not irrelevant to the subject. A partisan of Madame Geoffrin, the Paris Aspasia, was extolling her dexterity in sorting her guests. She set apart one fixed day of the week for entertaining *les beaux arts*, the artists and virtuosi; another for *les beaux esprits, les philosophes, les gens de lettres*. "*Mais hélas!*"—said a lady, who had no pretensions beyond being very pretty and very agreeable—"*N'y-a-t-il pas un jour pour les simples mortels?*" With us it is true, *les simples mortels* could not be thus wholly excluded; otherwise I must have stood without the door of the sanctuary. Young ladies followed their mothers and aunts as the by-laws of good old England enjoin; and, according also to these, if even the heads and oracles of the congregation happened to have wooden husbands or ignorant, insipid wives (no rare occurrences) they were forced to come with their encumbrances in tow. But then we who gained admittance upon this humble foot served to fill the stage, and knew it was our duty to keep silence—to break it, indeed, requiring as much intrepidity as to make a speech in Parliament.

The only bluestocking meetings which I myself ever attended were those at Mrs. Walsingham's and Mrs. Montagu's. To frequent the latter, however, was to drink at the fountain-head; for although Miss Monckton (now old Lady Corke), Mrs. Thrale, Lady Herries, etc., gave similar parties, Mrs. Montagu eclipsed them all. Nor was she a common character. Together with a superabundance of vanity—vanity of that happy, contented, comfortable kind—disturbed by no uneasy doubts or misgivings, which keeps us in constant good-humor with ourselves, and consequently with everything else —she had quick parts, great vivacity, no small share of wit, a competent portion of learning, considerable fame as a writer, a large fortune, a fine house, and an excellent cook. Observe the climax, for it is not unintentional: the cook may be the only one of the powers I have enumerated who could carry on the war single-handed. Thus endowed, she was acquainted with almost all persons of note or distinction. She paid successful court to all authors, artists, critics, orators, lawyers, and clergy of high reputation; she graciously received and protected all their minor brethren who paid court to her; she attracted all travellers and tourists; she made entertainments for all ambassadors, sought out all remarkable foreigners (especially if men of letters); nay, she occasionally exhibited a few of the very fine exclusive set themselves, at whom her less worldly visitants, country or college geniuses, with nothing but a book in their pockets, were glad to have an opportunity of gazing. But there was a deplorable lack of one requisite—of that art of kneading the mass well together, which I have known possessed by women far her inferiors. As her company came in, a heterogeneous medley, so they went out, each individual feeling himself single, isolated, and (to borrow a French phrase) embarrassed with his own person; which might be partly owing to the awkward position of the furniture, the mal-arrangement of tables and chairs. Everything in that house, as if under a spell, was sure to form itself into a circle or semicircle. I once saw this produce a ludicrous scene. Mrs. Montagu having invited us to a very early party, we went at the hour appointed and took our stations in a vast half-moon, consisting of twenty or five-and-twenty women, where, placed between two grave faces unknown to me, I sat, hiding yawns with my fan and wondering at the unwonted exclusion of the superior sex. At length a door opened behind us, and a body of eminent personages—the chancellor (I think), and a bishop or two among them—filed in from the dining-room. They looked wistfully over our shoulders at a good fire, which the barrier we presented left them no means of approaching; then, drawing chairs from the wall, seated themselves around us in an outer crescent, silent and solemn as our own. Nobody could be more displeased at this than the mistress of the house, who wanted to confer with them face to face, and not in whispers. But there was no remedy; we must all have died at our posts, if one lady had not luckily been called away, whose exit made a gap for the wise men to enter and take possession of the fireplace.

A circle such as here described, though the worst shape imaginable for easy familiar conversation, may be the best for a brilliant interchange of—I had nearly said *snip-snap*—of pointed sentences and happy repartees. Every flash being visible, every argument distinctly heard from one end to the other, the consequent applause may act like a dram upon bodily combatants, invigorating wit and provoking fresh sallies. As fitted for actors and an audience, it may likewise suit whoever has interesting anecdotes to tell and the talent of telling them well; or whoever can clearly and pleasantly explain something which the surrounding hearers wish to understand. If you had good luck, therefore, you might not only be greatly amused at Mrs. Montagu's, but carry away much that was well worth remembering. But then, alas! the circular form is not less convenient to prosers and people who love to hear themselves talk; so you might, on the contrary, come in for the most tiresome dissertations, the dullest long stories, the flattest jokes, anywhere to be found. All of which, by a sort of courtesy, or policy that seemed conventional, were listened to with a complacent show of edification, no one venturing to betray inattention or fidget in his chair, or recollect having heard the same thing (perhaps fifty times) before, or put in a claim to it on behalf of "Joe Miller."

Another entertainment you were pretty sure to meet with, unless the presence of some such wicked spirit as Horace Walpole or Soame Jenyns excited apprehensions of ridicule. When matters took their usual course, studied high-flown compliments were fired off on your right hand and returned with increase on your left, all the louder if no particular good-will subsisted between the complimenting parties. A *bureau d'esprit* never yet was the temple of sincerity.

And in this scene, among these people solely occupied with themselves, did I form a lasting friendship with the late Mrs. Alison, then Miss Gregory, whom Mrs. Montagu had almost adopted as a daughter—the perfection of strict truth, blunt honesty, and clear understanding. She verified the old Scotch proverb, "An ounce of mother wit is worth a pound of clergy." "That is a Natural," said Mr. Walpole, and the expression exactly suited her. Gifted with a great deal

THE FAIRIES' FROLIC

of humor, she enjoyed like a comedy much that passed before her eyes, yet would never permit a word to be said derogatory to Mrs. Montagu, at whom, I confess, I had sometimes a mind to laugh, but I never durst let Miss Gregory perceive it, although we were girls at the time, and soon treated each other with the freedom and familiarity usual at our age. It cannot be denied that constant pretension of some sort gave a tinge of pedantry and affectation to the bluestocking set, taken collectively: yet there were individuals, classed among them in common speech, wholly untainted with either. For instance, Mrs. Carter, upon whom the sound scholarship of a learned man sat, as it does upon a man, easily and quietly, and who was no more vain of being a profound Grecian than an ordinary woman of knowing how to spell. But the very humility and plainness of her character made it avail nothing toward simplifying the general tone of the rest, for she loved listening far better than talking; and as she had no quick perception of other people's failings and absurdities, much less any disposition to expose them, she sat still, honestly admiring what a livelier (though perchance a shallower) person would have criticised.

The name of "Carter" alone will prove that Mrs. Montagu was not without sincere and valuable friends. And even some of the men who diverted themselves most with her foibles would nevertheless, when speaking seriously, avow a high opinion of her abilities. Of this number was my brother-in-law, Lord Macartney, who piqued himself upon carrying compliments beyond the moon, and maintained that they were always acceptable to every woman without exception: although he paid them in a manner so glaringly ironical, took so little pains to look decently grave, that one wondered how the bait could possibly be swallowed by anybody who had the use of a pair of eyes. I have heard him laugh peal upon peal as he repeated behind Mrs. Montagu's back the compliments he had made, or intended to make her, bringing in (would you believe it?) Venus as well as Minerva, extolling the personal charms of a woman nearly old enough for his mother, and one who (to do her justice) was quite free from the weakness of wishing to disguise her age. "Oh, never mind" (said he), "you all like hearing of your beauty to the very last." Yet when the laugh was over he would conclude with, "After all, though, she is the cleverest woman I know; meet her where you will, she says the best thing you hear in the company."

From these premises you will infer that she was likely to have many of those flatterers by trade, vulgarly termed toad-eaters, who are apt to abound wherever the possessors of power, wealth, or influence, or even the mere givers of good dinners, betray any relish for the commodity they deal in.

But besides the more common kind, there crept around her a species just one step above them—dabblers in literature, literary coxcombs, male and female, who, not rejecting with absolute scorn the beef and pudding, chiefly coveted her recommendation—the reflected lustre of her celebrity, and a repayment of praise proportioned in quantity and quality to the loads of it they came to lay down. In a word, she had toad-eaters from interest, and toad-eaters from vanity—poor paltry insects both, and both often furnished with a concealed sting.

But neither flattered her so inordinately as a very different race of beings—good, worthy, sincere people, who said nothing which they did not think, and would not have sworn to upon the parish Bible; gentry, in whose skulls the phrenologist (granting his science authentic) would infallibly have found the organ of admiration extraordinarily prominent, and that of discrimination almost imperceptible. Downright sycophants, whose encomiums the vainest of us must now and then in spite of self-love secretly mistrust, are perhaps companions less dangerous to persons eminently gifted than such excellent mortals as these. Their truth and integrity being unquestionable, the lavish, superlative, universal applause which they pour forth from their hearts—at first possibly declined, or put by with a compassionate smile—may in time grow so agreeable to the habituated ear as to make just approbation and distinguishing praise grate upon it like censure.

At Mrs. Montagu's, these kind souls used to take us young people under their especial charge, acting as flappers, for fear we should lose opportunities of improvement by our want of attention to what was passing. We were pulled by the sleeve—"My dear, did you listen?" "Did you mind?" "Mrs. Montagu said," "Miss Hannah More observed," "Mr. Harris replied." And it was well that none of us ever cried, "What then?" For since the most superior men and women must often discuss ordinary topics in ordinary language, it would sometimes happen that even Mrs. Montagu and Mr. Harris were only debating whether the clouds at sunset had threatened rain or promised fair weather.

I have rambled far and wide, flying off at every tangent presented by recollection; but this you must forgive. Old age has a right to be garrulous; and as I am little prone to abuse the privilege *viva voce*, I may let my pen run on with the less scruple; for reading is a voluntary act, hearing (I do not say listening) may be a painful necessity. The Spanish Queen in Dryden's play tells us her lover's words descended on the ear like flakes of feathered snow. Oh that those of some great talkers, equally noiseless, could descend only upon a sheet of paper!

Now for the point to which I ought to have come long ago. The sequel of my tale is nothing more than an extended comment upon a very old text; namely, the brief admonition of Pericles to the female part of the assembly whom he was haranguing. I forget how the words are given in history, but their plain meaning, familiarly rendered, I presume to be this: "The less that is said of you, the less that is heard of you, the better for you." Time was, I confess, when I thought this doctrine harsh, affronting, illiberal, savoring of barbarism and dictated by prejudice, if not by jealousy. So every woman who joins a high spirit to some degree of self-conceit will probably think it while on the bright sunny side of twenty-one. But what was thus indignantly repelled made itself remembered; it could not be quite got rid of. And why? Because it was grounded on truth. Strong doubts arose upon the subject ere youth had taken its leave; and when the fruits of time—observation, reflection, experience—began to ripen, I cannot say any *doubt* remained. It is too surely a misfortune to women to be rendered conspicuous even without their own consent, as in the case of transcendent personal beauty or a high and responsible situation. But if a woman labors to attain the dangerous pinnacle of power, fame, fashion, or any other species of distinction, she will find reason to pronounce the Athenian statesman not only a sage but a prophet. Talk of prejudice as much as you please, there are sentiments too general, one might say too instinctive, not to have some foundation in our nature. The indolent, inactive man who has passed his useless days without peeping from his shell cannot be respected, can hardly respect himself like him who, as Prior words it, "in life's visit leaves his name"—though but a shopkeeper whose industry and activity have raised him to the mayoralty of his native town. While for a woman to lead a quiet private life, fulfilling her duties and pursuing unnoticed her domestic avocations, is universally deemed matter of praise. The one has stayed in the place legally assigned her: the other seems in some sort to have shrunk from entering on his proper career.

Madame de Staël has justly said that love is but an episode (she might have added an insignificant one) in the life of a man; the whole poem, the main story in that of a woman. And whether it be love commonly so called, or friendship, or maternal, or filial, or sisterly affection, no one can deny that *some* affection, something belonging to the heart, influences female conduct and fate far more than male. What goes by the name of that organ is woman's vulnerable part, the defenceless side of her citadel. I do not say this in censure of men; I barely state a fact which the expression in daily use, *unmanned*, will certify. But such as men and women were created, such, I presume, is (in a certain sense) what they ought to be. "Why has not man a microscopic eye? For this plain reason—man is not a fly." Why has not he (generally speaking) feelings that melt his resolution, impede his exertion, weaken his reason, combat his interest, overpower his prudence? For this plain reason—he is not a woman. Were it otherwise, how could the business of the world be carried on? How a single step be taken in public life?

You may now perceive the drift of my argument. An animal whose make disqualifies it for climbing should keep upon level ground; a being whose heart is subject to become thus troublesome should avoid those ambitious or vainglorious pursuits in which it will both prove a clog, and be exposed to rougher usage than it can bear. But why, you may ask, are women who covet admiration and aspire at celebrity more likely than others to be unfortunate in what concerns their affections? I can only answer that they are more swayed by imagination, and remind you that our forefathers used Fancy and Love as synonymous terms— through no great error in language, for their kindred is near, their resemblance close. Whatever exalts and inflames the one will as surely tend to introduce the other as high living and spirituous liquors to fever the

THE FAIRIES' FROLIC 167

blood. Alluring forms play before the mind's eye; images of perfection which are soon supposed realized by some individual in bodily existence. The Zirphes picture to themselves nothing less than the leaders of the fashionable world, men for whom all other women are to languish and die; handsome, attractive, animated, full of feeling, full of delicacy, just inconstant and impertinent enough to make fixing them a triumph, but, when fixed, so capable of the most violent passion! The Orindas conjure up a phantom more shadowy still; they hope to find a man of supereminent talents, universally admired, yet gifted with such a candid and generous spirit that, while they glory in his superiority, their own endowments, fully appreciated, will be his proudest boast and principal delight.

All this would do very well if castle-building went on as merrily and a counterpart were as much longed for on the opposite side. But far from it: upon no point do the sexes differ so widely. Woman, conscious (whether owning it or not) of inferiority, unable to stand firmly alone, looks to man for support and elevation: therefore in her waking dreams she ever beholds him seated on an eminence above her. The vainer she is of her own qualifications, the higher she exalts the imaginary object of her preference. With men it is exactly the reverse. The more highly a man values his own merits, the more moderate are his demands for merit of the same kind in a mistress or a wife. He has enough for both, and something to spare. The exquisite fine gentleman can content himself with a homespun mate, even one homely in person, who, while he shines abroad, will nurse the children, scold the servants, and carefully manage the family concerns, without wincing much if treated with a little contempt. The man who piques himself upon his brilliant parts—unless so cool-blooded as to make a similar choice, that is, to take a housekeeper—goes in quest of the prettiest woman he can find, and is likely to consider the ornaments of her mind about as philosophically as the lover in an old Scotch song, of which I remember but this one stanza:

> "I took it in my head
> To write my love a letter;
> But the lassie canna read,
> An' I *like*[1] her a' the better."

We blunder wofully, then, when we deplore the hard lot of a man whose lofty character commands our own admiration, but whom malicious fate (as we settle the matter) has thrown away upon a partner so far from being fitted for his companion that she is neither capable of admiring nor of comprehending him. A most melancholy case, I admit; and in bewailing it we do but overlook one trifling circumstance, viz., that the

[1] "Lo'e" is the correct word in the song. The chorus at the end of the verse is:

> "Aye waukin' o', waukin' aye and weary,
> Sleep I can get nane,
> For thinkin' o' my dearie."

The previous verse is:

> "When first she came to town
> They called her Jess Macfarlane,
> But noo she's come and gane,
> They ca' her the wandering darling.
>   Aye waukin', etc."

man married himself. The High Chancellor of England, although his authority may sometimes hinder and sometimes help to dissolve a matrimonial union, decrees none whatsoever. Nor can the elders of our Church, as with the Moravians, peremptorily assign Sister Tabitha unto Brother Joseph. The woman for whose insipidity you pity your hero or your genius is that woman whom it was his will and pleasure to prefer; and if a brighter star had guided his choice to one as intelligent and high-minded as in your opinion he deserved, it is possible that your compassion would now have to flow in an opposite channel; for *she* might be the party undervalued and misunderstood.

I am aware that you will say (and with truth) that we often see women of sense—nay, what presses more directly on the point, women proud of their sense—strongly attached to men far their inferiors in understanding. This cannot be denied, yet I believe it almost always occurs rather from the imagination having seduced the heart, and the heart blinded the judgment, than from such an indifference on the subject as would have made the deficiency disregarded if really perceived. I dare own myself convinced that no sensible woman ever yet fell in love with a fool—or even a blockhead, which is a different thing—knowing and deeming him what he was. She must at first have been persuaded, or deluded, or bewitched into a contrary belief, before any familiar acquaintance could take place. The *glamor* cast, the flame kindled, passion came and effectually sealed down her eyes. Whereas a man who is captivated by a silly woman needs no self-deception, and seldom has recourse to any. Either her beauty, her good humor, her devotion (real or feigned) to him, or some other charm overpowers his objections to her folly, or else he has no objections to be overpowered. His pride may make him assure his friends that she has a better capacity than they give her credit for; but he cheats himself only by assuming that her lack of sense can do him no harm, and rests well satisfied until taught otherwise by experience.

Take notice, however, that we are here treating of inclination, of preference, affection, love—not of *marriage*. The motives for this last are many and various: Miss Jenny in the comedy—"hopes she shall marry a fool, for she loves to govern dearly." And without doubt some accomplished ladies agree with her.

To conclude: if I have at all effected my purpose, you will observe a shade of difference between the fates of the two Fairy-adventurers. Both repent of their rash project, both are disappointed, both unhappy; but Orinda is the most deeply so—"Thought brings the weight that sinks the soul to woe." The reflecting character, slow to admit passion, and admitting it only in the specious disguise of a just esteem for worth, or a propensity (secretly thought meritorious) to admire enthusiastically whatever seems to surpass the common standard in merit or in intellect, is the most completely mastered by it when once overcome. Besides, the gift of Beauty, coveted by Zirphe, though insufficient to do for her all she expected, had done something; and, at worst, had never operated against her. Her lover did not forsake her because she was beautiful. Therefore

THE FAIRIES' FROLIC 171

her dejected spirit could still in a certain measure rally and find some relief, some faint gleam of satisfaction, in her undiminished power of attracting general admiration. Not so that of Orinda, who had reason to think her boasted accomplishments the bane of her peace and to suspect that they rendered her distasteful to the only person she wished to please. In his eyes she had naturally flattered herself that they would appear peculiarly valuable. And from the moment she discovered her mistake it was equally natural that they should become worthless in her own. For, without supposing so strong a case, if those who are our constant associates, though but agreeable to us in a common way, have no taste for the particular art in which we excel, we gradually learn to hold it cheap ourselves; as a tradesman sets little value on the goods for which he finds he has not any demand. Diamonds and pearls, where unsalable, cease to be precious. And can we look for a less effect from the influence of the most imperious and absorbing of all passions? Surely not: surely Madame de Staël, in making Corinne exert and triumph in her extraordinary talents when actually dying of a broken heart, demonstrated that she herself understood Vanity so much better than Love as to be ignorant how entirely the one, if unhappy and unrequited, would annihilate the other.

"Humble as maiden who loves in vain,"[1]

a line big with meaning, fell carelessly from a pen, not like hers, professedly sentimental, but belonging to a closer observer of human nature.

[1] "Bridal of Triermain," Canto 1, Stanza 1.—ED.

NOTES TO THE DIAMOND ROBE

NOTES TO THE DIAMOND ROBE[1]

THE incident of the ambassadors is borrowed from a French fairy tale; the invisible robe from a story in the 27th discurso (chapter or section) of Balthazar Gracian's "Agudeza y Arte de Ingenio," a kind of treatise upon wit. He professes to give it from "El Conde Lucanor," an old book written by the Prince Don Juan Manuel, son of the Infant Manuel, and grandson of Ferdinand, the saint king of Castile and Toledo, in the thirteenth century.

Literal translation of the passage in Gracian: "Among many moral tales, he (Don Juan Manuel) produces this, to show how a general delusion may sometimes take place; how all men will follow the opinion of others against their own judgment, praising (without understanding) what those others celebrate, lest they should pass for persons of inferior capacity or of a worse taste. Yet at last the falsehood fades away, and powerful truth prevails.

"Three cozeners came to a king, offering to weave for him a sort of cloth, so gifted that it could not be visible to a person of disgraceful[2] birth, one illegitimate or

[1] The metrical tale will be found in the Appendix, p. 295.
[2] *De malaraza.* Perhaps it properly means of a mixed race—a race mingled with the Jew or the Moor, not *vieja Christiana*, old Christian.

wronged by his wife. The king, highly pleased, assigned them a palace for their work, and they, taking a profusion of gold, silver, and silk, set up their loom, and gave out that they were continually weaving. In a few days one of them informed the king that the work was begun, and the most beautiful thing in the world; if his majesty wished to see it he must come alone. For greater security he first sent his chamberlain, but gave him no charge to detect the imposture should it prove one. The chamberlain, hearing their account of the cloth's peculiar virtue, had not courage to avow that he beheld no such thing, but told the king he had seen both cloth and embroidery, and that all was most admirable. The king then sent another gentleman, who brought back a like report. In short, all his messengers affirming they had seen the cloth, he at length went himself. He found the cozeners pretending to be busy, and was told, 'Behold the cloth—look at the embroidery—this is such a history—this figure such a person—here we introduce such a color'; all agreeing in their description. Hearing this, yet finding that he could not see what had been visible to every one else, he was ready to expire. He now doubted his being his father's son, etc., etc.; but for that very reason he loudly praised the cloth, and, returning home, told wonders of its excellence and beauty. Three days afterward he sent his Grand Alguazil, who, afraid of disgracing himself, extolled the cloth as much as his master, or more. The following day another favorite was despatched, with the same success. In this manner the prince and all his subjects remained deluded,

THE DIAMOND ROBE 177

for no one durst assert that the cloth did not exist. And thus the matter passed until the approach of a great festival, upon which the king was advised to wear it. The weavers, feigning to bring it wrapped up, gave him to understand that they unfolded it, then took his measure, and made as if they were cutting something out. On the feast day they returned, saying they had brought the garment completed, with which they accordingly pretended to enrobe him. Thus apparelled, he mounted his horse, and, attended by all his grandees, rode through the court. As soon as the people saw him coming, and understood that whoever could not perceive the cloth must be a bastard, a Jew, or a dishonored husband, they all exclaimed they beheld it, and applauded with violence. At last a negro who took care of the king's horse, coming up to him, said, 'Sir, you are half-naked, going about in your shirt.' A man who heard this cried out something similar, and first one, then another proceeding to confess they saw nothing, the king and the nobles, losing their apprehensions, finally acknowledged themselves cozened. The jugglers were sought for, but they had already disappeared, carrying with them the gold, silver, and silk, besides a large sum of money given them by the king.

"Thus," observed Gracian, "do many deceptions succeed in the world, and such power has the dread of risking our credit by appearing singular."

1814.—Some years after this translation was made, Sir Charles Stuart procured for me in Spain that curious old book "El Conde Lucanor" itself. But the difference between the story as there told and as given (rather abridged) by Gracian is trifling, and in no way affects its purport. Perhaps I have only spoiled by attempting to embellish it. The simple original, like one of Esop's fables, affords a lesson adapted to all times, and worthy of being borne in constant remembrance. For who has not witnessed the reign of some enchanted robe or other; some epidemic disease of mind, spreading as if infectious, disordering every brain in its progress, and, when it subsides, leaving us in the bewildered state of patients just recovering from epileptic fits, scarcely conscious of what we have said or done? No matter whether such a mania rage for or against its particular object—

> Whether we hate, or whether we desire,
> In either case, believe me, we admire.

An eager and catching zeal about some absurdity, which at a soberer time would be too gross for our own belief, is its essential, characteristic quality. Accordingly, it was the cry suddenly raised against an imaginary evil which first made me think of amplifying Gracian's (or rather Don Juan Manuel's) tale, and tagging it with rhyme.

During the transient calm that followed the Peace of Amiens, a few French actors, stealing over, performed two or three plays very privately in London, so much to the satisfaction of their audience that it excited a wish to have a small French theatre here, if such a thing could be managed without giving umbrage to our sovereign masters—the mob. To effect this, somebody proposed establishing subscription assemblies at the Argyll Street rooms upon the plan of those held at

Almack's long before, and, like them, under the direction of ladies, whose admission of only a limited number of subscribers should exclude indifferent company and guard against a crowd. With these regulations, it was hoped that Molière and Racine might furnish part of the evening's entertainment, unknown to the populace. Vain were both the hopes and the precautions; the secret soon transpired and the theatres took alarm. There lay before them an obvious and easy method of crushing the whole scheme at once by setting up a genuine English hue and cry against encouraging foreigners, introducing French fashions, and so forth.

Nor perhaps would such resistance have much displeased some thinking persons prone to disapprove of anything, however harmless in itself, that seemed to betoken or forerun a change in our national habits. But Mr. Sheridan, the rightful leader of the theatrical forces as manager of Drury Lane play-house, belonged to a political party, with whose views resistance upon this ground did not accord. Ever since the French Revolution his friends had been laboring to cure John Bull of all narrow national prejudices, and instead of "Down with the French" teach him to hallo "Reason, philosophy, peace, and fraternity"; and they knew very well that one syllable denouncing the "*parly voos*" would operate as the squeak of a mouse did upon the cat transformed to a woman. There would be an end of fraternity and philosophy along with the French play. Yet, setting aside that main point, what was there to find fault with?—what harm, or novelty at least in a subscription ball and supper? Apparent difficulties produce the triumph of Genius. Mr. Sheridan's masterly hand aimed a blow just at the place which common minds would have deemed unassailable; and the project was attacked on account (truly) of its being perfectly new under the sun, and profligate beyond all former examples. The people were called upon to combat this monstrous device, this unheard-of dissipation, this disgrace of our age and country. If the uncorrupted vulgar did not oppose and overthrow it, decency would abandon Britain. So said Vindex and Verax, and a Foe to quality-vices, and a Lover of decorum, and forty more correspondents of the *Morning Chronicle*. These serious invectives were aided by numberless witty paragraphs upon the refined pastimes of our virtuous nobility, and both faithfully copied into all the other papers. The stage meanwhile defending its interest with its own proper weapons, every new farce abounded with similar sarcasms; peals of applause followed, and nine-tenths of the audience went home faithful believers, not in a robe of light, but in one of darkness almost as extraordinary, directly imported from the dominions of Pluto. Reasoning from probability only, not from fact and experience, could we ever suppose that the influence of newspapers extended beyond the bar of an ale-house? Yet it does in reality both reach and govern the minds of many respectable people who live out of the world, swaying them more than we imagine, nay, more than they themselves are aware of. We wonder at the ancient heathens for not having suspected that the voice of the priest uttered the oracle. But I have some worthy acquaintances who, I am tempted to think, must unconsciously harbor a private notion that the newspaper writes itself. For should John or Thomas bring them a surprising account of what was passing in the next street, they would consult their own reason, and examine how he gained his intelligence before they gave him credit. Not so when the omniscient newspaper details a secret transaction or confidential conversation that took place last week between a foreign prince and his wife, or his confessor a thousand miles off. Every particle of that oracle is accepted with a faith so reverential that assuredly it cannot be in earnest believed to flow from certain mere mortals frequenting certain coffee-houses, and upon a fair average not much better or wiser than the Johns or Thomases whom we personally know.

For the Argyll rooms once more. The precise cause that rendered them so dangerous and detestable remained all this while in awful obscurity, shadowed by a cloud of mysterious horror. No particular species of wickedness had ever been pointed out, no explanation vouchsafed of what was to be done in Argyll Street which was not done in Hill Street or Harley Street, or Pall Mall, or Whitechapel. Therefore several well-meaning people could not but conclude it something too flagitious to be expressly named, and were ready to cry, "Avaunt!" and "Avoid thee, Satan!" without investigation. It is true that a rumor had gone forth of *Picnic* Suppers. Picnic as expounded by the learned signifies a custom prevalent in Germany when familiar friends have a festive meeting. To avoid ceremony and expense, each furnishes his quota of provisions toward the entertainment. "You send in a cold ham, I a couple of chickens." An injudicious plan possibly for a large company, because likely to produce a bitter bad supper, but with what offence to God or man it would be difficult to determine, judging in cool blood. However, as the Cardinal de Retz told us long ago, in all party-work fixing upon a name is half the battle; and Picnic was a precious one for the purpose, being at that time quite new, uncouth, unintelligible, and of a ridiculous sound. The most opprobrious which we were used to and understood would not have done near so well. It fitted all the regular commonplaces to a hair. Queen Bess and Queen Anne encouraged no Picnics. Archbishop Tillotson never heard of a Picnic. Picnics were unknown to our immortal Lockes and Miltons, to Algernon Sydney, John, Duke of Marlborough, and General Wolfe. For which reason, if masters of families could tamely sit still and let their wives and daughters mingle in Picnic society, it was vain for the baffled moralist to contend. The doctors and the proctors at the Commons might rejoice and cry "Picnic for ever." The greatest lawyers, it is said, acknowledge it difficult to prove a negative: if so, how much more difficult must it become where there is no specific affirmative to disprove. The promoters of the Picnic stood in this predicament. They might have defended themselves against a charge of gaming, gallantry, or treason; but being arraigned for the *Lord knows what*, found hardly a possibility of pleading "Not Guilty." Had Mr. Sheridan been counsel on their side instead of the other, he could have taught

THE DIAMOND ROBE 183

them that nonsense should always be refuted with greater nonsense, and the cabbage as big as a house encountered by the porridge-pot bigger than a temple. Blessed with no such advice, for want of it they did nothing but blunder. They passed by the fictitious objection, and foolishly combated the real one; alleging that their scheme could not injure the regular theatres, because the French play was not to begin till an hour when the English one would be over. Now had they said that the proposed amusement would be of too serious a nature to clash with any profane diversion, and maintained that they should frequent Argyll Street to hear sacred music or to say their prayers, their antagonists might have been puzzled how to reply. But the unlucky truth was a club instantly snatched out of their hands and laid about their own ears without mercy. "How! Were they then sufficiently audacious to avow their design of turning night into day? Let the public judge what would be the tendency of such scandalous assemblings. If midnight orgies were to pass uncontrolled, if we were once come to that, then indeed farewell to every semblance of national morality." *Midnight orgies!* The words spread consternation. Not that late hours were prodigies first known in the portentous year 1802. Some of us could remember having even in our youth regularly repaired to Almack's at the very witching time of twelve. We had afterward extinguished poor Ranelagh by not choosing to go to it till one o'clock in the morning. And previous to the commencement of the present dispute, it was a favorite assertion with all croakers over the degeneracy of the age that the hours grew later and later every year. But this on a sudden enchanted us back to those good days when the House of Commons used to meet after an early breakfast, and, according to Lord Clarendon, once, for a great wonder, happened to be "still sitting at three of the clock in the afternoon." Had the zealous Anti-Picnickians been asked during the heat of the controversy whether they ever before heard of such a thing as dancing all night, I verily believe they would have answered, "Oh, no! never in our lives." One circumstance attending the affair was wonderfully humorous. The foremost and loudest in making the outcry were the very people who piqued themselves upon their virtuous abhorrence of its concealed instigator—those termed (for lack of a more definite phrase) *good sort of women*. They are perhaps always prone to regard Wit with suspicion as akin to something sinful, if not itself a sin; but they infallibly think much the worse of any other sin for being caught in its company; and as Sheridan had more of it than his neighbors, and led no very strict life, he was what the French would have called their *bête noire*. Little did they dream that he drew them, one and all, in a string; that they were going about busily publishing what he, like the mover of a puppet show, chose to put in their mouths. No absurd stuff could be grafted upon the reports originally sown by his emissaries but they were ready to take it for gospel, while at the same time, if he in his own person had attested any fact upon oath in a court of justice, they would have sighed, shaken their heads, and hoped that even Mr. Sheridan would not perjure himself—by way of charitably hinting that it was extremely probable he would. More than once did I happen to be questioned by some of these grave ladies whether I belonged to the Picnic? "No, Madam, not I." "Ah, I thought not" (brightening). "I was sure that such a project could never obtain your ladyship's approbation; your principles are too well known." Principles!!!

The first opening of old deceased Ranelagh, as I learned from my elders, produced almost as great a combustion; possibly with much more reason, such promiscuous assemblies being really an innovation in that less dissipated age. As usual, however, the clamor soon grew nonsensical; strange stories were circulated; people renounced their creed and stood upon their heads the moment they got into Ranelagh; Ranelagh would corrupt the morals and destroy the peace of the country; the clergy ought to exert themselves, the magistracy to interfere, and, in short, everybody was in such a bustle that the then Chief Justice (Ryder, I believe) resolved to go himself and be eyewitness of the enormities practised there, before he issued his warrant for their suppression. After taking half a dozen turns he stopped short, and, looking round, said to his friends, "Well, now, I profess I can see no harm in this place—*but* the folly of it." I expected to be like him, to see no harm in Argyll Street but the dulness of it. French plays I despaired of, and I well knew what kind of dissolute scene would be presented in lieu of them—to wit, misses and their mammas sitting upright ranged upon benches, young men lounging up and down, too lazy to dance, and the fiddles vainly playing the same tiresome tune over and over again to provoke a beginning. Such, in fact, were the worst orgies performed. But the renewal of war diverting men's thoughts, the Argyll Rooms were left to go on as they would, and the whole business sank into oblivion. Was not this a Diamond Robe?

I can give the history of another mania which prevailed in the days of my earliest youth—the outrageous zeal manifested against the first introduction of Ostrich Feathers as a head-dress. This fashion was not attacked as fantastic or unbecoming or inconvenient or expensive or anything else which a woman's wearing feathers or wearing fiddlesticks' ends upon her head might very well be, but as seriously wrong and immoral. Ladies have since gone almost naked without occasioning a similar uproar or any uproar at all. The delicacy of the practice has been a little called in question; a few jokes and caricatures have assailed it; but though frequently censured, it has never been persecuted: nobody has begun clapping his hands and hallooing it down. Whereas the unfortunate feathers were insulted, mobbed, hissed, almost pelted wherever they appeared, abused in the newspapers, nay, even preached at in the pulpits, and pointed out as marks of reprobation. The good Queen herself, led away like the rest of the world, thought it her duty to declare how highly she disapproved of them; and consequently for two or three years no one ventured to wear them at Court, excepting some daring spirits either too supreme in fashion to respect any other kind of pre-eminence, or

THE DIAMOND ROBE 187

else connected with the Opposition, and glad to set her Majesty at defiance. So an *Ostrich* Feather, in addition to the inherent evil of its nature, had the glory of becoming treasonable, or at least disaffected.

Note added in 1835.—About this time poor Marie Antoinette and her gay court were amusing themselves with inventing new dresses every day, all which came over to us, no doubt, very curiously exaggerated and giving abundant cause for laughter; but people chose to be *angry*. A passage in Hannah More's "Letters" (lately published) will show you what grave indignation they threw away upon such worthy objects as caps and petticoats. One lady appearing with a tree in her head, another with a bunch of kitchen vegetables; Miss More, shocked and scandalized, invokes the shade of Addison to arise, and wishes anything could shame Englishwomen back into modesty. *Modesty!* Immodesty in dress implies, I take it, an undue exposure of the person. And at no time, before or since, has *that* ever so fully covered—indeed so effectually disguised—as when Hannah More wrote this philippic. If a North American Indian had seen a well-dressed lady's stiff stays, round hoop, and high-heeled shoes, her hair stuffed with bushels of powder and paste, and her neck overlaid with ruff, puff, frill, and tippet, he would never have suspected that an animal shaped and limbed like his own squaw lurked within the structure. Modesty then had no more concern in the business than Justice, Mercy, or any other cardinal virtue; and as for Sense and Taste, the parties really aggrieved, perhaps they were as much set aside by those whose wrath flamed thus against the foolish fashion as by its followers or its inventors.

At length there issued from the press a most wise and solemn quarto pamphlet, entitled "A Letter to the Duchess of Devonshire," taking that poor lady severely to task for her eager pursuit of pleasure, her want of thought and reflection (*N.B.* She was then in her twentieth year), and many other errors, but representing it as by no means her least offence to have adopted and promoted a mode so blamable. The author did indeed allow dress to be in general an indifferent matter; yet, observed he shrewdly, it was rather a suspicious circumstance that women of high rank should assume as ornaments the known emblems of lightness and frivolity. When we saw feathers waving without, we might be apt to judge unfavorably of the brains within. Nevertheless, were the said feathers plucked from the tails of hens and turkeys, sober domestic birds, something could be urged in their behalf. But before we decided on the propriety of the plumes now fashionable, he bade us consider the character of the ostrich. Now this was no easy thing to do, considering how little we knew of his life and conversation, for nothing, good or bad, could we deduce from his digesting iron, were it ever so well ascertained. But then his female leaves her eggs scattered in the sand. And what kind of wives and mothers were those ladies likely to prove who borrowed their favorite decoration from a creature thus unnatural? There was something in this—not exactly *sense*, to be sure, but so like it, so easily mistaken for it, that the effect was prodigious, especially among Mr. Sheridan's friends, the good sort of women. The Feathered Race became their war-cry, and each of them would have chosen a she-ostrich itself for her daughter-in-law rather than one of the depraved girls guilty of wearing its abominable feathers.

Thus we may learn how much good or ill luck has to do with the reputation both of persons and things. When buckskin was first used as the material of an unnamable garment, profound thinkers might have asked with great parity of reason how courage or any manly virtue could be supposed to exist in him whose clothing was supplied by that quaking animal, emblem of cowardice, the deer? But nobody chancing to give the matter this moral turn, buckskin breeches innumerable went about and prospered, and are still held to bear an irreproachable character.

The silly things here recounted came to pass in that trifling circle which those who move in it style the world, where a mania is almost always a comedy more or less ludicrous to the quiet stander-by. But human actors, whether they move on a wide or a contracted stage, must be human actors still. Therefore, take the word World in a larger sense as the mass of one nation or more, the world of politicians, the world of history, and this, too, has its manias, although seldom of a comic cast, or, to speak more correctly, seldom producing comic effects. For the Picnic, remaining the very picnic it was, without the smallest difference in itself, might have been made the instrument of shaking the Commonwealth to its foundation, if laid hold of at a fit time by any political or religious faction. Its partisans might have been pursued to the stake or the scaffold as rebels or tyrants, or heretics, or aristocrats, or democrats, or criminals of what kind you will, still merely for subscribing to the Argyll Rooms, and still by the very same process which we saw actually employed against them. We may find sufficient examples to prove this, though civilly steering clear of our immediate contemporaries (just as the company present are excepted in polished conversation), and yet not going too far back, for fear of entangling ourselves with lepers, and knight-templars, and, above all, with the First Crusade. The French Mississippi madness and our own South Sea, both precisely Diamond Robes, are the least tragical on record. As they escaped being dyed in blood, they may be contemplated without shuddering, notwithstanding the ruin they occasioned. Indeed, when run mad for love instead of hatred, our passion can grow ferocious only in its recoil. And this it did upon the bursting of the English bubble. Read the annals and speeches of the time; you will find that no man condemned himself, blushed for the folly which had made him aspire at impossibilities, or repented of his rapacity in seeking immoderate gain. On the contrary, we behold in the conduct of our ancestors—our Lords and Commons, ancestors in Parliament assembled—the self-same spirit which would have actuated their footmen in hunting a pickpocket, and not much more consideration of law or justice. If the cozeners, or South Sea delinquents (whose guilt is now said to be very doubtful), had not placed their persons in safety on the Continent, some summary bill of attainder might have disgraced us for ever by awarding capital punishment without trial. As for the mania in its most terrific form, surrounded by dread suspicion and fury, suspending the reasoning faculties, bearing away the wise along with the foolish, and during its prevalence turning man into a wild beast, Modern History supplies few instances of it more striking than the New England witches and the Popish Plot. While the former frenzy raged, no girl could have a fit of the vapors without endangering the lives and characters of all who had the misfortune to live in her neighborhood. Still, however, the full extent of human credulity can never appear where supernatural agency is admitted. To admit it in such a case may be grossly absurd, but this one absurdity franks and justifies all the rest. It is quite rational to conclude that the devil would not come abroad for nothing, and to expect from his immediate interference a few feats beyond mortal power or ability. On this ground may we not pronounce a good simple faith in ghosts and witchcraft to be philosophical compared to belief in alchemy, astrology, or any other imposture, past or present, that deals in jargon and pretends to work miracles by mystical yet not miraculous means? But in neither way can we lose our wits so completely as where our own species alone is concerned. Earthly motives and proceedings only were to be considered in the Popish Plot; therefore that astonishing transaction, above all others, best evinces the nature of a mania: a whole people seeming then to adopt by consent the principle which I once heard expressly avowed with regard to the strangest quackery of our own days, Animal Magnetism. An unbeliever in that mystery presumed to talk of common sense. "Common sense," exclaimed a proselyte, "oh, but I tell you common sense must be altogether set aside in the first place." Dr. de Mainaduc would have died worth millions could he but have brought this about as effectually as Lord Shaftesbury and Titus Oates, common sense being a stumbling-block that seems never to have obstructed their path for a moment. Whatever else the plot, if real, might aim at, Charles the Second was to be murdered. That his death was (in law language) *compassed* could not be disbelieved without discrediting the whole. For this criminal purpose, solemnly sworn to, were numbers condemned and executed, and if it never existed, their innocence and the perjury of the witnesses must have been self-evident.

Yet those enthusiastic Protestants whose unlimited faith in the plot made them account it just and pious to bring every Jesuit to the gallows, by no means questioned Charles's partiality to the papists or doubted his secret furtherance of their designs, nor did they suppose the Catholics themselves were ignorant of either. But the more reason they saw to suspect such a mutual good understanding, the more sacredly true they held the plot. Although this was no other than believing that his own friends and confederates, those to whom his life must be of most value, were combining to take it away—nay, and had some thoughts of despatching the Duke of York, their fellow-papist, after his brother —their secret suspicion of the king only led them to entertain a confused, shapeless sort of surmise that he himself had some share in the dark conspiracy. Which put into words would run thus—Charles is perhaps secretly plotting to dethrone and assassinate Charles. But when once men's brains are thoroughly heated they never do put anything into words. Whoever has seen the sea in a storm knows that it is usually obscured by a mist arising from its own foam, which prevents our discerning any object distinctly. So apt in every particular is the comparison implied in that sublime sentence, "He stilleth the rage of the sea, and the noise of his waves, and the madness of the people."

Bewildering as the hurricane was, one man at least (meaning one honest man) kept his senses in the midst of it—the cool-headed, impartial Sir William Temple, who, although he gives no direct opinion of the plot— indeed says he was absent when it began, and knew not what to believe one way or the other—yet so repeatedly protests against having anything to do with it, or with its chief prosecutor Shaftesbury, that we may divine his private sentiments. He evidently suspected the king of secretly favoring the Catholic party, and probably had little doubt that the papists were machinating to re-establish their religion; but it was not for this that wretched men were daily hanged, drawn, and quartered. We find him hinting to the Marquis of Halifax that the plot was too mysterious a matter to be comprehended except by those who had been at the beginning of it. A man not desirous of martyrdom could hardly speak plainer. Nor did Temple himself speak so plainly till, as he tells us, "provoked into some heat of temper." For the moment he recommended a little common justice and humanity toward Catholic priests (the mad dogs of the hour), Halifax—the head, be it observed, of the moderate party —threatened to represent him as himself a papist. And this after making the following memorable declaration: "We must handle the plot as if we believed it, whether we do believe it or not"—language which assuredly none of its sincere believers would have condescended to hold. Mr. Hume, after giving the history of the Popish Plot, says that "its memory should be perpetuated in order to warn posterity, if possible, from again falling into so shameful and barbarous a delusion." The peace-making particle *if* may reconcile opposite propositions as it does adverse persons; otherwise I am afraid he might as well have concluded his account of the sweating sickness by bidding us take warning and never again permit the spreading of an infectious fever. The next pestilence which Providence may send upon earth will in all probability differ from the disease of Henry the Seventh's days, and the next frenzy that overpowers our intellects prompt us to persecute neither witches nor Jesuits; but both the bodily and mental distemper may break out with virulence in some unthought-of shape to-morrow morning; and which of us can dare to call himself certain that he shall resist the contagion of either? As a sound constitution and habitual temperance would give us the best chance of escape in one case, so might steadiness of mind and the habit of always thinking for ourselves in the other. Nor would it be unwholesome to keep in mind this maxim—that though units make a sum, it can never be made by noughts, however multiplied; therefore the foolish story which we hear with contempt when whispered by one foolish individual deserves no better reception when shouted out by ten thousand tellers of the same class in understanding.

After all, this and every other precaution may fail when the mania reaches a height correspondent to that stage of the plague at which the very physicians sicken apace, and the people in despair shut up their houses and write "Lord, have mercy upon us," over the doors. No better resource remains in a mental epidemic when men of sense begin to catch the disorder and recommunicate it to the multitude. The poor citizen who is, notwithstanding, left by some rare chance uninfected, may learn from Sir William Temple to forbear struggling with his delirious neighbors, and to seize any plausible pretext for relinquishing the subject as one above his capacity. The humility of such an avowal must, however, be proved unfeigned by solemnity of tone and aspect, and even silence itself, qualified with "Alas!" and "Heaven defend us!" ejaculated at intervals. Otherwise the jealousy always attendant on redhot zeal may be aroused; and those who never know either doubt or medium, who, because they look at only one side of an affair, are confident that it has but one face, and can admit of but one way of thinking, will take alarm and whet their offensive weapons. Like that model of party-women who wore Dr. Oates engraven upon her fan and pocket-handkerchief, "The silent man must be against the doctor in his heart. She suspected as much by his saying nothing."[1]

Where effects are great enough to astonish us, we cannot help looking for a cause bearing them some proportion in importance; yet seldom indeed shall we find this to have been the case with the most raging manias.

To raise a popular cry is a thing so analogous to the act of raising the mob themselves, that we may judge how easily the one could be accomplished from the suc-

[1] *Spectator*, No. 57.—Supposed to glance at the more recent mania for Sacheverell.

cess of an experiment formerly tried on the other. Mr. Garrick once laid a wager that he would gather together a formidable crowd in ten minutes' time without uttering a word. He posted himself at the corner of a well-frequented street and looked earnestly up at the heavens, using, we may presume, all the power of his matchless eye and countenance to denote that he saw something extraordinary. The first man who passed by stopped, very naturally, and began looking up likewise. So did the next, and the next, and the next, and the next. Presently the whole neighborhood was in commotion, and every window filled with gazers; women and children ran flocking to the spot; the alleys poured forth their swarms, the dingy inhabitants of underground dens ascended into daylight; gentlemen stopped their horses and ladies their coaches to inquire what was the matter. The bet thus clearly won, Garrick flapped his hat over his face and stole away. Had he chosen to carry the jest one small step farther, no doubt the good people would have perceived in the skies any ousel or whale pointed out to them. And if led by a person of worse intentions, they might have knocked down an inoffensive passenger, or set fire to a house, before they dispersed, just to satisfy themselves that they had not assembled in vain. Would it require any greater effort to produce a mania? Let it be tried. Lay a wager that in such a time, say a week or fortnight, you can make a blue coat the object of universal abhorrence; declare it the token, the rallying signal of some unpopular opinion; give out that some ingredient in its dye will generate the yellow fever, or no matter what else you can invent most absurd. At present the Press must be employed; you must disburse a few pounds for the insertion of lies, and grave reasonings upon the lies, in the newspapers, so that your joke may cost more than Garrick's; but in a fortnight's time he will be a bold man who dares defend a blue coat, and a rash who ventures to wear one.

Enough—and, I fear, far more than enough. It is high time to end this unconscionably long rambling dissertation, and, returning homeward, see what can be said for the alterations of the original fable. In point of taste, perhaps nothing. Its simplicity, consequently its beauty, may be spoiled by making the jugglers weave diamond thread instead of silken, and converting them into pompous adepts who pretended to be five hundred years old. But—I know it will appear a paradox—but by doing so I have brought the story nearer to probability, and rendered it more like what might really pass in the world—in England, in London, or Westminster—were such a cheat attempted now. Yes, I maintain the assertion: there must be no modifying, no moderating where a wonder is concerned. Those inclined to open their mouths for it at all will stretch them to any size, and the more marvellous a marvel can be made, gulp it down the more readily. If you would practise as a mountebank, yet scruple administering physical impossibility, you betray want of genius, but if you stop at moral, hide your head for a coward and a bungler. The name of Count Cagliostro, once so famous, being now almost forgotten, it may hardly be recollected that after his French adventures he paid a short visit to this country, partly for refuge, and partly to try what he could do with us in the way of business. He found us for the major part upon our guard against him. His character and history were then so notorious, so fresh in our remembrance, that he could not venture upon any eminent exploit, such as enacting the Wandering Jew, or calling up the Mighty Dead, like Swift's governor of Glubdubdribb. So he condescended to utter nostrums in medicine after the manner of ordinary quack doctors; yet even thus contrived to hook in a few converts; and I had the good fortune to know two or three of the number, persons by no means deficient in understanding. They put on most significant mysterious faces when you mentioned Cagliostro. "That was a point one could not tell what to think of. Some circumstances respecting him were very odd. He had powerful protectors somewhere." "There were bankers in town upon whom he had unlimited credit." "Could draw for a hundred thousand pounds." Which, by the customary progress of repetition, soon grew into half a dozen millions. Now these people were not conscious of believing in the Philosopher's Stone. Nor did they, to their own knowledge, think Beelzebub the invisible potentate who dispensed the treasure. Nor had they retained from their days of childhood a fond lingering faith in Fortunatus and his purse. What it was which they thought and believed, they themselves probably could not have defined; but as long as the thing remained formless, an *Ombre Chinoise*, "half seen, half hid," all was well; they beheld it glimmer with great complacency and a grain or

THE DIAMOND ROBE 199

two of awe. But, for argument-sake, let us suppose that Cagliostro had contented himself with giving out what would be deemed a more plausible story, one shaped as follows: "However it has come to pass, he is secretly protected by the Empress Catherine of Russia. His ample supply of money must proceed from some such source. It is certain that he has brought over letters of credit upon 'Child' from the Hopes of Amsterdam for ten thousand pounds." Why, this rational, credible, probable lie would scarcely have found a single believer. Not simply because any clerk in Child's house could have contradicted it, but because, dazzling no one's imagination, it would have left every one's reason undisturbed, free to act, and each would have assailed it with a doubt or a cavil. "This vagabond worth ten thousand pounds? If he were, would he be a vagabond still? How should he have obtained the Empress of Russia's protection? If as a spy, when has she employed him, and where? Besides, ten thousand pounds would make a thundering sum in roubles. She bestows land and jewels, but has no such abundance of ready money, etc., etc., etc."

Such would have been the consequence of attempting to weave a miraculous robe with possible materials. Don Juan Manuel was a wise man, but he flourished nearly six centuries ago; and there lie before the present age six hundred volumes of experiments upon the nature and actions of man which he never saw and we have the power of perusing. With their aid we may carry our researches farther than he did; just as a smatterer in natural history, assisted by the "Philosophical

Transactions," may look beyond the theories of Boyle or Bacon. If the Castilian Prince had witnessed half the absurdities that have taken their turns to reign and been deposed since he wrote "El Conde Lucanor," he might have forestalled any additions by making his cozeners weave air and fire, and the cozened, instead of recovering their senses on the first flash of detection, wage a seven years' war with the detectors in defence of his invisible imposture.

NOTE.—The reader will probably recognize that the plot of this tale is the same as that used by Hans Andersen in his tale of the "Emperor's New Clothes."—ED.

HISTORY OF
THE FORTUNATE YOUTH

ADDED AS A POSTSCRIPT IN 1819

HISTORY OF THE FORTUNATE YOUTH

ADDED AS A POSTSCRIPT IN 1819

THE above reflections were written some years ago; yet little more than a twelvemonth has elapsed since THE FORTUNATE YOUTH presented us with a case so precisely in point that I myself could almost believe it the circumstance which suggested them. Therefore "meet it is I set it down," and at full length as it deserves, beginning at the beginning. Namely, some slight mention in the newspapers of an odd occurrence: a young man of the middling class having inherited a large property by the will of an old gentleman not at all related to him. Few people noticed the paragraph and fewer seemed to care. Presently we got further details. *The Fortunate Youth*—for this became his established title, as the young Roscius had been Master Betty's—the Fortunate Youth was now about eighteen. While still a schoolboy, he had by chance travelled in a stage-coach along with an elderly gentleman unknown to him, who in conversing with the other passengers advanced some opinions which he took the liberty to oppose. A dispute ensued: the lad maintained his argument so resolutely and ably that the liberal old man, more pleased than offended, praised his manly spirit, shook him by the hand at parting, and requested that their acquaintance might continue; although, for certain reasons of his own, he insisted that it should be kept a secret from the boy's parents and every one beside. They had private meetings afterward, the gentleman supplied him handsomely with money, and at length told him—still upon condition of the strictest secrecy—that having no relations in the world, and being charmed with the independence of his character, he had resolved to adopt and make him his heir. He was now no more; and the youth, inheritor of all his wealth, had used a part of it worthily, according to some of the papers, by providing for a venerable father. Others lamented that the joyful surprise, overpowering his reason, had left him in a state delicately termed one of nervous debility. Others made him consumptive and sent him to Bristol. Others consoled us with assurances that his health and his intellects were equally unimpaired. In short, they played the tune with a set of harmonious variations.

Thus far the tale, though romantic and singular, had in it nothing incredible. There might be a rich man without heirs; he might be a humorist; he might adopt a stranger-boy, or endow a hospital, as he liked best: who could tell? And *a great fortune* was a commonplace, vague, uncertain phrase, sometimes signifying fifty thousand a year, sometimes only five: so whether the acquisition of it had or had not unsettled its possessor's wits, the sound produced so slight an effect upon ours that, as long as the story rested there, it excited small attention. People said coolly: "It is very extraordinary, if true; but perhaps it is not true

HISTORY OF THE FORTUNATE YOUTH 205

—very likely a fiction from beginning to end." This sober-minded indifference was put to flight in a curious manner. Some county gazetteer published, and the London papers copied, a document which, they were persuaded, must afford their readers the highest gratification, a genuine authentic letter, dated at ——— (*one dash*), written by ——— ——— (*two dashes*), Esquire, a gentleman of great eminence and known respectability in the law (name withheld from motives of delicacy), to Mr. ——— ——— ——— (*three dashes*), at ——— (*one dash*), minutely stating the particulars of the Fortunate Youth's inheritance. It consisted of millions in the English funds—"not one or two millions" (were the words), "but millions, many millions," of immense mortgages at home and abroad, of considerable estates in almost every shire in England, and vast tracts of land in several foreign countries, especially Poland and Spain. I think there were also hoards of inestimable jewels. Briefly, all Aladdin's riches, without the lamp and the genie: that is to say, without the means of accounting for them. For, again, be it humbly suggested that we had better believe in magic than in nonsense. Yet how many grave grown men listened to these marvels, who would have pulled a little boy's ears and called him a simpleton for supposing Princess Scheherezade a reciter of true history.

When the flight of a few more years shall have converted this anecdote into "*an auld warld story*," there will not be two opinions among its hearers. They will unanimously conclude that the foregoing detail set the subject completely at rest, and made the whole kingdom exclaim in the words of Prince Harry, "Why, these lies are gross as a mountain, open and palpable." Oh, what different creatures are we at sea or on shore! Actually engaged in life's bustle, or viewing it at a distance! The moment this stupendous stride was taken from the surprising to the impossible, the moment the Fortunate Youth indulged us with this peep into unsearchable mines of countless treasure, he became an object of general curiosity and interest, about whom all grew eager to hear and to repeat fresh wonders. The mighty THEY, accepting it as a retaining fee, heartily espoused his cause. THEY said—*this, that,* and *t'other. They* labored hard to perform their accustomed office of each throwing the ball a pace or two beyond his neighbor. And notwithstanding the meritorious endeavors of the hero himself to render exaggeration impracticable, one must allow that even his story did not lose by the telling. What astonishing things (it was observed) one does hear of this boy's fortune! "Do you know, *they say,* that the interest of what he has in our funds alone amounts to three hundred and forty thousand pounds a quarter?" If you answered with an interjection, or cried for mercy, or held up your hands, you were silenced by a more serious and solemn appeal to the same great authority—"Nay, now, in earnest I assure you *they* really do say so." After which, who could presume to doubt any longer?

Who indeed can dare to contest *their* immemorial privileges, the exemption *They* claim from that tedious process of weighing and calculating, of spelling and putting together which common sense prescribes to in-

HISTORY OF THE FORTUNATE YOUTH 207

dividuals? That two and two make only four, that nobody can be in two places at once, that black is not white, nor ice fire, are propositions that *They* have an undoubted right to disregard. Yet let us just hint that the stocks were high at the time, therefore the principal yielding such interest must have been above forty millions sterling. A pittance forming only part of the miraculous old man's bequest. Most of the European sovereigns owed him enormous sums of money. And no tradesman ever spoke more handsomely of a lord who pays his bills at sight, and whom he wishes all noblemen resembled, than our young hero of the magnanimous Alexander's august mother, empress-dowager of Russia. Honorable woman! She was punctual to a day—though, to be sure, in a matter of trifling importance. For every virtue has its drawback: these exact old ladies, so scrupulous about paying, will be scrupulous about borrowing also; there is a narrowness, a shabby economy, in their notions, which prevents their dealing largely and nobly like their high-minded sons and grandsons. However, five thousand a year, the interest of the pitiful hundred thousand pounds which she had ventured to borrow, ever found its way, with love in the ballad, "over the mountains or under the waves," the very instant it was due. Certain other crowned heads, he acknowledged, gave him a great deal of trouble. And in truth he found the management of his immense continental property cruelly perplexing; the weight of his whole business almost insupportable. He warned his friends against the mistake of believing wealth a source of happiness. His spirits, he said, were depressed; the cheerfulness of youth had forsaken him; and, worst of all, he candidly confessed that he could perceive the love of money gaining ground upon his better disposition; so close and cool an observer was he of the workings of his own mind But the evil influence of riches spread yet farther; revenge crept in as well as avarice. Along with his actual possessions, he had inherited certain rights, his claiming which by law might bring ruin upon many families now unconscious of their danger. He could legally dispossess two great noblemen, whom he prudently forbore naming, of their whole estates. To one of these he owed no ill-will, so perhaps he should leave him unmolested; but the other had given him offence, while his condition was humble, by some piece of aristocratical insolence, and he did not deny exulting at the thoughts of effecting his downfall.

After all, the Fortunate Youth (to do him justice) was himself a phenomenon almost as wonderful as the fabulous tale he made us swallow. It would be scarcely three degrees more extraordinary to light upon a benevolent ancient in a stage-coach, worth fifty millions of consols, and owner of half the territory in Spain, than to find a lad of eighteen gifted with such a knowledge of the world, and deep insight into the weaknesses of human nature, as his conduct of the imposture seemed to prove. Well aware, by whatever revelation from above—or below—he came to know it, that Mystery is ever the *sine quâ non*, the grand ingredient without which no dish of the kind can have its right flavor, he did not let it be wanting. He was far from telling outright and straightforward all that I have related. He hinted one circumstance; he betrayed another when apparently off his guard; a third was drawn from him against his will. He would begin a confidential statement of his affairs, check himself abruptly, and shut up again. The newspaper puffs made him so angry that there was no suspecting he had written them himself; yet he led you to think him displeased, not because they asserted falsehoods, but because they told truths which he wished to keep concealed. Nor were the names of the two grandees in jeopardy the only secrets he withheld from his nearest friends. He never revealed whereabouts his estates in England lay, and never could be induced to show his benefactor's will. Everybody knows that a will, to take effect, must be made as public as an act of Parliament. Everybody did know it, but nobody chose to remember it. You would have sworn that the whole testamentary law had been repealed in his favor, and that he alone stood exempted from the legacy-tax of ten per cent.; for not one of those busy in discussing the subject ever appeared sensible that there was anything to hinder his slipping the windfall into his pocket, as quietly as he might have done a handful of rusty coins which he had picked up when digging by himself in his own garden.

And yet—and yet—and yet—will it be credited?—will it be deemed possible?—his chief dupe was a lawyer, a solicitor in good practice!!!—One cannot help thinking of the giant fishing—

His hook he baited with a dragon's tail,
And sat upon a rock, and bobbed for whale.

Such a whale (or rather shark) once taken, no wonder the net he proceeded to throw should sweep away multitudes of us poor shoal-fish, naturally prone to swim blindly one after the other, whichever way the current may carry us. The eagerness of tradesmen to secure his custom, supply his wardrobe, build his carriages, and furnish his palaces can excite no surprise. But the gamesters at the clubs, and the jockeys at Newmarket, began speculating upon the chance of having so magnificent a pigeon to plume; bankers solicited the honor of keeping his cash, and the voters of independent boroughs tampered with his confidants to learn how much of it he would be willing to exchange for parliamentary influence. I heard a man well versed in business and the world affirm that to his knowledge the sale of a large estate in Norfolk had been deferred, and a fair price for it refused, in hopes that the Fortunate Youth might fancy the purchase, and bid a higher. Nay, as in this country politics are sure to meddle with everything in return for every one's meddling with them—even the ministers of the day were said to have paid him a little secret court, or at least showed some desire to ascertain what party he meant to embrace—a point about which their antagonists would no doubt have been wholly indifferent. But these rumors did not spring forth till all was over, till the youth and his millions had vanished from our sight, and each man, woman, and child among us were (according to custom) protesting that—"*For my part I always thought the story very absurd.*"—"*And for mine, I never believed a word of it.*" That we never had believed it soon became our own steadfast faithful persuasion; and ill fared the impertinent remembrancer who insisted upon bringing back our forgotten words to prove the contrary.

In one respect the termination of the affair was singular, it dissolved instead of exploding. The young gentleman, after complaining heavily of his agents abroad, found himself obliged to visit his foreign dominions in person, and no sooner did he embark for the continent than all mention of him seemed to die softly away. Very possibly those whose purses had enabled him to maintain the cheat so long learned wisdom late, and thought it better to sit down in silence with their loss than to risk making themselves objects of ridicule by proclaiming it. However this might be, no explanation of his motives for inventing the romance, no account of the advantage he reaped, or sought to reap, from it ever transpired: the waters of oblivion closed over his head, and not a trace of him remained. Peace and mirth go with him! He has established, beyond any of his predecessors (always excepting the bottle conjurer), the certainty of this position—that there is nothing which men may not be brought to believe; that even where the engines most powerful in moving our nature, religious zeal or political, the desire of health or of wealth, the force of interest or passion, are in no way employed, yet still *marvel, for itself marvel*, has an attraction which human beings cannot withstand.

One more observation (grounded on this last story) and I have done. On considering any remarkable deception, how often do we find it accomplished by seemingly inadequate means?—truth lying all the while in the sight and at the feet of the parties whom some unaccountable impulse prompted to leap over it with their eyes shut, and leave it unperceived. Thus, also, the riddle hardest to guess is seldom the most ingenious, but often conceals a meaning so silly, so flat, so obvious, that when told it we turn away with a peevish "pshaw!"—disappointed and half indignant. No wonder we should be mortified at hearing a question of greater moment expounded as follows: "Look you, there is no such thing—dispute no more about circumstances, quantity, or quality, for the substance does not exist. I tell you there is no such thing."—Let this relieve us from ever so much perplexity, we shall still hear it with a blank aspect, and dislike to be convinced that we have been pondering, arguing, perhaps quarrelling, perhaps fighting, about positively and veritably *Nothing*. Of course we are always slow to make the discovery by our own voluntary efforts. Not the vulgar or ignorant *We* only, but men of talents, men of science themselves, if once imposed upon. And that they sometimes are so with regard to the subjects they understand best, the Fortunate Youth's attorney does not stand single as a proof. Were the old history of Elizabeth Canning[1] now related, every lady who attends

[1] An account of Elizabeth Canning will be found in "Chambers's Encyclopædia" and Paget's "Paradoxes and Puzzles." Briefly, the story is this: Elizabeth Canning was a girl in service in London. On New Year's Day, 1753, she went for a holiday to her parents in another part of London. She disappeared on her return to her master, and nothing was heard of her, till on January 29th she appeared at her home, half-starved and in rags. Her

the Royal Institution, every flippant boy and girl tolerably well read in "Beauties and Abridgements," would be sure to cry, "How foolishly our ancestors were duped! The world is rather wiser at present." Yet who was one of the dupes? Henry Fielding, the eminent wit, the acute observer of manners and character, and (what comes more home to the purpose) the able and active magistrate.

I shall conclude with another instance warranted by the "narrative old age" of an excellent old man familiar in my father's house when I was young. He had been chief surgeon to the court and the army, and intimate with the highest characters of his time, being as much beloved for his humanity as respected for his integrity and skill. He loved relating anecdotes or (if you will) telling old stories, and here was one which, I have heard, made no small noise when the event happened. A young lady of quality fell ill of a strange disease. Blotches broke out on her face, arms, and neck, suddenly appearing and disappearing, and perpetually shifting from one spot to another. A surgeon, particularly

story was that she had been kidnapped in Bloomsbury Square by two men who blindfolded and gagged her, and carried her to a house in Epping Forest, where she was confined in a garret, with a few crusts and a pitcher of water, till she contrived to escape. Popular excitement grew till, as Lady Louisa says in a letter, "John Bull ran bellowing mad." Owing to Canning's evidence a gipsy-woman named Squire was condemned to death. Doubts of Canning's story, however, caused a new trial, which ended in Squire's release and the transportation of Canning to New England for perjury. Some idea may be formed of the obscurity of the story by the fact that thirty-eight witnesses were in favor of Squire, and twenty-seven against her!—ED.

attached to her family, attended her long with the greatest assiduity, but, as he wrought no cure, all the principal doctors were called in to assist, and all were alike unsuccessful. They could not remove the obstinate humor. Yet her pulse continued regular, her tongue clean, her strength unimpaired; and, what perplexed them most, some powerful medicines which they administered with fear and trembling did her neither good nor harm. At length came an unexpected crisis. One fine morning, off together went the patient and the confidential family-surgeon in a post-chaise and four; the formidable medicines were found untouched in her closet, and the learned brethren of the bridegroom remained confounded like the king and courtiers in our Spanish tale. "Now," said the good old man, "do not go and fancy, from what you read in the 'Bath Guide,' that we came with our canes at our noses, and pocketed double fees for talking politics over the fire. We were all, I assure you, very honestly and really puzzled; indeed, unusually anxious to get to the bottom of a case so extraordinary. We racked our brains, and tumbled over our books—and so might we have gone on doing to the end of our lives—for" (proceeded he, chuckling) "not one of us—great blockheads as we were!—ever bethought himself of the effectual remedy close at hand —*videlicet*, dipping a clean towel in a basin of fair water, and *washing her ladyship's face.*"

UNPUBLISHED LETTERS

UNPUBLISHED LETTERS OF SIR WALTER SCOTT AND LADY LOUISA STUART

I

EDINBURGH, *7th Feb.* 1826.

MY DEAR LADY LOUISA,—I am flattered and delighted with your kind inquiries just received. Were I to say I was indifferent to losing a large proportion of a hard-earned fortune I should lie in my throat, and a very stupid lie it would be considered as an attempt to impose on your sagacity. But yet it is inconceivable to myself how little I feel myself care about it, and how much I scandalise the grave looks and grasps of the hand and extremity scenes which my friends treat me to to the tune of a Grecian chorus, exclaiming about gods and fates, and letting poor Philgarlick enjoy his distress all the while.

Every person interested, so far as I yet know, are disposed to acquiesce in measures by which they will be at no distant period completely satisfied. We shall only have to adopt some measure of economy of no very frightful nature, and which we meditated at any rate, for the number of visitors made Abbotsford very untenable during the autumn months. Now, those who get in must bring battering cannon, for no *billet-doux* will blow open the gates, come from whom it may.

My children are all well provided for, so that I have not that agonising feeling, and we have ample income for ourselves. I am ashamed to think of it, and mention it as a declension, knowing so many generals and admirals who would be glad to change fortunes with me. My land remains with me, being settled on my son, and I look round and round and do not see one domestic comfort abridged, though I shall willingly lay down some points of parade of servants and equipage and expensive form (which I always detested), and all the rout of welcoming strange folks, which, my age advancing a little, and the want of my sons to do honours, made very annoying last season. I have everything else—my walks, my plantations, my dogs great and small, my favourite squire, my Highland pony, my plans, my hopes, and my quiet thoughts. So, like the upholsterer, Mr. Quidnunc, I ask myself, *How are we ruined?* I shall make play, too, in the language of the turf, and try what I can do to recover my distance. None can calculate on the public favour, yet I have had a pretty strong hold of it, and have done more extraordinary things in my day than recover my whole loss within three years. This, however, is not to be much counted for, because novels and works of imagination are not like household bread, in fashion all the year round, but, like minced pies and hot-cross buns, have only their season. Such is my plan, and the only unpleasant part of it is that giving up my house in Edinburgh, I must necessarily live at my club, where we have excellent accommodation, for such time as I must attend the sittings of the Court. But there are plenty of convey-

SIR WALTER SCOTT AND LADY STUART 219

ances to Abbotsford, so once a week or a fortnight in summer I can make my wife and daughter a visit, and in winter we may take lodgings together for perhaps a month or six weeks in the gay season. This is the worst part of my retrenchment; but I am rather a solitary monster, and sit much by myself at all times. I am sure you are very good to think half so well of me as you do, my dear Lady Louisa. I am conscious of meriting it so far, that I have done good to some people, and never willingly injured a human being in my life. I will soon have to send you three volumes. The fates have not smiled on them, for you may be sure they have been written at disadvantage, even much greater than "Ivanhoe," much of which was dictated while I was in agony with the cramp in my stomach, and scarce able to utter two words without a pause. But there are some sort of vexations worse than bodily pain. Thank God! they seem all settled with me, and no unforeseen obstacle intervening, a fair field lies before me. When your ladyship can honour Sophia with a call she will be found at 25 Pall Mall. The loss of her is very serious at this moment, for had they remained keeping house in Edinburgh it would have been a great comfort to me. But if it proves in the end for their advantage I must be satisfied. They have a little boy about whose health I am truly anxious, an only child as yet, and very clever, from being so much talked to and fondled. I do fear London on its account not a little. But we will not anticipate evil. God bless you, my dear Lady Louisa; you have been since I knew you the ready and active comforter of much distress.

Indeed I think that things have happened to exercise your feelings in the behalf of others merely because you really have that sincere interest in the griefs of others which so many people make the ostensible show of. Do not think upon my losses as a thing to be vexed about, but let me have the great pleasure of hearing from you now and then, which will always enhance the pleasure of fair weather, and make this which is rough the more endurable. I heard from Morritt lately, which I was very glad of, as his letter contradicted an ugly report of his nephew's illness.—I am always, dear Lady Louisa, most truly yours, WALTER SCOTT.

II

DITTON PARK, 11th March 1826.

MY DEAR SIR WALTER,—Your welcome letter, together with the particulars Lord Montagu gave me, partly dispelled the anxiety that had prompted me to write in a manner which perhaps it was very kind in you not to take ill; for report, according to custom, magnified the evil twentyfold, and I dreamed of nothing less than utter ruin and desolation. Mr. Morritt, who at first did so too, vows this shall cure him of ever believing half what the world says, which before he thought a good safe proportion. Still, the truth, such as it is, would be overwhelming to most minds; and were I to tell you how your calm fortitude affected me, and how often I read over with admiration the little you say on the subject, I should be afraid of your thinking I dealt in the figure of speech called palaver. But there is something that makes one's heart glow when one meets with a character, even in books,

> "that is not a pipe for Fortune's finger
> To sound what stop she please"—

and the effect may well be stronger where one knows and values the person. I do own that if I had not checked myself I should have returned fire and expressed all I felt directly. However, by delaying I can speak on a theme you will like better, and give you a late account of Mrs. Lockhart, who has been here for two days of this week. I saw her in town just before I left it (a month ago); her looks are mended since then, and though her situation is pretty apparent, she did not seem the worse for a whole morning spent in viewing Windsor Castle within and without, old part and new, the most fatiguing thing in the world. At night she sung us two or three of her wild songs, and I wish you had seen the eager eyes of some of the younger listeners, to whom she was a huge lion as your daughter, and who had been sucking in whatever she said of you. I find her the same Sophia she ever was, as natural and as engaging; and her husband just what you described him, a Spanish nobleman, or suppose we say the Master of Ravenswood, with a face for painters to study, but a brow rather awful notwithstanding its beauty. It was a delight to me to renew acquaintance with her; twelve hours in a country house, you know, do more than eight-and-forty morning visits in London, therefore I looked forward to her coming as my best opportunity; and she was so glad to breathe some fresh air and meet her old friends Lady Anne (Scott) and Lady Isabella (Cust) that I believe she enjoyed her visit as much as we did her company, although pulled back by her poor little boy. He seems a fine lively spirited child. I am sorry his constitution is so delicate.

I do not know what may be the case with "Woodstock," but I am sure Malachi Malagrowther *ne ressent pas de l'apoplexie.* Who would have expected amusement from anything any human being could write upon banknotes and currencies? So I rest perfectly satisfied that the master-spring remains unbroken, 'though I feel a cowardly dread of the nest of hornets Malachi is drawing about his ears; some mighty to sting, however unequal to answer.

I write this before I go away, which I shall do early in next week, having made them here a visitation. They are to be in town themselves after Easter. With kind remembrance to Lady Scott, believe me, most truly yours,   L. STUART.

III

ABBOTSFORD, 13*th April* 1826.

MY DEAR LADY LOUISA,—For some time writing has been painful to me saving what I must needs write, and that being the discharge of a duty is always a sort of pleasure—at least you are interested while about it and contented when it is over. But of late I have had and still have terrible anxiety on Sophia's account and that of the poor child. I hardly ever regarded him but as something lent to us from another world, and viewed with terror the doating anxiety of the poor father and mother. The sweet little boy was in himself very taking, and I have frequently hardened my heart as well as I could to prevent its twining itself around my own heart-strings as it did about theirs. It is very clever, perfectly natural, and good-humoured; in short, the thing you would most wish to see at your knee had it had less of the stamp of early fragility fixed upon it. They are now, the mother and baby, as your ladyship probably knows, at Brighton, and I own to you my best hopes are that God will conduct my daughter through her approaching confinement, and permit her to be the mother of a healthy infant before

> "the bird is flown
> That we have made so much of."

My wife, too, the faithful partaker of much weal and woe, and who has in judging of what is upright and honourable the spirit of a hundred princesses, is very unwell. She is obliged to take foxglove, a terrible medicine in its effects, but which alleviates very considerably the disease and gives me hope to see her restored to tolerable health.

My own affairs assume every day a more comfortable aspect. My chief and only subject of impatience is the regret that requires people to wait a little for their due so far as I have been involved in the misfortunes of others. But my agent John Gibson, whom I four or five years since recommended to Lord Montagu, has done among the booksellers more in a few weeks than I have done in many years. He has sold the impending novel of "Woodstock" for £8000 and upwards, and has similar offers for my sketch of Napoleon. If these hold, a year or two's labour will place me in the happy alternative called *statu quo*. But I am very easy about that matter so long as I see the speedy prospect of getting rid of debt. I feel much like my friend John Hookham Frere, whom they could not get out of the lazeretto at the expiry of quarantine. I could not help telling said John Gibson that if he would maintain my establishment, which is very comfortable, in the present style and leave me my pleasant walks at Abbotsford I would, *to chuse*, remain as I now am, with every rational and many irrational wants supplied, and let the rest go to *Colin Tampon*, as the French song says.

But write I must—it has become a part of my nature, and as I become daily more solitary the pen and reading are, of course, my best resources. Every sort of society which I cared for is very much diminished by death and absence. The only man in this country whom I could regard quite as a companion from his taste and accomplishments, poor John Scott of Gala, is I fear very ill. I saw a letter from him to his man of business signed with his initials only—and such letters! I had a sincere love for him. We spent part of a little tour in France together, immediately after Waterloo, and I shall never forget his matchless good-humour, and on one or two occasions, where there really seemed serious personal danger, his ready gallantry and spirit. One night we were apparently in the predicament of fighting for our lives. I was even then a horse in point of strength and fearless by constitution, and

SIR WALTER SCOTT AND LADY STUART 225

yet with his delicate person and softer breeding he was the foremost of the two, let me do what I would. Poor, poor fellow!

I am delighted that Lockhart passes current with you. He really is a fine fellow, a scholar, a man of taste, and *point de vice* the gentleman. I am sometimes angry with him for an exuberant love of fun in his light writings, which he has caught, I think, from Wilson, a man of greater genius than himself perhaps, but who disputes with low adversaries, which I think a terrible error, and indulges in a sort of humour which exceeds the bounds of playing at ladies and gentlemen, a game to which I have been partial all my life. You would see, dear Lady Louisa, that I commenced politician for a start in a small way, incensed all my friends for pointing out their egregious blunders, and raised a racket of which I had not anticipated the least idea. I had half a mind to have followed up the controversy, for I had the cards in my hand, but, after all, I thought it as well to let it stand after I had *said* my *say*. It is not worth while to vex old friends about the past, and if they do not look better to their bats in time to come it will be their fault not mine. But they are playing a bad game in Scotland, if not in England, and turning people's heads round with such a constant succession of experimental changes that those to whom the vertigo is communicated will become incapable of remaining still; and when that time comes, Scotland, with her love of theory, her depth of brooding long and sullenly over her plans and the many clever *revolutionists*, for that is the word, whose game they are playing in mere wantonness, will some day *wind them a pirn*. I hope this will not happen till I am dead and gone, for I am too old to have any share in the *row*. I was not (between you, my dear Lady Louisa, and myself be it said) a bit sorry for this *turn up*— as the blackguards call it. My friends were some of them poor manning me a little too much for one who was asking nothing from them, and had asked nothing during my pilgrimage for myself, though I have been often a suitor for others. But I don't like they should think I am fallen out of the line. But this is all nonsense again, says my uncle Toby to himself.

I have had this lying by me till I should have occasion to write to Lord Montagu, which has suddenly and unexpectedly occurred through the very unexpected death of Sir Alexander Don. It will be a great shock to Lord Montagu, and would have been a still more severe one to his poor dear brother. As for me, I think the world is gliding from under my feet,

"For many a lad I loved is dead,
And many a lass grown old,
And when I think on those are fled
My weary heart grows cold."

But this has been, will be, and must be.

All health to you, my dear Lady Louisa, and all happiness.—Believe me, most truly and respectfully yours,   WALTER SCOTT.

You will have difficulty, I fear, in reading this, but my eyes are failing me fast. I cannot charge them with idleness.

IV

GLOUCESTER PLACE, 24th April 1826.

YOUR letters are always so acceptable, dear Sir Walter, that I wish it were not painful to you to write. Yet since it is, I would fain have it a thing understood that you need not answer mine, especially as I dare say I am not the only foolish woman who plagues you in this way. I trust your mind has been partly relieved since you wrote by Mrs. Lockhart's safe confinement, which I was most heartily glad to hear of. For the poor little boy, it must be as Providence wills, and at best I fear a source of long and wearing anxiety; but sometimes children such as you describe him live and do well at last. I am sure one might have used your very words—"something lent to us from another world" —about Lady Harriet Scott,[1] who is now as likely to live as any of her family, and rather less liable to illness than some of the rest. It gives me still more concern that you should have cause for uneasiness on account of Lady Scott's health. May God restore it and preserve her to you! How well I understand the indifference you feel about mere worldly matters when objects so dear are in any kind of jeopardy; then the probe reaches the quick, and all before goes for nothing. Still, I must rejoice these secondary things go so well, the more from its being a proof that the public mind is not changed nor the public appetite cloyed. Another thing pleases me, the general approbation of the

[1] Married 1842 Rev. Edward Moore and had ten children.

last *Quarterly Review*, Mr. Lockhart's first, I believe, and one in which your cloven foot is visible. It had something to set it off, however; for I think verily the temporary editor of the work during the *interregnum* must have been bribed into his extreme degree of dulness. By the by I have lately had a long bad cold, such as reduces one to trash and slops, novels and barley-water, and amongst the books my friends kindly sent me to while away time was the first volume of one puffed in the newspaper, "The Last Man," by the authoress of "Frankenstein." I would not trouble them for any more of it, but really there were sentences in it so far exceeding those Don Quixote ran mad in trying to comprehend, that I could not help copying out a few of them; they would have turned Feliciano de Silva's own brains. For example:—

"Her eyes were impenetrably deep; you seemed to discover space after space in their intellectual glance, and to feel that the soul which was their soul comprehended an universe of thought in its ken."

And this: "The overflowing warmth of her heart, by making love a plant of deep root and stately growth, had attuned her whole soul to the reception of happiness."

I amused myself with turning the metaphor to matter of fact. The overflowing warmth of the stove, by making the geranium strike root and grow vigorous, tuned the pianoforte to the reception of God save the King. Since the wonderful improvement that somebody who shall be nameless, together with Miss Edgeworth and one or two more, have made in novels, I imagined such stuff as this had not ventured to show its head, though I remember plenty of it in the days of my youth. So for old acquaintance-sake I give it welcome. But if the boys and girls begin afresh to take it for sublime and beautiful, it ought to get a rap and be put down.

The Montagus settle in town the end of this week for the remainder of the season, which the expected dissolution of Parliament is likely to abridge, therefore I wish they had come sooner. Poor Sir Alexander Don's death is a sad shock to them. I have not heard anything lately of Scott of Gala, but think his uncle, the admiral, was to visit him or be visited by him a week or two ago. I am going to stay a few days with the Scotts at Petersham previous to their setting out for Bothwell early in May, and if I can pick up any tidings of the nephew more satisfactory than what you seem to have had, I will send them you on my return, provided that if I do you are not even to say thank ye. I can easily conceive the blank his absence must cause in your neighbourhood. But alas that you, who as Canton says in the play[1] "are chicken to me," should already talk of the world gliding from beneath you! Certainly it must be one day, but indeed 'tis *o'er soon*, and I hope there will come brighter moments tempting you to retract the hasty word. God bless you! Dear Sir Walter, I say it from my heart.

I was going to conclude, and forgetting to mention Mr. Morritt, whose domestic happiness remains unabated. He trundles his whole cargo of nephew and

[1] Coleman's "Clandestine Marriage."

nieces down to Rokeby on the fifteenth of May, and if all should go well, builds upon the hope of luring you to come so far in summer. Now farewell. Believe me, always affectionately yours,   L. STUART.

Tuesday.

P.S.—Since I wrote the above I have called in Pall Mall, and Mr. Lockhart, who was at home, sent word that all was going on well at Brighton.

V

GLOUCESTER PLACE, 5*th May* [1826].

DEAR SIR WALTER,—I should have written again the moment I returned from Petersham if Admiral and Mrs. Scott had told me anything of their nephew which it would have given you pleasure to hear, but alas! this was not the case; and finding "Woodstock" on my table when I came back, I could not help reading it first. Scott of Gala and his wife had been some days at Petersham the week before I went there, and I am sorry to say they think his health and spirits little improved. *My* Mrs. Scott, commonly called Car, is as partial to him as you are, and grieves to see him so unequal to any enjoyment of society. After talking agreeably for half an hour he is forced to get up, go to his own room, and remain a long time entirely quiet and inactive. One evening he made her play to him some of Handel's music, and was so delighted, he said, "Well, I cannot resist it; I will fetch my flute and try to accompany you"; but before he could get through one tune, the pain in his head came on and drove him away. It is the same thing when he attempts any solitary occupation, he can read only for a few minutes together. The medical man he consults is of opinion that the stomach, originally deranged by the injury of the head, now reacts on the head in its turn; therefore he is applying mercurial remedies. Dr. Baillie told Admiral Scott that time and nature must act for themselves, medicine could do nothing. I hope this man— I think they named Abernethy (the surgeon)—will prove the contrary.

Lord Montagu desires me to tell you that the Duke of Buccleuch left London to go abroad yesterday, and the day before was privately presented to the king in the uniform of the Dumfriesshire militia, the first time in his life, it seems, that he had ever had on the utterly unnameable garment (for one may talk loudly of pantaloons), and he was as awkward and as much ashamed of showing his legs as any young lady. His Majesty, perhaps, would be still more so, having the gout in both feet, though otherwise well. He received the uncle and nephew very graciously, and told the latter that he was sitting for his picture to Lawrence, and meant to give it him, if he chose to accept of it, for Dalkeith House. The Duke returns home in August.

Now let me thank you a thousand times for " Woodstock." All I shall say about it is this, that I felt as anxious for Charles the Second's escape, and held my breath, as if I had not known he did escape, and been sure he must. I may add, too, as if he had been better worth saving. It was wise of you to refrain from reading "Brambletye House," for after reading it you would yourself have blushed to bring it into comparison; the coarse caricature, the vulgarity, as evident in the book as in the author, whom I have seen and heard sing his buffoon-songs! I read it first, and to be sure it set off not only your cavaliers, but your Cromwell and your Presbyterians. It is impossible, I think, that "Woodstock" should not have brilliant success.

What you will care more for, I trust, Mrs. Lockhart and her children are going on well. I called in Pall Mall yesterday, but Mr. L. was absent, and they had no later news than I learned there some days ago. Lord Montagu says you wrote him a far better account of Lady Scott, which I am sincerely glad of, hoping so marked an amendment will be followed by recovery. Remember you are not to answer this letter, nor even to read it except in a very leisure hour; but always believe me yours, with the truest regard,

L. STUART.

P.S.—I rejoice to hear young Harden[1] comes into Parliament.

VI

CHISWICK, *4th Sept.* 1826.

I FORBORE writing to you when I wished most to do it, dear Sir Walter, for there are moments and feelings upon which none but the nearest friends, and hardly they, ought to intrude; but God knows you were as much in my thoughts all the while as if I had told you how I felt for you. I saw Mrs. Lockhart in town, and

[1] Scott of Harden, the late Lord Polwarth.

SIR WALTER SCOTT AND LADY STUART 233

afterwards heard from her, for I could not help asking whether the newspaper story of your being King's Printer had any truth in it. By her answer I found out it was what Lord Montagu calls a mare's nest. However, she wrote me a comfortable account of you, and spoke of her poor little boy hopefully, as likely to outgrow at last the mischiefs that threatened his infancy. I trust it will be so; and may every cloud pass over him harmless! The Montagus talk of going to Brighton, where they will find her out if still there. You know, perhaps, that the hooping-cough in their family hindered their journey to Scotland, or rather delayed it, for I think they are likely to take it some weeks hence. When I asked Lord M. for a frank, he bade me tell you he had been on the point of writing to you himself, but hearing of you very fully from the Drumlanrig party, he put it off till another occasion.

Now to say honestly why the spirit moves me to plague you with a letter at present. That French *pirate*, Galignani, has gathered together in two small volumes your Prefaces to the British novelists, and published them at Paris, whence some copies have been brought over hither. Everybody who opens the book is charmed with it. To use the French expression, *on se l'arrache;* and nobody that I have met with seems ever to have heard of the prefaces before, but all are eager to get it from France. Were it to be got in England at double or treble the price, they would send to the next bookseller, but they will not lay out a large sum for the "Gil Blas'," "Clarissas," and "Tom Joneses" they have by heart already. The whole collection can only be a library book, furniture for a country house, like the " Bibliothèque de Campagne." Surely it would answer to Ballantyne himself to publish the Prefaces apart, and if there were two more volumes added (or four if you will) it would run like wildfire. Either Galignani has not printed all, or many are wanting whom you certainly do not mean to pass by: Moore's "Zeluco," Godwin's "Caleb Williams" and "St. Leon," Charlotte Smith, Miss Burney, Miss Hamilton, Miss Edgeworth, Miss Austen, and may I petition for a word in favour of Charlotte Lennox, Dr. Johnson's favourite, whose female Quixote delighted my childhood so much that I cannot tell whether the liking I still have for it is from taste or memory. General Burgoyne took the plot and characters of his admired comedy "The Heiress" almost wholly from another novel of hers, "Henrietta," and when he printed the play did not name her in the preface, which, considering he was a great man and she a starving authoress, I thought ungenerous.

I am lately returned from a friend's house where these prefaces have been *devoured* by man, woman, and child. One evening after they were finished, a book was wanting to be read aloud, and what you said of Mackenzie made the company choose the "Man of Feeling," though some apprehended it would prove too affecting. However, we began. I, who was the reader, had not seen it for several years, the rest did not know it at all. I am afraid I perceived a sad change in it, or myself, which was worse, and the effect altogether failed. Nobody cried, and at some of the passages, the touches that I used to think so exquisite

SIR WALTER SCOTT AND LADY STUART 235

—oh dear! they laughed. I thought we should never have got over Harley's walking down to breakfast with his shoe-buckle in his hand.

Yet I remember so well its first publication, my mother and sisters crying over it, dwelling upon it with rapture! And when I read it, as I was a girl of fourteen not yet versed in sentiment, I had a secret dread I should not cry enough to gain the credit of proper sensibility. This circumstance has led me to reflect on the alterations of taste produced by time. What we call the taste of the age, in books as in anything else, naturally influences more or less those who belong to that age, who converse with the world and are swayed by each other's opinions. But how comes it to affect those who are as yet of no age, the very young, who go to an author fresh, and, if one may say so, stand in the shoes of his first original readers? What instinct makes them judge so differently? In my youth Rousseau's "Nouvelle Heloise" was the book that all mothers prohibited, and all daughters longed to read; therefore somehow or other they did read, and were not the better for it, if they had a grain of romance in their composition. Well! I know a young person of very strong feelings, one "of imagination all compact," all eagerness and enthusiasm, she lately told me she had been trying to read the "Nouvelle Heloise," but it tired and disgusted her, so she threw it by unfinished. I was heartily glad to hear it, but I own a good deal surprised, for if she, the same she, had lived fifty years ago, she would have been intoxicated and bewildered and cried her eyes out

Now do consider and expound this, not in a letter to me, but in the next Waverley novel, or Preface, or Review. It is a theme well worth your handling as a curious trait in human nature, and I should very much like to see how you would account for it.

Remember no answer is required. I only venture to write upon that condition; otherwise I should abstain, as your eyes are far too precious to be worn out and wasted in correspondence.—Believe me always, with the warmest good wishes, most truly yours,

L. STUART.

VII

DITTON PARK, 1st *March* 1827.

AND so the murder is out, dear Sir Walter! I have been reading the newspaper account of your meeting for the Theatrical fund, and dislike only one ominous expression—"that the rod of Prospero is broken and buried." I hope—"that's poetry, Miss"—as Mason said to an old friend of mine who quoted his own words to him in opposition to some opinion he was giving,—I hope the rod will still work miracles under ground.

The Montagus and I have been comparing notes on the subject; they had no notion that I knew it, nor I that they knew it, which I think speaks us a good trusty honourable set of people, considering how much and often the novels used to be canvassed amongst us. The poor late Duke was their informer, to whom, by the by, you must know you gave your word of honour

SIR WALTER SCOTT AND LADY STUART 237

that you were *not* the author, in so serious and solemn a manner, that it was quite impossible you could be so, unless indeed you had given up all regard to character. This is one of five hundred stories I have heard positively affirmed since you owned the fact to me a dozen years ago, many of them supported by such evidence as there was no refuting. One work had been actually read in Canada, and another certainly heard of in Germany long before they appeared in print here, and this person knew, and that could swear to proofs, not presumptions, but clear proofs that you wrote none of them. Then, too, in reasoning on the books themselves: "Old Mortality," for instance, was plainly written by three or four different hands; people could point out traces of the patchwork, which it was perverseness or want of taste not to distinguish. One had nothing for it but to assent peaceably to whatever they chose to say, and without denying one's own belief, allow that they supported theirs by very strong arguments.

It has increased my knowledge of this world we live in a hundredfold, and I must confess gone far to convince me of the truth of the proverb "truth lies in a well"; for, without intentional falsehood, how most people do lose sight of it in the heat of an argument, and how very inaccurately most stories are told! It has *garred* me make some reflections on myself too, as well as on my neighbours. When inclined to be eager and vehement, in maintaining or combating any point, I have recollected that on this, which I was *sure* of, I said as little as I could, and took care not to attract notice. And I have thought to myself, "perhaps some silent person is now sitting in a corner who has the same certainty of the present matter, and to whom my prating is a comedy." I shall like to see how those that were so certain will eat up their proofs and their knowledge. The usual way, I know, is by forgetting all, and flatly denying they ever thought so and so; and in that case they never forgive you if you put them in mind of their former assertions.

I have been here above a fortnight, but managed things so awkwardly as to pass most of the time in my own room confined with a bad cold, which is the harder, as I had had a pretty severe one just before I came. I was in great hopes to have met the Lockharts, whom Lady Montagu proposed asking to meet me. Now I am well again, she says she will still try, but I cannot stay here for ever and aye. I suppose you know Mr. Morritt has inherited a considerable property from an old uncle of eighty-seven, who, I believe, was a determined miser. I hear the nephew, to be quite sure of not hoarding in his turn (though in no great danger of it), has portioned his two nieces most handsomely, added nobly to young Morritt's income, and so forth. Very like himself, and I dare say all true, as his own words are that this acquisition has enabled him to render those about him as comfortable as money can make them. These repeated stupifying colds have prevented my answering his letter (now five or six weeks' old) and asking further particulars. You see I have bestowed all my tediousness on you instead; but remember our bargain—no answer required.

I wish I could have any reasonable hopes of your

SIR WALTER SCOTT AND LADY STUART 239

coming up this spring, and bringing Napoleon out in your proper person. I am afraid that short spurt in the autumn is all we are to have of you. Wherever you are, may all that is good attend you!—Believe me, always your obliged and sincere, L. STUART.

P.S.—My lord and lady are gone for two days to Richmond, so I have no message to give you from them.

VIII

EDINBURGH, 8*th March* 1827.

MY DEAR LADY LOUISA,—I have your kind letter, and as I love contradiction as well as other folks I proceed to answer it immediately. The avowal of the novelist character was a mere accident. The circumstances attending Constable's bankruptcy placed the secret such as it was in the hands of too many persons to suppose that a denial could any longer be taken at my hands, and whenever that became the case I only looked for some decent opportunity to lay aside the mask, which was grown as thin as my aunt Dinah's. Besides, the joke had lasted long enough, and I was tired of it. I had not, however, the most distant intention of choosing the time and place, where the thing actually took place, for making the confession. Lord Meadowbank, who is a kind and clever little fellow, but somewhat bustling and forward, said to me in the drawing-room—"Do you care anything about the mystery of the Waverley novels now?" "Not I," I replied; "the secret is too generally known." I was led to think from this that he meant to make some jocular allusion to "Rob Roy." I trusted to find something to reply when I should hear, being willing on such occasions (like an old cudgel player as I am) to take up the baskets at any time for the amusement of the good company. But when, instead of skirmish of this kind, he made a speech in which he seriously identified me with the author of "Waverley," I had no opportunity of evasion, and was bound either to confess or deny, and it struck me while he was speaking it was as good and natural an occasion as I could find for making my avowal. And so out it came to the great astonishment of all the hearers. My secret was just in the case of Jack Meggot's monkey, which died just when Jack got completely tired of him. Besides, I was sorry for telling lies which were not believed. A lawyer, like Fag in the "Rivals," never cares for telling a lie either to serve himself or his client, but it goes against one's conscience to be found out. In fact, as to my denials, I could not have kept my secret a moment unless I had shut the mouths of people who thought themselves entitled to pry into what they had no business with. Your ladyship knew the parties too well to suppose poor Duke Charles would press for an instant on the secret of any friend. He was the person in the world who observed most delicacy on such occasions, and the way that his Grace came to know the circumstances was precisely contrary to those in which I was said to have denied them. The subject being brought on by some inquisitive person at Drumlanrig, I could not help saying the next time we were alone together that I was surprised his Grace had never testified any curiosity on the subject, and told him the secret at the same time, although I do not believe he ever doubted how the thing stood. There was a singular circumstance the other day, like some of those which happened with respect to omens, dreams, etc., corresponding with the original. Two gentlemen of Cambridge had a wager depending upon the question whether I was or was not the author in question. The bet remained unsettled for twelve years till of late that the gentleman who maintained the negative gave up his wager as lost, from the result of some inquiries, I suppose, and a day was fixed for announcing a handsome entertainment suitable, as the newspaper says, for the importance of the occasion. Just as the party were going to dinner, lo! arrives the news of the formal avowal. Was not this a very odd coincidence? To conclude, I think I must say some few things about the confession, and put them into a printed shape. Your ladyship is well entitled to hear all how and about it. I put it off till I should get to the country, out of the way of being farther poked or plagued about it. I am delighted with Morritt's good fortune. I remember the worthy defunct opened his hoards, and gave Morritt at some Jewish sort of interest the price which he purchased Brignal with, and which acquisition brought him so much amusement. Fortune is in her brightest mood when she bestows her favours on those who are sure to make a good use of it. He has had in some part of his life great anxiety and distress, as your ladyship and I well know; I hope and trust it will be made up to him in the love and gratitude of his adopted children. I have rarely seen any one more improved than young Morritt. It was my advice which sent him into the army, as the best way of teaching him some knowledge of the world, where he got rid of all the conceit and nonsense of a young genius, and is now a pleasant, gentlemanlike, sensible young man.

If this finds your ladyship at Ditton, pray have me most respectfully and kindly remembered to the lord and lady, and all the young ladies. I understand the Duke and his sisters are to be down here in summer. He is likely to be indulged in his wish to keep the Midlothian pack of hounds at his own expense, and it will probably bring him much to Scotland, which is devoutly to be desired for his own sake and that of the country. I send this to Sophia to forward as she may. —Ever your ladyship's truly obliged and most respectful humble servant, WALTER SCOTT.

I go to Abbotsford Monday.

IX

GLOUCESTER PLACE, 1st *July* 1827.

DEAR SIR WALTER,—I know not how to thank you enough for your present, which I received on Friday afternoon, and *fell to* without a moment's delay. I have finished the first volume. What others think of it I am entirely ignorant, and I feel it almost an impertinence to give my own opinion upon such a work; but this I can truly say, I have read it with just the same avidity as I ever did any of your novels, and I think enjoyed it much the more, instead of the less, from knowing, from having in a manner witnessed, the events it records. We do not see distinctly what is too near our eye, or judge calmly of things while they are actually passing before us. Various reports, different versions of every story, let alone party disputes, tend to confuse the mind and leave it in a sort of uncertainty. It is therefore most agreeable (I speak for myself) to see the intricate road one has actually travelled laid down in a good map, to have a fair, clear, candid, luminous statement of the momentous scenes that, when present, only bewildered one's faculties. And if ever I met with a statement deserving these epithets, I protest it is yours. If ever I beheld the causes leading to the French Revolution traced with a masterly hand, it is in your first and second chapters, where you have steered quite clear of the rock on which I had some fear of your splitting, *i.e.* too partial a regard for aristocracy, and so expressed yourself, that I shall wonder if even a real Whig can find fault, though a Radical may like your sentiments all the worse for being both moderate and just. I also admire particularly the description of the National Assembly and that of our House of Commons in the fourth chapter; and throughout am delighted with those flashes of poetical genius which, by one happy allusion, sometimes only one word, light up a complete image in the mind and, what is more, illumine the subject, render it better understood. I am going too far, and deserve you should recollect Dr. Johnson's speech to a bluestocking lady: "Consider what your flattery is worth, madam, before you *choke* me with it." But I affront myself by naming flattery, for I never flattered anybody in my life, and 'though I may judge mistakenly I do it honestly, as this *naïve* remark of a young friend, who chanced to meet with me Friday evening, and to whom I read some of these passages, will prove—"Why, Lord! you read it as if you had written it yourself." She meant *con amore*, and indeed I believe it was true.

You have made a mistake in calling the Emperor Francis, Leopold's *brother*, instead of his *son*, and have followed false information in your note, page 327, which you may think no great matter; but I can tell you it will serve to ascertain one point. Depend upon it, no ghost ever does, or did, or will walk, if poor Lord Sheffield's has not paid you a fearful visit by this time. He, as Colonel Holroyd, was the person who said to Lord George Gordon he would stab or shoot him on the first entrance of the mob into the House of Commons, and further, threatened to tear the blue cockade out of his hat, unless he put it instantly in his pocket, which Lord George, quailing, submitted to. Colonel Holroyd's fencible cavalry was one of the regiments whose coming up saved the town, and for his activity at its head Lord North made him an Irish peer. In his last years, when I knew him, these matters had grown exactly "His sacred Majesty's *isjune* at the Tower of Tillietudlem," and put all his friends to flight in the same manner. Whenever we saw the riots of 1780 impending, one person slipped out of the room, another spied a thunder-cloud in the sky, another even asked questions about his own pamphlets on the Corn Laws— nothing would do. As his newest acquaintance I was a favourite victim. In vain did I plead that I was grown up and in London at the time, and had had too hearty a fright to forget a single circumstance—our house being on the condemned list. No matter, I must read the old newspapers and magazines treasured up in his library, because containing the most accurate accounts of all that passed. For Cosmo Gordon[1]—no *General*—nor, I believe, ever an M.P.,—I remember no person (of a gentleman) so generally despised in society, or rather out of it; for a strong suspicion that much dirty scandal in the *Morning Post* about the Duchess of Gordon, Lord William, and others of his connections, came from him, sent him altogether to Coventry, whence he never returned.

I am afraid you will begin to think Lord Sheffield dropped his mantle on my shoulders when he left this world, yet I cannot help retailing an old story he was fond of telling, it seems so pat to what is going forward in the world at present, to Mr. Brougham's high opinion of Lord Eldon, and twenty other things happening, now that people are every day eating up their words— "with *any* sauce that can be devised." Oh! how I wish I could hear you for half an hour on these points!

Well! The old gentleman said he was a youth on his travels, Ensign Holroyd, when Wilkes came to Geneva during his outlawry. All the young men there were fond of his company as a remarkable person and a man of wit, and *he* made up to him still more than the rest; of course was in his favour. One day he took the liberty of saying to him—"Mr. Wilkes, may I ask

[1] To whom the story was erroneously attributed.

you what gave you such a hatred of Lord Bute?" "I a hatred of him," returned Wilkes very coolly. "Nobody could hate him less: I am sure he was always very civil to me; and for that matter, I protest, I thought him a very good minister."—"You!!! *You* thought him so?"—"Ay! Why should not I?"— "Good God! Why did you attack him so violently, then?"—"Why?" repeated Wilkes, turning round and staring, "Why, because it was my *game*, to be sure; I wanted to be somebody, and as matters stood, I had not much chance of getting anything from Government, so you know my business was to attack it."—"And had you no scruple of throwing the whole kingdom into confusion?"—Wilkes squinted at him with a look of fun.—"Why, if I *had* had such a scruple, I should not have been JOHN WILKES, but a *vaa-ry vir-tu-ous* Holroyd." And so the conversation ended.

Will you remember me in the kindest manner to Mrs. Lockhart; it does me good to know you are now together, and her little boy in so fair a way of complete recovery. I wish *she* would write to me and tell me all about you and herself, for I grudge your pen and ink being wasted, therefore do not desire any answer. I meant to have enclosed a note to her to this purpose, but the hour is too late to permit me writing it. I can only add that I am, ever truly yours, L. STUART.

X

July, 1827.

MY DEAREST LADY LOUISA,—I cannot devolve on any other person, however confidential, the task of returning my best and warmest thanks for all your kindness. Venturing to make a considerable allowance for the partiality of old friendship, there remains enough in your kind approbation to give good hopes that I have been in some degree successful in concluding the most severe and laborious undertaking which choice or accident ever placed on my shoulders. I positively felt last week like Christian when released from his burden, and could willingly have sung when I went on my way. My way too was a pleasant one, for I got holiday for four days from the Court, and Anne and I went to spend it at Abbotsford among my plantations and in the company of my dogs and rustics. I beg pardon of the human dignity for the collocation, but both classes are great additions to my happiness. I do not think I ever saw the earth look so beautiful, the weather neither too scorching or too chilly, but the air smelling and feeling like balm itself, the turf more highly embroidered with wild flowers, and spreading a fresher and a greener turf than I ever before observed, and being at once velvet to the step and the most beautiful embroidery to the eye. Then the delightful recollection in the morning that I was quit of my late yoke was something like the holiday morning of my schooldays, when I wakened at six to remember that I was not obliged to rise.

However, this springtide of pleasurable enjoyment could not last long, and my return to Edinburgh and to my official duty was attended with some anxious apprehensions as to the reception which my finished labours might find with the public. I could not quite view the matter *couleur de rose*, knowing with what haste the work was executed and the number of inaccuracies which it must necessarily contain, so that your kind letter, my dear Lady Louisa, came as a cordial, when a cordial was a little wanted; for though I am resolute in not worrying myself about what I cannot now help, yet I do not profess to be so entirely beyond the ordinary feelings of authorship as not to accept with the utmost gratitude the applause of those whose judgment I must needs value so highly as I do that of Lady L. Stuart. I was aware of the blunder about the Emperor Francis. It had slipped from me more in a mistake, for certainly I knew the fact very well. In that respecting Lord Sheffield I was misled by Burke's and Dodsley's annual register, which ascribes the anecdote to Gordon; but if a second edition be called for assuredly I will give Lord Sheffield his due. The trait was worthy of the stout old Lord Mayor who knocked down Wat Tyler, and would no doubt [be] executed as bravely as it was said. It is odd what straws a *free and a thinking people* will draw before them. I have often thought that either the absolute knave like John Wilkes, or the positive madman like Lord George Gordon, will succeed in making use of the popular credulity much better than men that are decently honest or reasonably sagacious, who fail in leading the animal to the utmost from uncertainty of the immense quantity of nonsense which may be imposed on it. I am glad your ladyship thinks I have attained the high praise of impartiality. I have certainly endeavoured to do so, and however incompetent I might be to judge of so comprehensive and powerful a character as Napoleon's, I have always endeavoured to regard Napoleon as a person upon his trial, and I myself one of his jury who was of course to condemn or absolve him. I should be particularly sorry to do injustice to Lord Sheffield, because I knew him a little in his latter days, and was much delighted with his spirit and urbanity at a late period of human life, and particularly with the spirit with which I have met him riding his pony in the park. I must never have been very high in his favour, for we never came so close together as to get the story of the Riots, and I rather wonder at it, for I remember the surprise and resentment of my father at the impertinence of the mob who took the Protestant reformation for their watchword, and more especially the supine negligence and cowardice of the magistrates who suffered such infinite disorder to take place. I was always a willing listener to tales of broil and battle and hubbub of every kind, and now I look back on it, I think what a godsend I must have been while a boy to the old Trojans of 1745, nay, 1715, who used to frequent my father's house, and who knew as little as I did for what market I was laying up the raw materials of their oft-told tales. My choice friend was a certain Alaster Stuart of Invernahyle, a leader of no ignoble portion of your ladyship's royal clan of the Stuarts, namely of

Appine, which he led on many a bloody day. I shall never forget one of his answers to me. I was, I suppose, about ten years old, and seated on his knee, listened to his warlike exploits, of which he was no loath narrator. "O Inver (this was his familiar and pet name in the family), will you tell me if you were ever afraid?" "Troth, Gurdie mavourneen" (Walter, my darling), said the old man, "the first time I gaed into action, when I saw the red coats rank opposite to us and our people put up their bonnets to say a bit prayer, and then scrug their bonnets down ower their een and set forward like bulls, driving each other on and beginning to fire their guns and draw their broadswords, I would have given any man a thousand merk to insure me I wad not run away." Poor Alexander Stuart, I saw his son the other day, a grey, drinking, half-pay captain, who has spent the little estate, and is now an idle stupid animal, and yet I can never help feeling kindly to him and stopping to talk to him about the memory of the high-souled enthusiastic old man. All this is very little to the present purpose. Sophia has stuck herself into one of those lodging-houses in Portobello, where she pickles the children, duly I hope to their advantage, for certainly it is not to her comfort or theirs either. The place is a stew-pan in hot weather, a watering-pan in rainy weather, and affords the accommodation of a piggery at all times, when she might live at Abbotsford like a princess, up to the ears in flowers and vegetables and as happy as a cow. There is no accounting for tastes, and I have suffered too severely for interfering in matters of health. For, after all, a fellow who has

SIR WALTER SCOTT AND LADY STUART 251

had the constitution of a Bonassus for the greater part of his life is no very capable judge how women and children ought to be treated. I expect my youngest son to-morrow from London dignified with the title of Master of Arts, and I hope like to turn out intellectual. Walter fills his own place very well. He has good sense and the most perfect good temper, *bel cavalier beau sabreur*, a very kind husband to his little wife. He is, besides, mathematical, however he picked up this quality, and a good draughtsman. All this does well for a youngster who hath land and beeves, but the younger brother has or ought to have more stirring qualities, and accordingly Charles I think has a decided turn for reading, and a good deal of something like talent that may turn out dross or good metal as God pleases. He has, however, like his brother, a generous and noble heart, and I have good hope of him and of both from their great affection to me, their sisters, and each other. Such is papa's tale. I have no mind to say anything about the public except that looking as an individual

"My friends by turns my friends oppress,
Betraying and betrayed."

And thinking as one of the public I can only say—

"A plague of both your houses."

They are teaching the world at large to call them all self-seeking knaves, which the world, as Mother Quickly observes, will do fast enough of itself. It is a sad scene of party passion.

I will put my sheepish nonsense like Win Jenkins

under my lord's own *kiver*, for certes it were hard measure to pay postage for it. Should it find your ladyship at Ditton I need hardly beg to be most kindly and respectfully remembered. I have hardly left room to say how much I am your ladyship's respectful and obliged humble servant, WALTER SCOTT.

XI

DITTON PARK, 31st *Jany*. 1828.

THREE months have stolen away, dear Sir Walter, since I begged for the little bit of paper I enclose, meaning to send it you directly; but various melancholy and untoward circumstances (to borrow the word my betters are squabbling about in Parliament) occurred one after the other to prevent my writing. Mind, I make no excuse for that—excuses are more wanted when I do write. But to explain the merits of the scrap. It was part of a letter my sister-in-law received from her brother Granville Penn, a man of letters and an author, chiefly on theological subjects. A year ago he had an overwhelming misfortune—his favourite daughter, happily married, was carried off by a week's sudden illness. Struggling to recover this by plunging yet deeper in his Greek studies, in order to finish an elaborate work for the press, he so injured his eyesight that the oculists prohibited all use of it whatever, and, like most people accustomed to read much to themselves, he could not like being read to, until your "Life of Napoleon" so riveted his attention that his children declare it has been a perfect blessing, for which they

SIR WALTER SCOTT AND LADY STUART 253

shall thank you as long as they live. He sat listening to it from morning to night.

Now, though I firmly believe you as free from author's vanity, as you say in the introduction to the "Tales of the Canongate," is not there a something in you quite distinct from that (or vanity of any sort), a something to which the praises of the poor half-blind, afflicted man will give sensible pleasure? I will not think otherwise, for it seems to me that none of the French mountebanks who crowned Voltaire at the theatre paid him so gratifying a compliment.

The next thing to it is the delight of the children in the "Tales of a Grandfather." I have made two or three sets very happy with them, but they have carried away my copies too fast to let me read more of them myself than the first volume, which, indeed, Mrs. Lockhart lent me before they were published. *Apropos* of her—now in some degree my neighbour—I saw her during the very few days I was in town before I came here last week, and have seldom seen her looking so well. Little Johnnie, whom I found at the door just getting into his wicker-coach to go out, had a healthy, fresh colour, and as for his next brother, he was standing manfully on his legs, one of the finest, sturdiest fellows I ever beheld. I bade her give you hints of some trifling matters to be minded when the new edition of "Napoleon" is printed. People complain bitterly for want of the years marked on the margin, as is customary in most historical works; and they would also thank you greatly for a general index. I know this is a very troublesome demand, but have you not what Dean

Swift calls some under-spur-leather, some drapery-painter, to do such drudgery for you? If not, I should for one grudge its taking up your own time, and very much prefer a few more Tales of the Canongate. You may suppose that having known Mrs. Anne Keith added to the interest I felt in them. She once passed a winter in London with Lady Hardwicke, and we made some acquaintance through the friend to whom I owed (and owe) most of the bright gleams checkering my life, and amongst whose papers—bequeathed to me in sacred trust—are many of Mrs. Keith's letters. I can therefore fancy I hear the latter tell her own stories, although it is so long since I saw her; latterly, I believe, she hardly ever left old Lady Balcarres. In town I remember she was thought to *prose*, a propensity on which sentence is always passed without mercy, for very few people stop to distinguish between prosing about something and prosing about nothing, 'though froth and plum-pudding are not more different. . . .

I say nothing of the two [the Duchess-Dowager of Buccleuch and first Lord Douglas] that have finally closed a chapter in the families united here. For I should say too much if I entered on the theme at all, and it is still a painful one to me as well as to those more nearly concerned. Both Lady Montagu and Mrs. Scott are sadly dejected. The thing is the decided break, the line it draws along the middle of life—and then having kept what you loved and revered longer than you could hope, does not make you the more willing to part with it. Lord M., too, was deeply affected by the death of his mother. You will rejoice to hear that nothing could be more amiable, more feeling throughout than the conduct of the young man, or more fervent than the gratitude he expressed (on coming of age) to his uncle. But, an you talk of prosing, I am sure I have prosed long enough; so farewell.—Ever truly yours, L. STUART.

P.S.—Pray how do you approve of my nephew's title, Stuart de Rothesay? H.M. laughed, and called him "a sly fellow for stealing one of his names."

XIII

GLOUCESTER PLACE, *4th June* 1830.

DEAR SIR WALTER,—When I bespoke the frank, Lord Montagu bade me give you a message, but I was afraid of blundering, so he has put his own words in the cover, where you will find them.

Excuse my annoying you with a letter. As I enclose one to Sophia, longing to know how she accomplished her voyage in that tempestuous weather, and how she does after it, I own I cannot resist saying a word or two to yourself. However, it will require no answer. I, like many others, felt cruelly disappointed at your not coming up in the spring. Next year or this seems all one to young people, but at my time of life *puttings off* are most uncomfortable. Not that youth, alas! is much more secure. The Montagus, Scotts, etc., have just put on mourning for Lady Charlotte Stopford, Lord Courtown's youngest daughter, who has been several months wasting away in a consumption, like her cousin Lady Anne Kerr, and has now followed her to the grave, at Hastings. Thus have gone five cousins-germain of the race in two years—these two, the other Lady Charlotte, Robert Stopford, and poor Isabella.

With regard to the king, in whom I know you take a deeper interest than most of his subjects, he is undoubtedly better for the present, whether relieved by nature or art. One hears both affirmed so confidently, one knows not what to believe. If it were the former it would show a strength of constitution that might almost lead one to hope for his recovery; yet this nobody ventures to talk of as possible.

Well, no more on melancholy subjects; it is but a sad world, and we owe the greater thanks to those who, while we do live, make life pass pleasantly, withdrawing our minds from its cares and sorrows. Whom can this apply to, if not to you? It has been particularly good in you (or your publisher) to let us have the eleventh volume of the new edition (of the poems) separately. At least I think so, because I have two editions already, yet could not have rested without what that volume contains. By the by, one of your reasons for abandoning poetry I deny to be valid. Pray, had not Pope the same fate? For half a century after him did not man, woman, and child write smooth ten-syllable couplets, copying, *tant bien que mal*, the tone of his versifications? And do we like his poems the worse for all the dull, heavy things in Dodsley's collection? Nay, *an you go to that*, has your favourite, Lord Byron, escaped any better? The Annualist Companies, who cover our tables with volumes in red silk, have

SIR WALTER SCOTT AND LADY STUART

learned to write so like him that till one falls to examining the meaning of their stanzas one sees little difference. Just so I remember a certain Mrs. Powell on the stage, who had caught the voice, tone, and manner of Mrs. Siddons so exactly that I was more than once surprised into thinking: "How comes Mrs. Siddons to act so ill to-night?"

Yet it did not spoil Mrs. Siddons herself to me the next time I saw her. If we cannot now delight in Cowley as our ancestors used to do, surely it is because the style of his poetry was vicious and unnatural in itself, not because his imitators, the metaphysical poets, as Dr. Johnson calls them, were innumerable and unreadable.

Mr. Morritt, who is in great feather this year, leaves town next week. I dare say he will either visit you at Abbotsford or seduce you to Rokeby ere long. May no visitation of Wranghams or Hugheses, no invasion of impertinent tour-makers disturb the comfort of your meeting. I wish I could be of the party, but steam-carriages are not yet brought to perfection, and I had enough of steam-vessels in my last summer's excursion to France. Adieu, with every prayer for your health and prosperity, always yours most sincerely and affectionately, L. STUART.

XIV

GLOUCESTER PLACE, 25th October 1830.

DEAR SIR WALTER,—I have been feasting upon the Demonology and Witchcraft; yet some stories freshly rung in my ears, and I am sure fully equal to any of those you tell, give me a longing to attack you for civilly supposing the present *enlightened age* rejects the superstitions of our forefathers because they were absurd, though I grant it has dropped them because they are out of fashion. Vanity and expense in dress were not left off along with hoops and bag-wigs, nor credulity with the belief in hobgoblins. And I own that I think, of the two, it is more rational to ascribe a miracle, a supernatural fact, to the agency of a devil or even a fairy, than to imagine it effected by itself without any agent at all, divine or diabolical. But hear what has happened in 1829–30.

You know, perhaps, that the mania of Animal Magnetism rages anew, and more than ever both in France and Germany. A lady, by name Miss Stevens, went from Cheshire to Paris, I am told, and there was cured last winter by a magnetising doctor of some inward disease. This is nothing, a straw in the balance: mark the next. The process, performed before a large circle, who carefully noted down what passed, cast her into a deep sleep, a trance, a state of total insensibility, during which she was unconscious of anything she uttered. However, on being properly questioned, she described her complaints most accurately, using the scientific anatomical terms that none but a professional person could understand. I did not hear that she talked Greek, but you will agree that she might as well. This done to everybody's edification, they began to think she might give them information on other points. So an English lady asked her if she could tell where a certain Captain Smith then was, and what he was doing.

SIR WALTER SCOTT AND LADY STUART 259

Now, Miss Stevens, alive and waking, knew nothing of Captain Smith, not so much as that such a person existed, but Miss Stevens entranced answered readily that he was in Ireland and had lately had a dangerous fall from his horse, which has since been ascertained by exact comparison of dates as a positive truth. And this is credited by people who are enlightened up to the throat, who subscribe to London Universities, frequent Royal Institutions, and who would have the face to laugh at a Cock-lane-ghost; nay, who, I am afraid, would take a contemptuous tone about things of more importance. For one is often enough reminded of Charles the Second's exclamation: "Odds fish! This learned doctor believes everything but the Bible." My dear Sir Walter, it is not for you to toad-eat the March of Intellect when it can counter-march in such a manner.

What you say of the disorder that presents apparitions to the eye interests me particularly, for I knew an instance and had an account of it from the person herself, an old Mrs. Middleton, widow of the once great surgeon David Middleton, and the last of the Yorkshire family of Fairfax. She was past fourscore, but in clear possession of a very sound understanding, and, having lived much with medical men, saw the subject in the light they would have done, without alarm or perplexity. She assured me she had no other symptom of delirium at the time, nor did she feel herself ill; though her servants, frightened at her asking why the garden was full of people, sent in all haste for Dr. Warren (the present one), who made her go to bed, and by bleeding her sent off the spectres. They, however, haunted her for three days, but were not troublesome or disagreeable; on the contrary, she said it rather amused her to lie and look at their figures and dresses, 'till one of them came and sate upon her bed. Then, growing displeased, she tried to push it away, and found that her hand went through vacancy. The same thing, she told me, had occurred to her once before, though in a far slighter degree—certainly from none of the causes you assign, for there could not be a more temperate person, nor a better regulated mind.

In the bushel of advertisements tacked to the *Quarterly Review*, I spy two from Cadell that I am very glad to see—"New Tales of a Grandfather" and "Robert of Paris." By the by, it has struck me that the review of Southey's "John Bunyan" bears some tokens of coming from that quarter. But Pope said of old, "Every coxcomb knows me by my style"—so I dare not be confident. And now I have told you the two stories your book made me wish you should hear, I will have done. I hope by your visiting Drumlanrig with the Lockharts you were all well. If ever you come again to London and find me living, there is nobody it will give more pleasure to.—Ever affectionately yours, L. STUART.

No answer required, you know.

[*The following letters to Mrs. Lockhart and Lady Montagu are added from their connection with Sir Walter Scott.*]

LADY LOUISA STUART TO MRS. LOCKHART

DANESFIELD, GREAT MARLOW,
24th *July* 1831.

MY DEAR MRS. LOCKHART,—You have no notion how grateful I was for your letter of July the 10th, though it may not appear from my delaying so long to answer it. The truth is, it came just before I left town, and at a very sad moment, when the loss of a very old and most valued friend, Mrs. Weddell, took up all my thoughts. This deprived me of the freedom of mind requisite for writing, and yet as in such circumstances one looks around with anxiety on those who still are spared to one, I was perhaps only the more glad to receive a pretty good account of your father. I thought it so, because I cannot but believe his spirits the most material point, and if they are improved I hope everything else will mend. I have been as cautious as you could wish, and mentioned the plan of his going abroad to nobody except Lady Montagu; only said that his family desired he should leave home next winter. There can be no doubt that if he has health enough to enjoy such a tour even in the least degree, it must be of infinite service to him, and this in every way, awaking new thoughts, giving new views; so Mr. Cadell may well recommend the scheme, and the world rejoice at it. I am sorry he has incurred your hatred, for I suppose it is by being in general troublesome and teasing and counteracting your endeavours to make Sir Walter lie by and give his mind some rest. I wish you could be of the foreign party, as well as your brother or Mr. Lockhart, though, if I live till another year, the wish is against my own interest; but I think it would do you good, and might do Johnny more. However, I know all the difficulties of moving from place to place with a young family, and can hardly hope you will be able to overcome them. You say nothing of the influenza, which has been raging in London, and, as far as I know, in the country too—whole families laid up with it. Lord and Lady Montagu and three of the girls had it a fortnight ago, and are now at Ditton to recruit. He suffered the most, being of a constitution easily knocked down by an accidental illness. With other people it has attacked their servants, and sent half a dozen to bed at once. And I hear it has been to the full as prevalent at Paris, where their name for it is *la grippe*. Still, there seems in it nothing dangerous nor permanently detrimental. It has entered my house, for my maid had it, but I escaped, by which I conclude it is not catching. You say you can send me nothing but a bulletin. This I am always glad to receive, and you will truly oblige and gratify me by renewing it from time to time, as little as I can offer you in return. Mrs. Scott and I are chiefly alone together, and learn no news but from the newspapers, which just now I sicken at and hate to read. And I own that my thoughts turn so much upon my poor friend, and the blessing and comfort she had been to me for near fifty years, that I have little heart for other subjects. But there never was so resigned a spirit, nor so peaceful and happy a death, undisturbed by pain of body (*that* had quite ceased for the last week) or uneasiness of mind. "I am on my passage," said she, "and should not at all like to be interrupted." One ought not therefore to repine at a change most happy for herself. Forgive what I have no business to trouble you with. The Stewart Mackenzies are in town, but I believe she is going soon to Leamington, where an old aunt of hers resides, who has taken the boys for their holidays. One of them, and she herself, had the influenza. She got out of her bed *to go to Court*, and returned to bed when she came home, therefore stayed in it longer than she would have done had she taken care of herself at first. As it is five years since I saw her, she looks, to my eyes, a good deal older than she did, but in all other respects is just the same, as entertaining and captivating as ever. Some minds have what one may call an elastic quality, and I am sure hers is one. A visitor from London for the Saturday and Sunday, engaged in Reform—that is, mischief—the rest of the week, gives me an opportunity, I am glad to seize, of sending you this stupid letter franked. My love to your father, and kind remembrances to Mr. L. and your sister Anne. God bless you all, my dear Sophia. Pray write again. I shall be here two or three weeks longer, but it is always best to direct to Gloucester Place.—Ever affectionately yours, L. STUART.

Mrs. Scott will be very angry if I do not say something very kind for her.

DITTON PARK, 18th December.

MY DEAR MRS. LOCKHART,—In the first place, I want very much to hear something of you, and have some account of little Johnny; in the next, Lady Montagu is much vexed that she has not yet dared to propose your meeting me here; but an untoward thing has happened. One of Lady Lothian's girls, who came down the same day I did, a fortnight ago, was immediately taken ill, and it proved the smallpox. She is lodged quite apart, and has done so well she will go away in two or three days, yet still Lady M. thinks you would not like to come till time enough has elapsed to have her apartment and all that wing of the house thoroughly aired, fumigated, and purified. She hopes by the end of the month all will be perfectly safe, and then nothing will make her so happy as to see you and Mr. Lockhart. Meanwhile she charges me to tell you, and bid you tell your father, how delighted we are with the new "Tales of a Grandfather," which I am reading aloud to the congregation in an evening, and have nearly finished. I protest I think few things he has written can surpass them. A book for children indeed! The account of the progress of civilisation in the first volume would alone mark a master's hand; and Lord Montagu was last night observing that in all which ensued respecting the political parties, no stranger would be able to guess to which the author himself inclined, so fair and impartial were the statements. For my part, what I chiefly wonder at is his power of making a subject that has been so hackneyed, so often trod over even in his own works, as interesting as if one had never read a word about it before. I have a crow to pluck with him myself though. Pray *dun* him for the information I asked him to send concerning the names of poor Queen Mary's attendants on the scaffold. Madame *Vanderbruggen* (née *Vanderstichill*) is still in painful suspense about her descent from one of them, and my friend at Ghent has more than once dunned me. I was in town for three or four days the beginning of this month, and should have called on you, but that the day I came a great surprise awaited me—a very pleasant one, however. I found a niece of mine was going to be well married, so she and her affairs completely absorbed my attention. Mr. Morritt writes me word he and Anne are going to usher in the New Year at Abbotsford, "hoping the lion will then be at rest from the hunters." Mother Hughes's persevering chase has made such an impression on him he cannot forget it. I wish he would not defer his journey till the end of the year, for it has hitherto been so unnaturally warm that my mind misgives me it will change all at once in the Christmas week, and we shall have a hard winter. Stainmoor and Mosspaul are ugly passes when it snows. Adieu. We shall all be very anxious for a favourable answer, including Miss Clinton, who is here, and desires to be particularly remembered to you. As I stay till the middle of January (unless my niece summon me sooner to her wedding), I am a party deeply concerned in your complying with Lady Montagu's request, and always most sincerely yours,

L. STUART.

GLOUCESTER PLACE, *Thursday Morning.*

MY DEAR MRS. LOCKHART,—I have not yet got horses, and the weather has been too bad for walking, which has hindered my calling on you. You will see by what I send with this that I have been engaged in a melancholy occupation, looking over the letters it once gave me such delight to receive. Those here picked out seem to me most characteristic, and also to explain most his purposes in the works he was planning. You will consider whether they can be of use to Mr. Lockhart. The first note relates to the history of "The Luck of Muncaster," which I had got for him from Mr. Morritt, with whom he was not then acquainted. King Henry the Sixth, after one of his defeats, took refuge in the old castle of the Penningtons, beyond Wast Water, the farthest of the Lakes, and stayed there several weeks. When about to flee farther into Scotland, he said he was too poor to offer his host any adequate reward, but he would leave him his drinking-glass, which he solemnly blessed, and prayed over it that, while it remained unbroken, the Pennington family might never want a male heir. Mr. Morritt saw it when visiting Lord Muncaster (Lady Balcarres's father and this lord's uncle); he describes it as a thick Venice glass, in shape like a Scotch *quaich*. Lord M. brought it out at a meeting of his tenantry, and the poor people all fell on their knees, attaching to it some idea of sanctity, derived probably from Roman Catholic times. I had mentioned the story to your poor father at Bothwell, when he read us the first canto of "Marmion"; he was mightily taken with it, and begged me to get him the particulars more fully. The paper at the bottom of the parcel (sent in the last letter I ever had from him) relates to a question of mine which, however, it does not directly answer—Why *very* young people, who do not yet know the existing world, should so far partake of the spirit of their age as to judge according to it of books that are as new to them as they were to their parents or forefathers when they first came out? What suggested it to me was this: In my own day all mothers strictly forbade their daughters to read Rousseau's "Nouvelle Heloise," and all daughters, of course, longed to read nothing so much. I knew one young lady who owned to me that she stole a reading of it standing on the top steps of her father's library-ladder; and another, who procured it and carried it into the country with her on her wedding-day, as the first fruits of being her own mistress. To say the truth, I believe no book ever did so much mischief. Yet within these few years I happened to hear a girl of very warm feeling, enthusiastic, romantic, just the person whose head it would have turned of old, declare she had tried to read it, but been so disgusted that she threw it away before she got through half the first volume. Forgive this long prosing. Let me add that you would be perfectly welcome to look over all the rest of his letters whenever you liked. If Mr. L. wishes to insert (or extract from) any of these I will beg not to be named. It is not that I am not proud enough of having been honoured with *his* regard, but I never yet saw my name in print, and hope I never shall.—Affectionately yours, L. STUART.

LADY LOUISA STUART TO LADY MONTAGU

Nov. 1835.

I HAVE learned the name of the lady, poor Sir Walter's first and perhaps only love, so beautifully touched upon in the "Life." You will be surprised to hear it was Sir John Forbes's mother, the only daughter of a Sir Gilbert Stewart. Her husband, mentioned, you know, in one of the prefaces to "Marmion," came forward in the handsomest manner, on the failure of Constable, with an offer of £50,000. Sir Walter was heard to say that after her marriage he withdrew his waking thoughts from her, but nothing painful ever happened to him that he did not dream of her before it. Remember the passage about dreaming we read the other day in the "Lady of the Lake." He read it to *us* at Buchanan in private, and I recollect spoke with a thrill about the renewal of feelings (long hushed) in a dream. . . . The *Mimosa* lines in "Marmion" were certainly applied to Sir William Forbes, son of the *good* Sir William, at the time of its publication, when I carried it to Mr. Alison's, and read it to the family.

24th Oct. 1837.

. . I HAVE now got half through my fifth volume of Lockhart. . . . Mark the scheme of letters of James the First's time; for, what will surprise you, I had a principal finger in that pie, though I never knew it was the origin of the "Fortunes of Nigel." When poor Sir Walter came up this time six years he brought the printed copy of the letters with him, and what passed, *till* I saw it, proved rather a disturbance to me, as I had so totally forgotten the whole transaction that I faced him down he was mistaken, and it must be somebody else he had confounded with me. A staring proof of forgetfulness is not at all pleasant at a certain age. . . .

APPENDIX I

THE FAIRIES' FROLIC
A TALE

APPENDIX I

THE FAIRIES' FROLIC

A TALE

WHEN swiftly with departing night
Had fled the goblin and the sprite,
While Demogorgon cracked his whip
Lest fairies should in daylight trip;
Two elves one autumn morn outran
Ev'n Ob'ron as he led the van,
And 'till next eve' conferring staid
Apart from all his cavalcade.
A princely pair; among the chief
Who worshipped Chaucer's mystic leaf;
In mutual friendship fondly twin'd,
But proud, and of a restless mind,
That mocked accustomed sports and plays
Bequeathed them by their grandame-fays,
Thefts, antics, gambols, roundelays.
They for a nobler frolic plann'd,
To burst the bounds of fairy-land,
Take female lineaments, assume
The cumbrous hoop, the lofty plume,
And ponder Woman's fate, the while
They led the fashion in our isle.
   Not new the thought; for manifold
Such metamorphoses of old;
From Pallas—Mentor with her friends—
And Jove—disguised for naughty ends—
With scores of other names at hand
Down to King James of *fayre Scotlande*.

But princes bent their pow'r to hide,
And heathen gods transmogrified,
Of borrowed stations did but taste,
And took their own again in haste.
Not thus the fairies' purpose; they
Have heard such tales of Beauty's sway
From straggling gnomes frequenting town,
Such wonders learned of Wit's renown,
That either gift they prize beyond
Possession of their monarch's wand,
And long as life in man may last
Aspire to act a part so cast.
 As friends, as sisters, still, they mean
To enter on their human scene;
One, lovelier than the morn ere rose,
To reign a despot o'er the beaus,
Break hearts, and madden heads, 'till all
On this side thirty victims fall;
The other, Wit's and Learning's pride,
Where-e'er these flourish to preside;
And 'though her subjects, past their prime,
May keep their wits whole all the time,
The mightier things they understand
To rule them with the higher hand.
Thus, cherished, celebrated, buoy'd,
Fed full with praise, but never cloy'd,
By lovers worshipped, sung by bards,
No change, no downfall on the cards
(For age nor sickness dares surprise
Your fairy, errant in disguise)—
A life like this may prove a feast
Some fourscore years, they think, at least.
 'Tis well for children, oft' they're told,
Their headstrong wills can be controll'd;
'Tis well for men, too, preachers cry;
And rash the voice that says they lye.
Perhaps great Ob'ron now might make
Some such reflection ere he spake;
For sans his nod their scheme's a vision;
And nod he does—but in derision.

—"Some fourscore years!" he cries—"When four
Are fairly finished, sue for more—
But mark me, 'till those four be past
You're aliens from your place and caste.
Examine earth by Us unsent?—
You shall—and you shall 'bide th' event;
Not use your fairy-pow'r and skill
To guard the woman with at will,
But take her heart as well as form;
That heart where griefs and evils swarm,
Which can be thrilled, and bruised, and pained,
And still will struggle though enchained.
Your course—you are not to foreknow—
Enjoy your four years' frolic—Go—."
  No more deterred than is the boy
From meeting Christmas-tide with joy
Because the pedagogue he fears
Pours a full warning in his ears,
They snatch the leave, forget the frown,
And straight are *Ladies*—come to town.

The shape that Zirphe chose to wear—
But epithet and trope we spare.
Take youth's own freshness, lightness, bloom,
The softness of the dove's own plume,
The head, the features, moulded, plac'd,
As Grecian art had willed when chaste,
The form all-exquisite, the whole
Alive, and flashing forth a soul;
You then have Zirphe—Zirphe 'spied,
And who flung half a look aside
At faces which but yesterday
Men flocked and panted to survey?
Their owners brooked this ill; but found
'Twas useless to contest the ground,
Whether with haughtiness or guile,
A pensive aspect or a smile,
Each gazer now to Zirphe flown,
They languished and they laughed alone:
Each gazer—all—whoever saw,

In purple fostered or on straw,
Like charmed birds, the multitude
Grew still and silent as they view'd;
The crone, who grumbling gave them place,
Looked up, and, startled, blessed her face;
The sober thrifty drudge in trade
Stood mindless that his bill she paid;
The beggar tend'ring open palms
Gazed, and examined not her alms:
Nay, ev'n the child's delighted eye
Showed nature felt true Beauty by.
Meanwhile a conscious glow betray'd
That what she was she knew and weigh'd,
Yet welcomed such full pow'r to charm
With wonder bord'ring on alarm.

How formed Orinda, ill or well,
Our story stands not pledged to tell.
Bright eyes and murd'ring dimples, hence!
Make way for talents, genius, sense,
Quick parts, and understanding sound
That felt no science too profound;
Not that whose wond'rous pow'r appears
To poise the stars and guide the spheres,
Not that which numbers herb and ore
And searches nature to the core.
What Tully spoke, what Homer sung
She read, and read in either's tongue;
Wrote she herself—'twas force, 'twas fire,
High eloquence, invention high'r;
Or did she speak—in every phrase
Flashed brilliant Fancy's clearest rays—
Her wit, resistless weapon, low
Laid pert opponents at a blow
Whene'er she chose; but that was rare,
It gratified her more to spare;
And this, and many a gift beside,
There were who'd face you down she tried,
And wished, and did her best, to hide—
But here cross accidents o'ercame;

THE FAIRIES' FROLIC

She always stumbled so on fame
That men of crooked minds believed
No fainter wish was ere conceived.
   Let's tell plain truth then; bound in honour
To take the *trade* compleatly on her,
She soon saw 'twould be driv'n but ill
If modest excellence sate still
Expecting, as good books advise it,
The Godlike Few to come and prize it;
The Many gained, she found the Few
Were apt to sneak in basely too;
And mountebanks (all said and done)
The field from fairer practice won.
She let her banner stream in fine,
Or, if you will, hung out her sign,
Encouraged puffers of her goods,
And had her whims and altitudes,
With some ostents, which, we're afraid,
Her better reason had withsaid.
Thus in her chamber she perhaps
Left medals tossed about, and maps,
Planted her telescope just where
You'd put your myrtles forth to air,
And (for gilt clock and china cup)
Set globe and bust and fossil up
'Till all the wicked laughed aside;
While plain well-wishers could have cried,
And simpletons abhorred the niche
Like the dread circle of a witch.
There, when buzz wigs and stockings blue
Did ape indeed a conj'ring crew,
We grant she mid' them sate elate;
And who had witnessed their debate
Might well have, in the cramp words utter'd,
Supposed some incantation muttered.

   Zirphe meantime consigned her hair
To grave Toussaint's adorning care,
Built up her head 'till with its plumes
It swept the ceilings of the rooms,

And wore, on Flamand's neatest stays,
The last invented polonaise,
Then, like a sov'reign newly crown'd,
Made wise alliances around:
Ma'ame Beauvais ne'er in anger bore
A slighted bandbox from her door,
Nor carried back Gobère decried
Th' embroid'ry France had last supplied,
Nor did loquacious King complain
That Zirphe's cash was hard to gain,
Nor yet had Vaugh'n a hint to spare
Expence and taste in Zirphe's chair.
Almack, Gallini, all their tribe
Proclaimed her aptness to subscribe;
And wisely, for, had she been miss'd
Desertion would have thinned their list.
Unless she deigned the dance to lead
Quadrilles themselves could scarce succeed;
Unless her voice the concert grac'd
One's list'ning proved one's vulgar taste.
   Rude is our age—their beaus, we're told,
Our haughty grannums more controll'd,—
But Zirphe ne'er was heard to cry
That men were rough, or scarce, or shy:
The brutes—if brutes were those she saw—
Gave her a down and velvet paw,
And scratched her neighbours (she believed)
But when they were misused or grieved.
If at a ball or masquerade
A word of dancing Zirphe said,
If, when the morning star arose,
She talked of seeking soft repose,
The sauciest son of Brooks's there
Would ask her hand or call her chair;
Would whisper compliments, and sigh,
And praise that love-inspiring eye,
Abuse all other females near,
And hint a passion—so sincere!—
   While cold hard self-conceit thus woo'd,
The burning youth, who silent stood,

THE FAIRIES' FROLIC

Would think—"If I like these could shine."
Or—"Oh! Did wealth and worth combine
To let me boldly cry—'Be mine!'"
For wealth gives courage, 'tis confest;
And, stout of heart, some forward press'd
By vet'ran rent-rolls flanked and nerved,
While jewels formed their corps reserved;
These set both *but* and *if* aside,
And cried—"Be mine!"—with fearless pride.

Thus feasted Zirphe; drank thus deep
Of that sweet bowl which lays asleep
Alarm and caution. Now let's ask
The flavour of Orinda's flask?—
Why, 'twas a rich one, one of pow'r,
Nor in the settling turned it sour,
Nor was there held to Beauty's lip
A cup could scorn its fellowship.
In short, if nectar be the phrase
By which old stories pictured praise,
Each sister at a draught took more
Than Jove could swill or Hebe pour.

Flutt'ring from bush to bush we see
Beauty—a butterfly—a bee—
But wit, a sob'rer thing, sits down
To chaw the cud of its renown:
And thus Orinda sate and chaw'd
I' th' centre of a crescent broad,
Thro' which, if she but stirr'd her fan,
Applause and expectation ran;
But if she smiled, tee-hees awoke
Prophetic of her unborn joke.
Then—talk she of whate'er she wou'd,
Tom Thumb's red cow or Robin Hood—
It charmed and edified all one.—
"Ma'am, there's no woman like her—none—
Hers is such real sense—always
Such profit to one's mind conveys—

That nuts are harmless 'till they're crack'd
Sounds obvious, a familiar fact;
But she gives things so new a turn
That something rare one seems to learn."
  So the wise women all averr'd
In bustling whispers well o'erheard;
While, for their dignity, wise men
Took snuff and seemed to think again.
Grave clocks, whose striking, you'd presume,
Set all the watches in the room:
To whom the ladies turn, when gravell'd,
To get perplexing points unravell'd,
Beseeching with a jury's awe
The bench would speak and give them law.
From these, howe'er, when once it came,
Burst adulation like a flame;
No speech they issued but to chime
"Minerva! Muse! Divine! Sublime!"—
No work to which they did not pin
Some note that lugged her merit in;
On law, on geography 'twas hung;
They preach'd, they quoted her, they sung;
Submitted, as her voice decreed,
This book to censure, that to read,
Besought her sanction for their toils
And owned themselves, at best, her foils.

  Thus, while with speed their moments flew
Nor care nor grief the fairies knew.
Life seems to post and these to creep,
Yet on so steadily they keep
That, pass it fleeter than a blast,
They track it and o'ertake at last.

  Like moths, who long work unperceived,
At first small evils lightly grieved;
With that grave gossip Form unite
The keen confed'rates Spleen and Spite,
Who scarce could in their beds take rest
While Zirphe went about so drest,—

"Ma'am, it's prepost'rous"—"Ma'am, it's worse;
It shows some folks a notion nurse
That they're above the world, and them
'Tis bound to cringe to, not condemn"—
"I hate affected airs"—"And I
Am modesty's declared ally;
Beauty (though I know those who think
Of ugliness she's on the brink),
Beauty the coxcomb's eye may gloat on,
But sense is what men ought to doat on."
 They ought; but with these graceless males
The old grand error still prevails,
While Beauty, with whate'er combin'd,
Finds neither judge nor bishop blind,
Their sons Orinda maul as follows—
"Now guard us, Jove, from female scholars!
Let boys for sapping famed at Eton
Her classic ground the lady meet on;
We tremble to be there entrapp'd
Who (lazy fellows!) never sapp'd.
This deep-read dame too, I conclude,
Must by her charter be a prude,
Sententious, and no doubt precise—
Has told eighteen, I take it, twice—
Looks down on us, unlettered crew!—
Zirphe! How she must envy you!"
 Then, for your busier steadier souls
Who know the price of soap and coals,
They listened but made no replies
When people thought themselves so wise.
They—and their taste they could not curse—
Liked prose: they understood not verse,
They but with *common* sense were blest,
But, humbly speaking, *'twas the best*—
For grant all science hers—compound for 't
(And half was puffing, they 'd be bound for 't),
To reckon stars and read Greek lives
"Is that what husbands want in wives?—
Then what she writes—say what she plunders—
Well *I* could never bear such *wonders*."

APPENDIX

But where consummate splendour reigns
We scarcely note how narrow brains
Are glorying o'er our specks and stains.
Men laugh, observes the saw, that win;
Beauty looks round, and Wit within;
Nor care they, gay and gratified,
How beldames carp or fools deride,
More than the sun for what may do
Those clouds he can at will break thro';
Disperse they, blacken, flit they, lour,
He knows eclipsing past their pow'r.

As time, howe'er, yet farther fled,
Malice clomb up from where 'twas bred,
From secret, sordid nooks (where long
In dirt it burrows 'till it 's strong)
And, helped by Envy, got installed
Where never reptile should have crawled.
In forms too sweet, in minds too high,
For such a snake to venture nigh,
Alas! it nestled. Zirphe found
The lie she laughed at could rebound
From lips that should have loathed and curs'd
Back to the mob who sped it first;
Haply in all its progress run
More welcomed and upheld by none
Than him who 'd wooed and had not won:
By none with more complacence heard
Than the fair rival not preferr'd;
Who, first of all, made notice sure
By whisp'ring with an air demure,
Then stole a meaning smile—then tried
The teller of the tale to chide.

If thus 'tis with that lighter school,
Vot'ries of giddy gay misrule,
Who, when their latitude offends,
Talk of the heart that makes amends,
How fares Orinda 'mid a train
Who boast themselves all head and brain?
In scenes where flatt'ry, 'though 't be doled

THE FAIRIES' FROLIC

With shovels, like a banker's gold,
Like that, is strictly summed, and meant
To bring in int'rest ten per cent,
May one bold hand unquestioned come,
And clear the table of a Plum ?—
No—wonder's motionless, but brief;
Soon the raised parish hunt the thief.
Soon hostile rivalry far off
Aims slander, epigram, and scoff;
Nay, ev'n the unsuspected band
Of warm admirers near at hand,
Adoring poets, prim divines
(Still for th' Amphytrion where one dines),
Ev'n these three steps beyond her hearing,
Vie with the vulgar crew in sneering,
And call good puddings, just like cits,
The worthiest works of female wits.

This damped, and did ('though slowly) bring
A trifle downward fancy's wing,
Dispelled some dreams, and taught the fays
That life must see some low'ring days,
But pride and hope, in vigour still,
Resisted and survived the chill;
And not one throb expounded yet
The scope of Ob'ron's parting threat.
That heart on which he laid such stress
Thus far had sought to meddle less
Than kings just castled do at chess;
Kept facing forward, tame and quiet
As nags are on a cornless diet,
Unable seemed to rear or paw,
And started not whate'er it saw.
But many a broken bone proceeds—
Young riders !—from these sober steeds;
On whom one feed of oats bestow'd
May make them mind nor rein nor road
But, frantic with the sense of pow'r,
Leap walls, and o'er the country scour.
Then, if you can, with bits secure,

Then pat 'em back to pads demure,
Starve them and curb, as heretofore;
Lie down they may, they pace no more.

The Fairy-prince, who, by the bye,
Still on his truants kept an eye,
Aware what shortly would succeed,
Now watched them with the closer heed;
And saw those sluggish hearts (supposed
Scarce living things because they dozed)
An inward quickening testify
By tremors he alone could spy.
Uneven grew their motion, late
So measured, equable, sedate,
They fluttered now, they paused anon,
Lay for a while as sense were gone,
Then lab'ring seemed beneath some yoke,
Mourned—fetched their first strong sigh—AWOKE.

We wake in fevers from the deep
Oppressive torpor, miscalled sleep,
Delirious wake, affirm we see
Bright forms and hear sweet symphony;
So at this hour of aweful change
Poor Zirphe hailed each feeling strange
As some bright beam from Heav'n, that threw
On life, on time, a colouring new;
As some sweet thrilling sound, that brought
Delight unfigured yet by thought.
She trembled; but not long she stood
In doubt what vanquisher pursued.
She recognised the wings and flame,
And called her master by his name.—
'Twas thou, O Love!—Adored—avow'd—
Of thy resplendent fetters proud,
Thy slave, intoxicated, spurned,
The peace which, parting, ne'er returned.

Not thus, audacious as thou art,
Cam'st thou to seize Orinda's heart
In all thy matchless might confest,

THE FAIRIES' FROLIC

Like Jove at Semele's request.
Unconscious she that aught assailed;
Thy voice was hushed, thy form was veiled;
Thy tread the silent thief's; and slow
Was thy light footstep fain to go
As crawls the burthened ant to gain
A sand-hill's summit with her grain;
But fail and backward slide may she—
No ground e'er crumbled yet for thee,
Who never mov'st but onward still,
Be sand or adamant the hill.

  By no fierce burning taught to fear
Revulsion or disorder near,
Orinda's soft'ning bosom opes
To wand'ring thoughts, to whisp'ring hopes,
That, indistinctly murm'ring, win
Small notice when they first begin,
But breathe a tale that holds at last
Her riveted attention fast.
They tell of quiet bliss conferr'd
By Friendship—false and fatal word!
Cool draught whose milky seeming hides
The deadliest poison Love provides.
Of mutual trust they tell, and aid,
Of truths from mind to mind convey'd,
Of Reason still supreme (Alas!)
And balmy hours that are to pass,
'Till, all relaxed and undermined,
Her spirit 's to the dream resigned.
  Yet Love, the tyrant that subdues
That sister whom she pitying views,
She still accounts a bugbear-ill,
Which they may put to flight who will.
Her calmer mind conceives not why
So sparkled Zirphe's raptured eye
As long as at her feet lay One—
Not worthiest sure beneath the sun—
Nor wherefore when the fop withdrew
A faith but valueless if true

There followed, 'stead of freedom, pain
That left the suff'rer scarcely sane:
While she, with a yet dormant pest,
A frozen serpent, near her breast
Warming to vigour day by day,
Is tranquil, confident, and gay;
Nor ever calls to mind or feels
The fearful inmate she conceals,
'Till, sudden, to her heart's deep core
Its tooth has pierced, and all is o'er.
Ay!—jealousy's envenomed fang
Then wakes her with so dread a pang
No fear illusion should remain;
She knows her foe, she feels her chain
And, as she strives against it, finds
It heavier weighs and faster binds.
Oh! Now with envy she could see
Those poor short hours of ecstasy
Enjoyed by Zirphe, while allowed
To credit all a false one vowed;
They flitted quick, were purchased dear;
But *she* has had no hour to cheer,
No happiness to make amends
For the long misery that impends.

"Now to the test," stern Oberon said,
"Your fame is, as you wished it, spread;
Bid fame a cure, a solace bring,
Bid Wit draw forth the barbéd sting,
Or Beauty's consciousness defy
The anguish of a hopeless sigh—"
And said his taunting whisper true?
Could Hope to Beauty bid adieu?—
Ah, worse!—Bewild'ring Hope long staid
To vex and harass, not to aid:
Hov'ring o'er Zirphe's glass each day,
"Look!—Look, and trust me," would she say:
'Till Zirphe, losing pow'r to trust,
Turned from that glass, and saw (unjust!)
Her lovely shadow with disgust.

THE FAIRIES' FROLIC

What cruel days ensued!—If brief
The period of impassioned grief,
Yet, oh! spectator of its throes,
Give it thy pity while it flows,
For life is brief—and life would fail
Ere told were ev'n our shortest tale,
Did some sharp wounds for aye withstand
Time's secretly assuaging hand.
Outlive thou may'st, serenely too,
The bitt'rest sigh poor Love e'er drew;
But if thou, ere thine end, maintain
'Twas light, and gave thee little pain,
Nor shudder inwardly, nor seem
Like one that's troubled at the theme,—
Why then thy memory, overplied,
Hath wasted, and before thee died.

As in some town, where midnight fire
Hath late revealed its aspect dire,
The frightened householder who fled
Half wild and naked from his bed,
Creeps trembling home again when told
The flames are quenched, the walls are cold;
Yet scarcely, whatsoe'er they say,
Can feel the peril passed away;
Sees all his goods, if left unburned,
Disordered, ransacked, overturned,
Finds bawling tumult at his door,
And sleep and safety knows no more.
To Zirphe thus, recalled at last,
Came Reason back, but came aghast,
Confused, and dizzy, to be braved,
And tremble while the passions raved.
And yet ere long, resolved anew,
Her own vocation to pursue,
Gay scenes again our Fairy sought—
Perhaps with half a lurking thought
That *one* deserter might, for shame,
Rejoin the standard graced by fame.
'Twas soothing, from long use, beside,

With vows and praises to be plied;
'Though, vapid now and void of zest,
These only whiled the hour at best;
And, every soft address she heard,
Remembrance like a thorn recurr'd—
"Thus fondly pleaded, thus complained,
The *One*"—ne'er rivalled, ne'er regained.

Nor was (as Ob'ron had forecast)
Ev'n this vain pastime long to last.
No house of cards, no rolling stone,
Unsteadier thing than Fashion's throne;
And (as some mining hand below
Were lab'ring for its overthrow)
It now beneath our Zirphe quaked
Like Etna when the Titans waked.
Unchanged, such beauty might despise
Contending with inferior eyes,
Nor grudge the newer face its right
Of hasty glance and homage slight,
But Magnanimity herself
Looks foolish laid upon the shelf;
And when did Fashion's turning tide
With pitying slowness gently glide
By halves from the forsaken shore?—
It rushed at once—it instant bore
Its gifts and glories back amain
To pour them on another's reign:
And that—oh, wormwood in the draught!—
That prosp'ring *Other*, she, whose craft
O'er Zirphe had already cast
The influence of an evil blast;
Whose charms, while yet accounted mean,
Had aimed one arrow all too keen,
And snatched from hers that only thrall
Whom wayward love held worth recall
When slaves and worshippers were All.

Then such fair riddance of the rest
Her drooping sister would have blest,

Whose heart ev'n sickens at the name
Of praise, of homage, or of fame;
Who shrinks, as from a blow, when told
How high the place her talents hold,
And nearly could give way and weep
When questioned on her studies deep.
The words convey, as if design'd,
Reproach and mock'ry to her mind,
And flatt'ry leaves a sorer sting
Than malice could have pow'r to bring:
'Though now no more unfelt the gibe
At she-philosopher and scribe
That malice flung, and levity
Rang changes on, it knew not why;
For self-upheld no more she stood,
But timid watched one hearer's mood,
If haply aught his eye exprest,
To avenge her of the paltry jest?—
And *He*—sate unconcerned (his smile
A cruel sanction gave the while)
Who tow'r'd above the lettered tribe,
And *was*, what authors but describe;
At whose cold glance, though scarce a frown,
Her vanity unnerved sank down,
Sank, not to rise with lessened pow'r,
But perish like the trampled flow'r.
   Despondent, but not yet debased,—
Ill-will and enmity she chaced,
And only with a sigh survey'd
The graces of his chosen maid;
A blooming girl, unfledged, untaught,
Who ne'er had read, nor felt, nor thought,
Who, pleased, approaching wedlock saw,
But prized not him, nor held in awe.—
Him—at whose very sight a spell
Like dumbness on Orinda fell,
Whose hand had been so dear a meed!—
   She broke from thought, and strove to read—
Ay, strove and strove—then cast a look
So bitter on the closèd book

It spoke what, noted and enrolled,
A volume hardly could have told—
"Away!" it sorrowfully said,
"And fye upon the choice I made.
The eminence whereon I plann'd
Alone and unapproached to stand,
While happiness beneath had been
Perhaps attained; perhaps, unseen,
Had never witched me with its mien.
Fye on the love that, dry and dull,
Thus frets the pain 'tis wooed to lull;
And doubly fye upon the Muse,
Who lent illusion brighter hues,
O'er vulgar virtue raised mine eye
To glories indistinct and high,
And seasoned, if not filled in part,
The cup whose poison slew my heart."

The wretched sisters! How they blest
The mercy of their king's behest,
The frown that first their scheme o'erthrew,
And limited their years to few.
Now past were three; yet they complained
A ling'ring century remained.
Linger it did, oppress, and weigh;
And as crept on each weary day
They met no wife who honouring eyed
Her kind protector, prop, and guide,
No maiden giv'n to household cares
Who fed the poor and said her pray'rs,
But inly—spoke a wishful sigh—
"Another choice—and such were I."

'Tis said (the word of pardon past,
And fairyhood resumed at last)
They pity still the thing they were,
Take Woman to their charge and care,
And hush the heart that heaves her breast,
And bid it value peace and rest;
Oft whispering (though not often heard)—

THE FAIRIES' FROLIC

"The shadier path—be that preferr'd,—
The ray will scorch, the gust will chill;
Let Man with firmness tread the hill,
Who, born to front them and to 'bide,
Must leave no rude extreme untried.
But thou, while hedgerow, copse, and bow'r
May screen thee from their searching pow'r,
Be mindful of thy feebler frame,
And shun, oh shun, the Heights of Fame!"

APPENDIX II

THE DIAMOND ROBE, OR THE MANIA

APPENDIX II

THE DIAMOND ROBE, OR THE MANIA

PART I

BRAVE is the man who in the breach can stay
The rushing victor and the sack delay;
Heroic he whom duty still detains
When fate upon the flaming vessel gains;
And great of spirit who serenely eyes
The wheel injustice for his doom supplies.
But he that on dry land, in days of peace,
Can thro' the world's wide common brave its geese,
Make onward sturdily for reason's hill,
And while with throat upstretched and op'ning bill
In gen'ral cackle all exclaim, "*They say*,"
Demand undauntedly, "And who are *they?*"
Nay, he that, but with passive courage blest,
Forbears a while to cackle with the rest
And keep a neutral eye or vacant ear
Where Common-sense may find one inlet clear
When she shall come (the hubbub hushed) again
To drive each silenced gander to his pen;
Valiant beyond the chief besieged is he,
The rack's contemner or the burned at sea.
Let only those who boast such valour theirs
Deride the narrative my muse prepares,
Or (fitter) borrows. Twice an age ago
Castile from subtle Gracian heard it flow—
Castile, the nurse of spirits grave and slow,

APPENDIX

Who never, by the gadfly sudden stung,
Caught random frenzy from each other's tongue,
But brewed their notions like their Xerez wine,
Closed up the cask and left them to repine.
Oh, had the sage who thus his Spain portrays
Seen us, and seen us in our mania-days,
Had he but witnessed how a word—and one
Of undetermined meaning or of none—
Could cheer us on to worship or attack
(As if a huntsman slipped his eager pack),
Away, head-foremost, open-mouthed and wild,
Still zealous woman first, then man and child,
What apt additions would the tale have known,
The pithy tale which we no more postpone:

There reigned a monarch once—(our author's pen
Is too concise to mention where and when),
A prince whatever clime beheld him sway,
Of pomp and pastime fond, and rich array;
Who let the sabre hang untouched and dry,
While castenet and lute 'twas loyalty to ply.
Benign as jovial, an auspicious lord,
None lacked his willing smile and free reward
Who piped, or harped, or capered well, or wooed
The muse of masque and jocund interlude;
Nor failed of recompense their humbler pains
Who wrought him costly trappings, spurs, and chains;
Nor dealt he less than royally when trade
Her gems and merchandise before him laid;
Bounteous to all. But did some sable gown,
Some venerable beard, approach the town,
Some worthy sav'ring of the sage occult,
Who bids a patient alchemist exult,
One with the stars who privy dealings held,
Or into bondage fiend and fay compell'd,
On such a wight, how people, court, and king
Would gold uncounted and unvalued fling!
For brains (as may be noted by the wise)
Were here no prodigies for strength or size;
Merry the crew, the pilot debonnaire,

But sounding deep they held not their affair;
And as for good old books that smelt of must,
Who prized them might peruse them—'twas but just.

Now soft sweet air the tender leaflet stirred,
And loud to carol was the woodlark heard,
And white anemones in tufts were pil'd
Beneath his foot who wandered thro' the wild;
For hard at hand was May—a month of joy
Which ancient usage bade the court employ
In banquettings and jousts, as consecrate
To splendid revelry and feasts of state.
But had it challenged from no former year
More honours than dull March, its gloomy peer,
A gallant welcome 'twould in this have won,
And all its plumed minstrels been outdone:
Outdone in song, in gaudy hues outvied
By the gay masquers and the ladies' pride.
This year was marked with more than common grace,
An heir bestowed upon the royal race
Drew tributary lords and knights unknown
From distant provinces to hail the throne;
And (looked for long) ambassadors were nigh,
Chief nobles of a potent proud ally,
On whose arrival May must overflow
('Twas purposed and proclaimed) with sport and show.
Fermenting folly thus had room to sway;
No goldsmith, no embroid'rer idle lay,
The tailor woke ere Phosphor shed his beams,
The courtier's wits were buried in his dreams,
New braveries to devise and colours blend
Which e'en his wayward mistress might commend,
When lo! alarm thro' all the city flew,
Each bade his toys and trifles quick adieu,
And hurrying ran, tho' wherefore no one knew;
Sudden as out of earth they just had sprung,
Or from a cloud been with the raindrop flung,
The outer gate and palace porch between,
Advanced three strangers of mysterious mien,
Whose shrouding garments, shapeless, dark, and wide,

Save a vast beard left nothing human spied,
Who slowly moved, in silence so profound,
That mute and solemn too grew all around,
And ev'n the guard, austere to every class,
As if afraid to challenge, let them pass
Unquestioned whence they came, for signs they made,
Refusing to be catechised or staid;
Arrived before the throne, they kneel and pay
Commanded homage, but with grave delay,
As conscious of their worth, tho' deigning to obey.
Yet ask they not (for welcome all to hear)
A private audience or a secret ear,
But let the chiefs surround their lord, and them
Be circled by a crowd of lowlier stem,
While list'ning warders bar but ill the door,
And menials peep, and in the burghers pour;
So swallowed all at first or second hand,
What thus the spokesman ladled to the land.
"O prince! O people! in each other blest,
May pleasure still embrace you, wealth and rest;
Long have we known, though distant our career,
The rev'rence paid to Mystic Science here,
And oft, as chiefest of her sons, design'd
To glad you with our presence, free and kind,
Ere that dread hour should close our pilgrimage
Which comes to all, though slowly to the sage,
The true adept, survivor doomed to be
While generations melt and ages flee.
Five have we numbered now, three toiling past
In unremitting study, prayer, and fast,
The rest in travel. We have dared to probe
The womb and burning centre of the globe,
Have heard the mermaid, seen the dragon coiled,
Gazed while the roc the mighty mammoth foiled,
Held conference with Druid, Brachman, Mage,
Enthralled—but peace! or we unseal a page
Forbidden to the unhallowed. Nameless Pow'rs!
Obedience was your bond, and silence ours,
Whereof to murmur, blab the when and where,
Tho' under earth or o'er this breathing air,

THE DIAMOND ROBE, OR THE MANIA

Revolt were to provoke, and deadly peril dare.
"No further preface. 'Tis enough that we
Have mastered secret Learning's inmost key.
Yet far be from us all unholy skill
And sorcery's wicked pride in working ill.
Nor aught, O king! we 'gainst thy crown contrive,
Nor would thy treas'ry of a mark deprive:
We come with gentler purpose—'tis to show'r
Fresh glories and delights on this fair hour,
Add to thy worthy fame of rich and gay,
And proffer, for the livery of thy May,
Such raiment, luminous and strange of hue,
As glistened on that fiend whom Delos knew,
That Phœbus, worshipped as a God erewhile,
Tho' but in truth the demon of the isle.
For him what craftsmen wove it, well we know;
Their loom is ours, and it again shall go.
Nor ask we aught but mere materials—toys,
The ruby, diamond, em'rald, pearl, turquoise,
Whence filaments we draw, and radiant thread
With sunbeams manufactured, seen to spread
Till robes of living light effulgent flow;
So thin, he feels them not on whom they glow,
Tho' close the web, and decency concur
With warmth that Scythians scarcely find in fur.
By these with sudden loveliness endow'd
Majestic grows the form, the stature proud,
The strength a lion's, the diminished age
Recedes to just on this side pupilage,
With beauty glows the cheek, with wit the eye,
Good luck and friends, and merits multiply.
"Well may ye marvel; but far more remains,
Or little would the work deserve our pains.
Stand all dishonour fearfully aloof,
Nor try the virtues of a charmed woof
That tries the gazer too. Alone the man
Who terror never felt nor truth outran,
Son of a matron chaste, and, if he wive,
Husband of her whose suitors fail to thrive,
He (and but he), from stainless fathers sprung;

No Jew, no Saracen the race among;
No felon, churl, on sire's or mother's side
Who died the death that angry laws provide;
He with unclouded eyeball shall behold
The sparkling texture, brighter than foretold.
His heart shall at the glorious vision swell,
And his wild praise all eloquence excel.
"But he whom fear hath mastered and disgraced,
Whose soul, or fraud or falsehood hath debased,
Whose helpmate, at the best not wholly true,
Grudges a frown when graceless lovers woo,
Who boasts a father he might disobey
If half his mother's secrets met the day,
Or harbours mongrel blood, whose course contains
One drop from Jewish, Moorish, Ethiop veins,
One blot of crime or slur of dastardy—
Invisible to him our work shall be;
Unmoved, unseeing, shall he pass it o'er
And question happier men what object they adore."
  The monarch paused, but scarce a thinking space;
Remembrance spake no act, no feeling base;
Consort and mother like Lucrese he deemed;
And, certes, with such fame and honour teemed
No other line that down from Adam streamed.
"Hail, Sages!" cried he, "to the proof—prepare
A robe which I shall view, I trust, and wear:
Waste all my jewels ere ye scant a thread."
Now owned the courtiers, think you, doubt or dread?
With grave demurring faces came they round
And argued out the point on reason's ground,
Or if not so, divine ye what restrained?
A spaniel soul! By you forsooth disdained,
The sycophants (you hold) belied their wit,
And the king's fiat made his knaves submit?
No, in good truth. Be lofty minds apprised
That judgement 's oft'ner wildered than disguised.
When sped the arrow, who shall countermand?
The floodgate opened, who the wave withstand?
The mighty wave, which, like the people, ne'er
Permits an obstacle to say forbear,

But, deaf and deafening, as it downward goes,
Whirls on the mounds and fences that oppose.
Nor mound nor mortal thus opposing now
Faces the tide and lifts a hostile brow.
All borne along, unanimous, and sure
That never prophets uttered truth so pure,
Revere the mighty strangers, burn to see
The robe, the lucid robe, the prodigy,
Bring with the crowns their jewels to be spun,
And hold the promised work perceptible and done.

PART II

Three suns had ris'n and set; now moments press'd,
And the king panted for his radiant vest.
To reconnoitre then the work, and bring
Full confirmation of the wond'rous thing,
He chose a counsellor of trust; one famed
For every gift the fiery trial claimed,
A saint-like spouse and ancestry unblamed.
  Serene and confident, the sages hear
His charge delivered with a steadfast cheer,
No time in useless parlying consume,
But manifest at once the vacant loom,
And teach their grave inspector how to gaze,
Nor risk a sudden blindness from the blaze.
"There, where the diamond beams, and beams alone,
Be this thin veil (they cry) a moment thrown;
'Tis safer viewing what we now unfurl.
Here rest thine eye, where, gleaming mild, the pearl
Athwart that lustre steals a greyer white,
And soft cerulean sapphire heals the sight."
Much more they said, but briefest tales are best;
'Twere wasting precious rhyme to give the rest,
Heard only by themselves; no ear He lent
Whose consternation figured for assent,
Who, all aghast and scarcely breathing, strove
To dream he saw and picture something wove;

But 'twould not be; pure emptiness was there,
And (dark or shining) viewed he not a hair.
Now creeping through some crevice of his brain
An humble doubt that feared to be prophane,
Just shook its head, just murmured "fraud," when down
'Twas instant knocked by all the rising town,
The mob of thoughts, who straightway rushing cried,
"The man that sees not, evil him betide—
To brand himself that man, confess he drew
Some thousandth drop of life-blood from a Jew,
Resign his pedigree, his honour wave,
Accept the blot of coward or of knave,
Or claim the crest no wedded front desires,
Or shame the buried brow believed his sire's,
What wonder if a shrinking heart said nay,
And hardly could a swoon be chased away.
 The crafty weavers of the viewless thread
Perceived how paleness quenched a burning red,
But termed it feebleness of nerve, th' alloy
That nature mingles with ecstatic joy,
And ministered (say some) a cure benign
In goblets filled from no ignoble vine,
Where Bacchus, missing truth, set courage free,
And drowned perplexing doubt and nice integrity.
But wherefore should we sift the means employed
To fortify the man or fill the void?
Whate'er the cordial or the charm, at last
A firm regard upon the loom he cast
And praised the splendour; coldly praised, 'tis true,
But, cheered and prompted by the wily crew,
Took better heart at every lie, arose,
Considered, and his course maturely chose,
Then issued, fitted to confront the throng
Of questioners and fools who, thousands strong,
Beleaguer now the porch, and testify
Their tow'ring expectations by their cry.
 'Twas well; a calmer audience might have marr'd
The piece at once, and borne the player hard,
Who, copying close his master-knaves, designed
To stun the faculties and storm the mind,

Rushed forth with such an ardour, eyes so keen,
Such lifted hands, and eagerness of mien,
That ere a saucy question could obtrude,
Exulting shouts from all and mad applause ensued.
Belief thus won beforehand, what remained,
The colouring of the tale, was soon attained;
For had the diamond cloth indeed been spun,
Or cloth of beaten stars, or cloth of sun,
No fiercer beams description could have cast;
It flashed, it glittered, while his breath would last.
Dismissing then the people, on he flew
To quell each doubt his anxious master knew,
To kindle the bright blaze of gems again,
Exalt the work, and magnify the men
(Or more than men), by Heav'n despatched to bear
Its fav'rite prince the garb that seraphs wear.
This drudg'ry done, our minister at last
Went home to ruminate on what had past.
Oft darted he that eve (report was rife)
An eye she knew not on his bosom's wife,
And when appeasing slumber shunned his bed,
Sang wayward requiems to those grandsires dead,
Of whose ill deeds or shame or coward stains
Thus lit on luckless him the penalties and pains.

This night, indeed, the lucid robe will keep
From many a courtly pillow quiet sleep;
Its fame hath, like an autumn vapour, spread,
Fills all the air and works in every head.
Ere morning reddens, up the nobles spring,
Impatient each to importune the king,
Though not, as usual, laden with demands
Of pow'r and gold, vice-royalties and lands,
Precedence and degree, but all on fire
For licence to survey the bright attire.
If certain of them quailed (they best knew why),
Sir Pride, that learned in the law, stood by,
Glossed o'er the evidence, and proved that still
Oneself might find the ordeal iron chill;
While Christian charity—Ah! snug sate she,
No loophole showed by which a friend might flee,

No journey-work beyond her threshold sought;
She bustled but within, as housewives ought.
In secret then each baron made a jest
Of his foolhardy neighbour's rash request,
Bade luck attend the perilous enterprise,
Wished but as safe his honour as his eyes,
At worst would warrant their escaping harm,
Then blest himself at self-deception's charm.
  Not so the gracious ruler of the train;
He triumphs in a court thus free from stain,
Approves their virtuous ardour, and agrees;
Whoe'er petitions gains a sight—and *sees*—
A convert each, whose clamours aid the fraud
And bind th' approaching novice to applaud:
For each came singly; 'twas a fixed decree
Discreetly issued by the mystic Three.
So throve they merrily and safe, deranged
By neither wink or syllable exchanged.
Did some—but, counts mine author, few were they,
Like hounds sagacious scent the coz'ner's way,
These weighed the risque, the warfare might betide
With folly schooled and knavery defied,
And ended by out-bellowing all beside.

  But when our mock magicians thus had fast
A score of thinking men and highly class'd,
Who, self-entangled in their net, were fain
The cheat for very prudence to maintain,
They felt themselves at ease, securely rode
Without a curb, and opened their abode
For all the tribe in such dilemmas sure
To rule their restive eyesight or abjure,
Those active stirrers in the world's concerns
Whom anything can drive, though nothing turns,
Whom once let accident or man's design
Speed with a touch along some given line,
And on they go till doomsday, if you please,
Convinced the moon's a pancake or a cheese.
A goodly phalanx, and a strong (I hold
Linked closer than the Macedons of old),

THE DIAMOND ROBE, OR THE MANIA 305

Round whose firm edge shall hover Wit in vain,
And Argument, dismounted, bite the plain.
These won, the fortune of the day 's secured;
The rest, some terrified and some allured,
Come in apace, no cavilling offends
A fact as sacred for its foes as friends.
For foes existed; spirits stern and sour,
Devout old crones abhorring Satan's pow'r,
The jealous vulgar, stomachful when told
Of sights that nobles could alone behold.
These roared for judgements on the Diamond Robe,
Thought dallying Heav'n too slowly smote the globe,
And fain would cleansing fires meanwhile have plann'd
To purge those wicked weavers from the land;
On this ran Party, as it uses, high;
But none stood boggling at the keystone lie.

Thus far triumphant, free from present fear,
In caution still our sages persevere,
Take feasts and gifts and honours as their due,
But keep one object like a star in view,
Th' expected embassy whereof we told,
Which summons all the court and clothes with gol
And which to welcome will the sovereign wear
The tissued gems and glories they prepare.
They watch its coming, as they sought to show
Their prowess on the frontier 'gainst a foe,
And dreamed that this pacific princely band
Would slay the peasant and lay waste the land,
Not cordial vows and costly tokens bring
To attest the kindness of a brother-king.
Soon as the panting courier speaks it near,
Our feigned adepts must shorten their career,
Nor stay, like fools with consciences at rest,
Till these untutored strangers spoil the jest,
Who, faithful to their senses, right or wrong,
May speak and startle the believing throng.
Enough—the fraud is ripe, th' event prepared,
Their flight resolved, their precious booty shared,
And to the royal dupe this saying borne,
"Thy finished mantle may at will be worn."

APPENDIX

Alas good Prince, it pities us for thee,
The meanest courtier crouching at thy knee
His eyes hath glutted and thine ears hath fed
With floods of light not twenty suns could shed;
No tongue hath murmured doubt, no blush betrayed
A conscience loathing what the lips conveyed;
All, all have gazed, and vainly not a man;
On thee alone is fallen the dreaded ban,
Thy single hand the lot of shame hath drawn,
What then! Asunder shall thy queen be sawn?
Shall she who bare thee, to the stake consigned,
Be roasted for the sin that made thee blind?

Such purposes at first confus'dly formed,
Before thy dizzy soul like atoms swarmed;
But these thy waking wisdom rose and chased;
The ill we cannot fly must be outfaced.
Veil, veil thine agony, thy weapon sheathe,
Thou too shalt transport, thou shalt triumph breathe;
To thee, as to thy servants, need shall waft
That sight-assisting tube, behoveful craft,
Through which thy sharpened eye shall view, no fear,
All they (beshrew the varlets) find so clear;
Thy voice, as fits it, shall out-trumpet theirs,
And gainsay them and thee let him who dares.

Yes, ev'n this final visit but concurr'd
To prop the cheat, and with a monarch's word.
The gale that might (had frowning planets willed)
Have made the navy mastless ere 'twas stilled,
Swept over lovingly, nor swelled a wave,
Nor from its moorings one poor pinnace drave;
This weathered, not a shelf or breaker now
Can harm our mariner's advent'rous prow,
And welcome is the whirlwind's self to blow
That, forcing from the shallows, leaves them free
And speeds with all their cargo out to sea.

The day arrives; before its matin bell
Th' ambassadors' approach loud clarions tell,
Awakening joy and bidding splendour rise
To grace the entry of the State's allies.
Th' impatient court they need not urge; 'tis all

THE DIAMOND ROBE, OR THE MANIA

Assembled at the palace ere their call,
In solemn still convention ranged around,
As grave as if the sov'reign yet uncrown'd,
Were first t' assume his regal honours now
And plight inauguration's aweful vow.
Still graver, as becomes his chief degree,
He enters last; forthwith the ready Three
From a rich coffer feign to pluck the vest
And fold that *Nothing* o'er his royal breast
Whose radiance straight each feeble eye forbears
And every lip to glowing Heav'n compares.
This done, mysterious duties early vow'd
Recall its rev'rend weavers from the crowd
To fashion pious rites and solemnise
What privacy must screen from earthly eyes.
Rites? ay in verity—they such perform
As age to manhood sans a spell transform,
Make raiment, beard, complexion disappear,
And do away all remnant of the Seer,
Unmarked they then their sev'ral journies chuse,
And many a league are fled ere aught pursues.

Nor was it strange if ceremonial's pace
Proved somewhat tardy for an outlaw's chase;
The marshalling was long, and many a cause
Disturbed and made the slow procession pause,
Beside that on its path the rabble burst,
Still gath'ring here again when there dispersed;
Parading squadrons, maidens strewing flowers,
Dull orators haranguing, took up hours,
And day well-nigh departed ere at last
The 'missioned nobles to their audience past.
But oh, that spectacle! Since time began
Was ne'er so tried the gravity of man.
Perched on his throne, an antic prince or mad
In unbeseeming garb succinctly clad,
While pomp and state and grandeur round him blaze,
And scarce an eye his prostrate subjects raise.
Though wise the stranger lords and stern withal,
A laugh they could not stifle shook the hall;
Yet kindling at the scorn they thought implied

(As ceased their merriment and rose their pride),
They willed the framers of that sport to know
'Twas an ill jest converting friend to foe;
Avenging arms might teach the scoffing king
Another mode of royal welcoming;
Defiance in his teeth and shame for shame!
Then, brandishing their swords, all parley they disclaim.
　Truth instant flashed, like light on objects dim
For which we sit devising form and limb.
Though brief the glimpse, tho' deep return the shade,
No longer we mistake them, once surveyed;
Not all the might of fancy can renew
Those shapes she gave them on a twilight view.[1]
Now look met look, demure, observing, sly,
And questions seemed to steal from eye to eye—
"Did you speak honestly?" "Said you your mind?
Or are we all but vermin of a kind?"
Signs followed next; then murmurs passage found;
The thread was clutched, and fast the clew unwound.
　As straight from brine by chemic process tried,
Its watery particles in vapour glide,
And leave pure salt—and crystallised—behind,
So now exhaling folly fled the mind.
—There halt, my simile. Alas! we view

[1] *Note.*—In Mr. Dugald Stewart's preface to the "Encyclopædia," published several years after these lines (which he certainly never saw) were written, he says: "This is remarkable in the history of our prejudices that as soon as the film falls from the intellectual eye we are apt to lose all recollection of our former blindness. Like the fantastic and giant shapes which in a thick fog the imagination lends to a block of stone, or to the stump of a tree, they produce, while the illusion lasts, the same effects with truth and realities; but the moment the eye has caught the exact form and dimensions of the object, the spell is broken for ever, nor can any effort of thought again conjure up the spectres which have vanished."

Unless Mr. Stewart and I both borrowed this image from some common original, forgotten by me, this is a singular instance of coincidence where there could be no possibility of plagiary.

No search commencing for the residue,
No poring to perceive if in the brain
Thy crystals, Wisdom (purest salt), remain;
For pride and fury, folks unapt to pore,
Have mast'ry of the time and lead the roar—
"The thieves—Pursue 'em, fetter, flay 'em, broil"—
The thieves, who, calmly treasuring their spoil,
Have left, to pay all forfeits in their room,
Their fearless effigies and empty loom;
Wherewith may sate herself (and welcome) Rage,
And a fooled nation play 'till waxèd sage.

When came that blessed hour is yet untold,
Or which way surfeited that rage grew cold;
But let old Gracian vouch it or deny,
Thus much for sequel might a child supply,
That soon as Time had o'er the story cast
His light beginning haze, and marked it past,
The robe became a proverb; never named
But this man moralised and that declaimed;
Told, laughing, how the world was once bewitched,
How cowards wavered and how blockheads preached,
Nor aught forgot, or sparingly detailed,
Save (ever) how with *One* the cheat prevailed.
Each had himself—dispute it if you durst—
Adhered to sense and reason from the first,
In prudence held his peace, for that was fair—
Who'd face a tropic whirlwind if aware?—
But, cool as morning, kept his own firm head
And smiled or sorrowed as the madness spread.

Experience! Pearl by Egypt's unsurpassed!
For thee we dive where line was never cast,
Our sole rich recompence declare thee still
For life's long struggle with the surge of ill;
Yet, half possessed, permit entombed to lie
In thine unopened oyster till we die.
Thus by a nation bought, and bought so dear,
Thro' lack of mem'ry wast thou prisoned here,
For when the next vagary, fresh and strong,
Came whirling brains and spurring tongues along,

The man who should have cried, "My brethren, hold,
To shun new errors, ponder well your old;
That drowsy reason who withstood them not
May chance to slumber through a second plot,
And leave you, when her lethargy is o'er,
A byword for the mockers as before."
Like Troy's poor prophetess, rebuffed and spurned,
This answer had he had where'er he turned—
That dark the age and weak indeed the mind
Which foolish fables, Diamond Robes, could blind,
But for the worthier thing about to draw
Within its vortex every stick and straw,
The point *now* clamoured for with might and main—
'Twas manifest—'twas certain—truth in grain—
What Time (were Time appealed to) would but tend
To fix and hallow, let alone defend;
For ere to-morrow's cry revoked to-day's,
The sun should see the owlet court his blaze,
Or hear the lark salute his evening rays.

By JAMES BOSWELL

LIFE OF SAMUEL JOHNSON, including Boswell's Journal of a Tour to the Hebrides, and Johnson's Diary of a Journey into North Wales. Edited by GEORGE BIRKBECK HILL, D.C.L., Pembroke College, Oxford.

Édition de Luxe, limited to 300 copies. Six Volumes. Large 8vo, Half Vellum, Uncut Edges and Gilt Tops, with many Portraits, Views, Facsimiles, etc. (Sold by subscription only.)

Popular Edition. Six Volumes. 8vo, Cloth, $10 00.

The student of the period, and the reader who has loved his Boswell with a life-long love, will thoroughly enjoy the intellectual treat provided for them by the editor of this beautiful edition. —*Spectator*, London.

By SIR WALTER SCOTT

JOURNAL, 1825-1832, from the Original Manuscript at Abbotsford. Two Volumes. Portraits. 8vo, Cloth, $7 50; Half Calf, $12 00.

Popular Edition. Two Volumes in One. Crown 8vo, Cloth, $2 50.

The "Journal" is a book to last. No king in literature has such a chronicle, and as Scott in his novels has made his principal characters now and again serve as heroes of the tale without being conscious of their heroism, so here, without egotism, without pettiness, yet with minute detail, he has drawn his own superb figure with a strength which is ineffaceable. It is cause for congratulation also that the editing of the work was intrusted to one so painstaking and so sure in his judgment and taste as Mr. David Douglas has shown himself to be.—*Atlantic Monthly*.

HARPER & BROTHERS, PUBLISHERS
NEW YORK AND LONDON

☞ *Either of the above works will be sent by mail, postage prepaid, to any part of the United States, Canada, or Mexico, on receipt of the price.*

By G. W. E. RUSSELL

COLLECTIONS AND RECOLLECTIONS. By One Who Has Kept a Diary. With One Illustration. Crown 8vo, Cloth, Ornamental, Deckel Edges and Gilt Top, $2 50.

It does not often happen that a volume of reminiscences presents so much interesting and attractive matter. . . . It is difficult to lay aside a book which contains so much of the salt which seasons life. Such a volume is a never-failing resource for the reader wearied of overmuch feeding on the solid viands of literature. Especially commendable is the spirit of kindness which pervades the narratives. There are no flings at living pygmies or dead lions.—*Brooklyn Eagle.*

THE RIGHT HONORABLE WILLIAM EWART GLADSTONE. (*Queen's Prime-Ministers.*) Portrait. Crown 8vo, Cloth, $1 00.

Mr. George W. E. Russell, who writes this book, has done a difficult task well. The personal biography is necessarily brief, because the plan of the book calls for a political biography, and because Gladstone entered public life at twenty-two, and has lived and breathed the air of Parliament ever since. Yet it would not be possible to measure his public career justly without that knowledge of his personality and his ingrained tastes. Mr. Russell has provided the needful information in a succinct form, and his final chapter, in which he analyzes Mr. Gladstone's character, is eloquent in its restraint and vigor of touch.—*Atlantic Monthly.*

HARPER & BROTHERS, Publishers
NEW YORK AND LONDON

☞ *Either of the above works will be sent by mail, postage prepaid, to any part of the United States, Canada, or Mexico, on receipt of the price.*

www.ingramcontent.com/pod-product-compliance
Lightning Source LLC
Chambersburg PA
CBHW030747230426
43667CB00007B/871